P9-DFI-601

THE
PUPPETEERS

Also by Jason Chaffetz

*They Never Let a Crisis Go to Waste: The
Truth About Disaster Liberalism*

*Power Grab: The Liberal Scheme to Undermine
Trump, the GOP, and Our Republic*

*The Deep State: How an Army of Bureaucrats Protected Barack
Obama and Is Working to Destroy the Trump Agenda*

THE
PUPPETEERS

The People Who Control the
People Who Control America

JASON CHAFFETZ

BROADSIDE BOOKS
An Imprint of HarperCollinsPublishers

THE PUPPETEERS. Copyright © 2023 by Strawberry C, LLC. All rights reserved. Printed in the United States of America. No part of this book may be used or reproduced in any manner whatsoever without written permission except in the case of brief quotations embodied in critical articles and reviews. For information, address HarperCollins Publishers, 195 Broadway, New York, NY 10007.

HarperCollins books may be purchased for educational, business, or sales promotional use. For information, please email the Special Markets Department at SPsales@harpercollins.com.

Broadside Books™ and the Broadside logo are trademarks of HarperCollins Publishers.

FIRST EDITION

Library of Congress Cataloging-in-Publication Data
Names: Chaffetz, Jason, 1967– author.
Title: The puppeteers : the people who control the people who control America / Jason Chaffetz.
Description: First edition. | New York : Broadside Books, [2023] | Includes bibliographical references and index.
Identifiers: LCCN 2022058541 (print) | LCCN 2022058542 (ebook) | ISBN 9780063034969 (print) | ISBN 9780063034976 (digital edition)
Subjects: LCSH: Liberalism—United States. | Political culture—United States. | United States—Politics and government—21st century.
Classification: LCC JC574.2.U6 C52 2023 (print) | LCC JC574.2.U6 (ebook) | DDC 320.510973—dc23/eng/20230130
LC record available at https://lccn.loc.gov/2022058541
LC ebook record available at https://lccn.loc.gov/2022058542

23 24 25 26 27 LBC 7 6 5 4 3

To the men and women who came before us. May we work hard and work smart to preserve the gifts you have given us.

I appeal to you to constantly bear in mind that with you, not with politicians, not the President, not with office-seekers is the question, "Shall the Union and shall the liberties of this Country be preserved to the latest generation?"

—President Abraham Lincoln

Contents

Preface

When I wrote my first book in 2017, I still thought winning elections could save us. That's how our system is designed to work. The voters should theoretically be able to punish government for failure through the election process. I thought freedom-loving congressional majorities could turn back the tide of the Obama-era administrative state. They could restore the liberty that has been the engine of world progress for more than two hundred years. That may have been enough at one time—but not anymore.

Our federal government is a conduit through which rules are written and policies are made. But not by the people we elect. Increasingly, the work of government is being done by people outside of government—people who are invisible to the American public, but who pull the strings, set the agendas, create the incentives, and write the rules we must all live by. They rotate their own people in and out of the bureaucracy, leverage their vast resources on behalf of the Democratic Party, and inject a globalist agenda none of us voted for.

The full extent to which voters have been displaced has revealed itself to me slowly. After stepping down from my role as congressman from the great state of Utah and chairman of the House Oversight and Government Reform Committee in the United States Congress, I was deeply troubled by patterns of partisanship I had seen in the allegedly apolitical federal bureaucracy. What I witnessed then was only a template for what we are seeing now.

In writing my first book, *The Deep State*, I exposed the extent to which I had seen America's federal bureaucracy politicized and weaponized on behalf of one political party. The lack of accountability was being deliberately built into our system. In the very first chapter, I described how Democrats had established a new agency, the Consumer Financial Protection Bureau (CFPB), that was unlike any agency ever before created. A foreshadowing of things to come, it was designed to circumvent democratic government and use the authority of the state to compel compliance with leftist goals. Looking back now, I can see that the agency was merely a pilot test for today's government-wide transformation from a representative government to a counterfeit version of democracy. Though CFPB was created by Democrats in 2011, it took eleven years before a court finally struck down its unconstitutional funding mechanism in 2022.[1]

The rerouting of power to circumvent popular opinion was the reason I needed to write this book. The playbook has changed. Our fight has changed. The battle is eminently winnable, but only if we understand how to fight it. We don't beat this back by simply campaigning harder during election season.

Using both government and nongovernmental institutions, Democrats have figured out how to bypass the legislative process to compel institutional compliance with partisan goals. The White House or the Congress may change hands, but the left remains in power.

Political puppeteers have infiltrated not just our government, but nearly every other sector of our economy. This, too, was a pattern I wrote about. In 2019, I opened my second book, *Power Grab*, exposing a scheme by tax-exempt nonprofits to funnel money into partisan get-out-the-vote operations in key swing states on behalf of Democrats. What would happen in 2020, with harvested ballots and "Zuckerbucks"—private funding of elections by "philanthropists" like Facebook founder Mark Zuckerberg—was all foreshadowed in that book.

Even then, I had not predicted the breathtaking magnitude of what was coming. All it needed was a crisis to light the fuse. In 2020, my book *Never Let a Crisis Go to Waste* explored all the ways the COVID-19 pandemic and Black Lives Matter protests were being used to consolidate power for the left, revealing the partisan capture of scientific and academic institutions.

The red flags I described in those three books have only multiplied since the election of President Joe Biden and Vice President Kamala Harris. With the fox once again in charge of the henhouse, the revolving door between increasingly woke companies, politicized nonprofits, a compromised scientific community, and partisan agency officials has rotated. Now we find ourselves in an epic battle to protect our constitutional rights, our economic well-being, and our national sovereignty.

It is because of what these strategies portend that I felt compelled to write this book. Both inside and outside of our government, institutions that once served a core function in our representative republic have been insidiously compromised. Large segments of the leadership of financial institutions, professional public employees, nonprofit organizations, labor unions, academia, and social and legacy media gatekeepers have been replaced with craven partisan activists with a common goal: controlling the thing they call a democracy. These puppeteers have learned to leverage their combined power to drive the American agenda. And they're driving us off a cliff.

Like a magician performing a magic trick, it's done using misdirection. While voters are focused on the "A Team" of federal, state, and local elected officials who are supposed to be running the country, the real work of governing is being handed off to the "B Team." Some of these are partisan puppeteers who revolve in and out of the executive branch, some of whom I'll highlight in this book. They are appointed, hired, or consulted not so much for their professional expertise or their commitment to serve the public, but for their ties and commitment to a globalist agenda that seeks to weaken America and redistribute its wealth.

It's a systemic corruption that can't solely be solved by voting differently in the next election. If we make the mistake of focusing exclusively on who wins elections, who donates to campaigns, and who counts the votes, we will lose. Powerful interests have concluded that the real power now lies in the substructure of American government—the bureaucracy and its many linked and loyal private sector appendages. Once-vaunted institutions of capitalism, charity, science, and justice have been infiltrated and transformed into political tools.

Who are these puppeteers who seek to control our democracy? This book will show readers who they are and how to recognize them. I'll help readers recognize the pretexts they use to grow their power and the ways they pervert the institutions they claim to represent. The bad policies are now on autopilot. And it's going to take a much broader strategy to reverse the damage.

We have the tools. They're enshrined in the Constitution. A federalist system calls for shared power between the federal government and the states. It is through states that we must challenge the compromised federal system.

Introduction: Establishing Perpetual Power

Over the course of the last two Democratic administrations, the left has politically weaponized many of our most trusted institutions. The federal agencies, American health care, the whole field of scientific research, the public schools, the mainstream media, the technology sector, academia, professional organizations and unions, the entertainment industry, and even the index fund managers could all be credibly accused of serving the interests of the Democratic Party.

The 2022 midterms were touted by Democrats as a referendum on democracy—at least that was the message from the president and prominent members of his party in the months leading up to the election. At a Maryland fundraiser in August, President Joe Biden implored Democrats to vote—implying that they needed to save our democracy from the people who want to Make America Great Again (MAGA). He demonized Donald Trump's seventy-four million voters as "extreme" and intimated that supporting Trump was comparable to "semi-fascism."

"They're a threat to our very democracy," Biden claimed. "They refuse to accept the will of the people. They embrace . . . embrace political violence! This is why in this moment, those of you who love this country—Democrats, independents, mainstream Republicans—we must be stronger, more determined, and more committed to saving America than the MAGA Republicans are to destroying America."[1]

The list of prescriptions the ruling party promoted for saving democracy was long. But all of it coincidentally aligned with the list of things a party in power would need to do to perpetually stay in power.

It's the classic playbook: rachet the alarm up to eleven and use the ensuing panic to seize control. In reality, Biden's puppeteer-friendly administration had already been laying the groundwork to minimize voter control of the levers of power. If ever there was a figurehead for a puppet politician, it was this president.

There was a certain irony to Biden's messaging. The calls to action were almost all decidedly undemocratic. Think about it. To Save Our Democracy, we just need to change all the rules to ensure the ruling party can govern unobstructed by pesky voters, checks on power, or partisan minority voices. But those changes don't save democracy. They save Democratic majorities. None of these policy prescriptions are on the agenda when Democrats find themselves deep in the minority.

The Problem with the Word *Democracy*

By its own definition, China is a democracy. That's what the government claimed in a December 2021 white paper released in response to the authoritarian regime's exclusion from the U.S.-sponsored 2021 Summit for Democracy. The Chinese Communist Party (CCP), which governs the world's most populous nation, made this audacious claim attempting to soften and legitimize China as another kind of democracy. They called it "democracy with Chinese characteristics."[2]

Among those characteristics of Chinese democracy are censorship, civil rights violations, religious crackdowns, and one-party rule. Basically, it's a system that stacks the deck in favor of the ruling party. Hardly a democracy. If I ever travel to Hong Kong again, I could possibly be arrested under the terms of China's national security law for simply having criticized the CCP.[3]

China doesn't even hold a federal election. Having removed term limits from China's constitution, President Xi Jinping can presumably serve for life, never having to answer to his voters.[4] China is surely the furthest thing from a democracy as it is normally defined. It lacks key characteristics of democracy as defined by the United Nations.[5] It has been a one-party state for seventy years, lacks the signature separation of powers that characterize democratic governments, has no independent judiciary or protections for speech and expression, and holds only periodic elections. Even local elections lack the competitive opposition candidates that are typical of Western democracies. But that doesn't stop China's ruling elite from appropriating the term.

Likewise, Vladimir Putin rose to power in 2000 with the promise of what he called "managed democracy" in Russia. It was a promise of power to the people, except when authoritarianism would better solve a problem. The Carnegie Endowment for International Peace describes managed democracy as a system where "Putin has replaced the institutions outlined in the constitution with those of his own design." In Russia, it "controls society while providing the appearance of democracy."[6] What if an American ruling party could do something similar? What if they already have?

Democracy with Progressive Characteristics

Insulated from the volatility of frequent electoral pendulum swings, the permanent government here in America—with its ancillary private support structure—makes the consequential decisions while the elected lawmakers become mere figureheads. Power is shifted from the state and local level to the federal level, from Congress to the bureaucracy, and in some cases from the bureaucracy to partisan outside institutions.

It's a "heads I win, tails you lose" form of "democracy" in which elections, by design, will eventually become largely irrelevant. The permanent government, with the assistance of loyal interest groups, will write the rules. They will decide who must play by those rules.

Turning over his government to partisan puppeteers may be President Biden's lasting legacy. It's one in which financial institutions compel corporate investment in Democratic-driven climate schemes. It's a legacy of schools that become political indoctrination centers and data-gathering services. It's a story of nonprofits and federal agencies that become get-out-the-vote operations, of unions and professional associations that set public policy, regulators that usurp the role of elected officials, and tech companies that become the government's proxy speech censors. But it's all dressed up as the only possible solution to problems many agree are urgent.

No longer is the A Team in charge. The traditional three-ring government, with its checks and balances, separation of powers, public disclosure requirements, and election-day accountability, is slowly being marginalized.

The B Team

The transition from a true representative republic to a fake democracy starts with the growth and empowerment of the federal bureaucracy.

I recall an urban legend during my time in Congress that rings all too true. As the story goes, a congressman set up a meeting with a Senate-confirmed cabinet secretary to answer his questions—a process with which I am very familiar. But when the congressman arrived at the office of the secretary, to the lawmaker's chagrin, he found the secretary absent and senior staff prepared to take the meeting. The congressman, frustrated and offended that he was relegated to meet with staff rather than the high-profile secretary, expressed disappointment. He told the staff it was unacceptable for the secretary to skip a meeting specifically booked for the two of them. He didn't want to meet with the staff. He wanted to meet with the one in charge. He thought it was a waste of his time to meet with the B Team.

He expressed his irritation until one of the senior staff finally spoke up and told the congressman the audacious reality. "It's true—we are the B Team," he reportedly said. "You are meeting with the right people. We 'B' here before you, we 'B' here after you, and we 'B' the ones to make the decisions. If something is going to get done, we 'B' the ones to decide, and we 'B' the ones to do it. We will give the secretary your regards."

When I wrote *The Deep State*, I thought of the B Team largely as federal bureaucrats. And they are that. They exist at every level of government—gatekeepers, decision makers, people who write the fine print. Many times, they design the studies, choose the consultants, fund the research, highlight the data they want seen, and frame the argument before your elected official or cabinet appointee ever dives into an issue. They are professionals who wield a lot of power and a lot of expertise.

But the B Team is more than that. Especially in today's political environment. They are also the subsidiary institutions who vie for lucrative contracts, offer lavish postgovernment "revolving-door" positions to those bureaucrats who have served them well, and otherwise benefit from a big-government agenda. The whole woke-industrial complex works together to hijack the power of government to reward allies and penalize opponents, as this book will show.

For us as individual Americans, the difference between A Team governance and B Team governance is stark. While our elected officials get more power by complying with the will of the electorate, the B Team gets more power by growing government. They get power by choosing which outside vendors will get government contracts, creating relationships with those vendors, and potentially later being hired by them. The B Team within government gets more power by insidiously annexing power from state and local government (the Department of Education is a case in point[7]). For them, federal power is the best kind of power.

Voters get to hold accountable only three out of the 535 members of Congress—their two U.S. senators and one U.S. House member. The rest generally won't even take a meeting with someone outside their district. They are lucky to make time to meet with a few of the hundreds of thousands (and in some cases millions) of people they officially represent. Your ability to influence an act of Congress is much less potent than your ability to influence your city council, school board, state legislature, or even your governor. The B Team prefers it that way.

Government by the B Team is inevitable as power becomes more centralized at the federal level. It's not new. It's not even partisan. But what is new is the deliberate effort by progressive lawmakers to delegate their authority to the B Team, structuring government programs in ways that insulate those programs from public influence.

Yet this is how prominent Democrats propose to "Save Our Democracy"—by stifling the power of the A Team in favor of a B Team approach that is, in many ways, insulated from popular pushback—aka democracy.

Supreme Court justice Neil Gorsuch, in his dissenting opinion on Occupational Safety and Health Administration (OSHA) mandates in 2021, wrote, "If Congress could hand off all of its legislative powers to unelected agency officials, it would 'dash the whole scheme' of our Constitution and enable intrusions into the private lives and freedoms of Americans by bare edict rather than only with the consent of their elected representatives."[8]

Why the B Team Agenda Is a Leftist Agenda

While the growth and empowerment of the B Team was a bipartisan creation, there is good reason to focus special attention on the left. Republican administrations have stepped on the toes of blue state governments on issues like federal gun rights legislation, but that is comparatively rare. The right tends to champion state and local government over federal solutions. In this book we specifically scrutinize what's happening on the left side of the aisle, for three reasons:

1. **The left prioritizes federal power.** First, leftist elected officials overtly push for more decisions to be made at the federal level, ensuring that the public has less control over the way they are governed. When it comes to elections, health care, resource extraction, gun restrictions, abortion, or K–12 education, the left largely supports a top-down, one-size-fits-all approach. They share an antipathy to the kind of state government for which the Constitution, except in the case of very specific enumerated powers, explicitly calls.

2. **Insulating government from the people.** In addition to their big-government agenda, as this book will show, left-wing elected officials are intentionally creating programs designed to be untouchable by future Congresses. That means the government becomes less responsive to the people, less accountable, and less representative and democratic.

3. **Bureaucratic bias.** The third reason the left requires special scrutiny in these matters is that the federal government bureaucracy is largely populated with progressives.

During the Obama and Trump administrations, this became painfully obvious. We watched a weaponized Internal Revenue Service (IRS) go after conservative groups. We saw a politicized FBI vow to "stop Donald Trump" with a hoax investigation. And we later learned from whistleblowers that the FBI warned agents not to investigate the damning material on the Hunter Biden laptop ahead of the 2020 election.[9] House investigations in the 118th Congress will likely uncover more about FBI efforts to control the Biden laptop narrative. During my service on the House Oversight Committee, I routinely heard from federal employee whistleblowers complaining of hidden efforts to screen out conservative job applicants, silence conservative perspectives, or fire known conservative employees.

That's not to say that Republican presidents might not be subject to a similar temptation, but it's a tool that hasn't been available to a Republican president by virtue of the bureaucracy's overwhelming left-leaning partisan bias. Technically, federal employees are barred by the Hatch Act from raising money for political campaigns. But they can donate. And in 2016, 95 percent of contributions by federal employees from fourteen agencies analyzed in the presidential race went to Hillary Clinton.[10] Their unions demonstrate a similar lopsided partisanship. For example, in the two years preceding the 2022 midterms, the National Treasury Employees Union PAC, which represents IRS employees, sent almost 99 percent of federal candidate donations to Democrats, and just over 1 percent to Republicans.[11] These are the people who decide which Americans get audited, which research gets funded, which narratives social media companies will be asked to suppress, and which nonprofits get lucrative government contracts.

The pandemic was a perfect demonstration of how this new style of puppeteer-managed democracy is designed to work. As I wrote in my last book, the left spent two years using public health as a pretext for usurping power. They used the pandemic to shut down the economy and the schools, to empower loyal allies at the teachers unions, to adopt voting practices for partisan advantage, to punish dissent, and to censor scientific truths they feared would threaten their grip on power. And they did it all with a Republican president.

Though there are many pretexts being used to justify shifting power away from voters and toward a weaponized bureaucracy, we'll look at the three biggest ones in this book.

Social justice, in which subgroups of Americans are turned against each other in a competition for victimhood, is overused as a pretext for policies that reward and privilege loyal Democratic constituencies. It has become the justification for double standards that undermine equality and justice.

National security, which the left once derided, is becoming an important pretext for silencing dissent. This pretext is used to justify mass surveillance and to paint political opponents with a domestic terrorist brush.

But the most valuable pretext to date is climate change, which has enabled the ruling class to divert the flow of capital out of the productive economy and into their own pet projects and institutions. This powerful pretext allows globalist puppeteers to exert unprecedented control over the markets. It destroys pluralism and ideological diversity by bifurcating the economy into companies that comply with the prevailing agenda and companies that don't. For the noncompliant, access to markets and capital will be narrowed.

PART I

The Pretext of Climate Change

CHAPTER 1

America's New Social Credit System

magine trying to buy a train ticket and being rejected because you were, unbeknownst to you, added to a government "untrustworthy" list. It sounds crazy, but that's what has been happening in China since the implementation of the country's social credit system.

One of the CCP's novel initiatives for controlling its 1.4-billion-member "democracy with Chinese characteristics" is the evolving social credit system. Using extensive surveillance and data-gathering tools, the CCP collects vast amounts of information that enables various levels of government to reward and penalize corporate and individual behavior. Using a system that assigns "personal trustworthiness points," the program ranks both businesses and citizens in order to maintain social control.[1]

Though it appears to be patterned after the credit scores used in our American financial system, the Chinese version is much more sinister. It's not just about assessing creditworthiness and financial risk. It's about control. In China, the social credit score determines who can travel and at what comfort level, who can borrow money, and who can have fast internet.[2] The social credit system seeks to regulate all sorts of everyday behaviors—the sorts of things we consider well outside the purview of centralized control. And the consequence for these small infractions is hugely disproportionate. People who don't visit their parents on a regular basis, who jaywalk, who walk their dog without a leash, or who cheat in online video games could find their children banned from higher education, their names added to a blacklist for certain jobs, or their companies targeted for more audits.[3]

Couldn't happen here, right? Think again. Rather than exporting democratic governing principles to China, the United States appears to be importing elements of China's top-down perversion of democracy to American shores. A disturbingly similar "social credit" system is coming to a financial institution near you if the American left gets its way. But they don't call it a social credit score.

Here in America, the scoring system has started in the financial sector, where we call it an ESG (environmental, social, and governance) score. Entities seeking investment dollars—think states, municipalities, and companies—are now scored by ratings companies for their compliance with certain political dogma. It's sometimes referred to by the feel-good moniker of "sustainable investing." These ESG ratings haven't morphed into personal credit scores . . . yet. But don't think they aren't talking about it. Nonetheless, what we're seeing in the financial world borrows heavily from the principles underpinning China's social credit scores.

Instead of a system imposed by government, this version is controlled by incredibly powerful private actors. It may seem like it's just capitalism in action at first, but the reality is the organizations imposing ESG scores are profoundly hostile to a healthy competitive market. We'll talk about the ringleaders in the next chapter. But for now, let's explain the system.

By implementing the ESG standard, the green activist movement seeks to fundamentally alter the relationship between businesses and shareholders. ESG alters the underlying criteria by which businesses—and eventually consumers—are evaluated by investors. Rather than using standard metrics like profitability, demand, or quality of goods and services, scores are calculated based on a company's responsiveness to the requisite progressive cause of the day—whether it be climate change or social justice. ESG metrics are conveniently flexible, shifting to accommodate what Tesla CEO Elon Musk popularized as "The Current Thing."[4] Companies aren't expected to invest in mitigation for every potential immediate catastrophic contingency, but they must invest in preventing one specific prediction for the distant future—climate change.

Indeed, one writer calls ESG a covert war on fossil fuels. In his op-ed for the *Hill*, Paul Kupiec predicted that the abuses have only just begun. "Once a voluntary movement that prioritized investment in companies that adopt policies and practices that promote the progressive left's environment, labor and human rights causes, ESG investing is about to become a regulatory tool they will use to achieve specific objectives."[5] And all of this is accomplished without the help of elected officials.

Though this ESG score is ostensibly about justice, former House Speaker Newt Gingrich surmises it is really about power.[6] It's a way to shut off access to credit and services for the politically noncompliant, redirect capital to more politically favored industries, and position progressive political priorities as global consensus.

But the consensus is not real.

The Great Reset

The so-called environmental, social, and governance rating is marketed as a service to help people who want to direct their investments toward "socially responsible" companies. In reality, it is a tool that conflates what is "socially responsible" with what is politically progressive. Hence ESG scores reward those who overtly demonstrate obeisance to progressive political goals and cripple those who don't without politicians ever having to get their hands dirty.

Referred to as "the Great Reset" by German economist Klaus Schwab of the World Economic Forum, the implementation of this system sounds like a conspiracy theory. But it isn't. According to Schwab it is designed to "revamp all aspects of our societies and economies, from education to social contracts and working conditions."[7]

Some great books have been written about this plan that are worth spending time to read. But for our purposes, we just need to understand how activists use climate change as a pretext to police the private sector, crippling free trade with onerous progressive policy checklists.[8]

The *E* in ESG relates to all things environmental, with an emphasis on climate risk. For example, companies that demonstrate plans for transitioning their business to net-zero carbon emissions score better. The result is that company decisions are driven less by economics and more by the impact on the company's ESG score. Companies are rewarded for implementing solar panels or wind energy into building designs. However, long-term environmental damage from nonrecyclable solar panels and windmills or depleting the global supply of rare earth minerals for electric car batteries are not part of the calculus.[9]

There is no standard list of metrics, leaving rating agencies to choose their own.[10] Companies wishing to score well with large credit rating agencies may disclose factors such as the company's energy efficiency, carbon footprint, greenhouse gas emissions, biodiversity, climate change mitigation, pollution mitigation, waste management practices, or water usage.

In a practical sense, what this means is that companies who can afford to go green get a competitive step up. And for "green," substitute "whatever environmental goals progressives deem good." Organizations that naturally don't produce greenhouse gases—tech companies like Facebook, for instance—easily get a good score. But for critical sectors of the economy like energy, achieving the same result would require significant sacrifices.

Those sacrifices are ultimately borne by society. Unreliable electric grids are one primary example of this phenomenon. Texas invested heavily in wind and solar energy. When snow fell across the state in 2021, power went out just when it was needed most. The wind stopped blowing. Clouds covered the sky. The demand for energy skyrocketed, exceeding the supply, and the grid gave out. The political pressure to adopt renewable energy at the expense of cheap, reliable, and plentiful fossil fuels predates the almost ubiquitous use of ESG scores today. Those promoting the adoption of these scores rarely deal with the messy results. The Texas citizens had to bear that cost.[11]

There are also social milestones to meet ESG standards. The *S* in ESG includes social justice factors. Disclosures may include labor standards, wages and benefits, workplace and board diversity, racial justice training programs, pay equity, and human rights. If you institute a White Fragility workshop, that could improve your score with the companies who provide ESG scores to the investment community. But these factors, too, are selective. One analysis of ESG metrics identified 1,700 different social metrics among just twelve ratings frameworks.[12]

Finally, the *G* stands for governance and addresses traditional shareholder activist items like executive compensation and board independence. However, new measures include board diversity, corporate political contributions, and sustainability initiatives.[13] Interestingly, board diversity does not mean ideological diversity—the kind that has merit and is valuable for companies. Nor does it mean inclusion of a military veteran. Perhaps too many of them lean conservative. Rather, the required diversity relates to gender, race, and sexual orientation, demographic data points that do little for shareholder value.

Shareholder activists push companies to disclose contributions in the name of "transparency." They may also say contributing to the wrong causes could create reputational risk. This is all done in an effort to get companies to disclose what organizations they support. If the causes are right of center, then the activists put pressure on the company to stop supporting them. We've seen this script play out when advertisers are attacked for supporting shows the left hates. It's a classic bullying tactic designed to harm those with different views.

The governance criteria can be used to privilege companies whose boards have the most skin colors and the broadest range of gender identities, those who fund leftist causes, and those who adopt hiring quotas for marginalized groups. Notice that none of this has to do with America's traditional meritocracy. No longer are we rewarding the best and the brightest. We are now implementing criteria that reward discrimination and pander to victimhood, rather than performance and achievement.

As the once-voluntary ESG standards become more and more coercive, they look less and less like free market capitalism. Already American companies are being scored to help investors identify "sustainable" institutions.[14] Of course, that means other companies are on the ESG naughty list. You would never guess which industries! For example, in December 2021, Moody's, a credit scoring and research corporation, released new ESG scores that "have an overall negative credit impact on most automakers, oil & gas companies, and utilities, reflecting high carbon transition risks in these sectors."[15] Despite the fact that electric vehicles are not a practical alternative to trucks, jets, and heavy equipment used in much of American industry, or that intermittent renewable power generation is currently incapable of supporting baseload power supply, companies dependent on those technologies would receive low ESG scores, and thus pay a higher cost for capital than they have historically paid.

Using a scale of zero to one hundred, the scale weighs compliance with selective goals to assess ratings. The left would like us to think that these analyses are just objective, fair assessments of virtue. But in an analysis of ESG metrics, the Competitive Enterprise Institute pointed out a host of metrics that "simply assume that the progressive policy positions called for are universally desirable," even though many of those goals are "highly controversial and far from universally accepted." For example, CEI gives positive results to companies with employer-sponsored abortion coverage and restrictions on promising energy investments like nuclear power that many believe are the key to a low-carbon future.[16]

When the Russian invasion of Ukraine led to sanctions on Russian energy, the impact of U.S. investors allocating capital based on ESG scores suddenly became painfully evident as American energy companies scrambled to meet the need. Kathleen Sgamma, president of Western Energy Alliance, explained one reason American energy companies couldn't scale up to quickly meet the demand: "We can't get capital because they're putting so much pressure on banks not to lend to us in the name of climate change."[17]

But once Europe was cut off from Russian energy supplies, ESG and the global climate agenda were about to hit two critical bumps in the road. One would come from nations that embraced the idea. The other would come from states that did not.

Europe Can't Heat Homes with Good ESG Scores

Germany was on track to become the first industrialized nation to wean itself off fossil fuels, with an ambitious plan to abandon nuclear power by 2022 and coal power by 2038.[18] Even this zealous goal was criticized by environmental groups as insufficient to meet the demands of the 2015 Paris Climate Accords.

The great green utopia was on the verge of realization. Europe had rid itself of all that icky fossil, nuclear, and coal. What could go wrong?

This dream world shattered with the Russian invasion of Ukraine in early 2022. The European sanctions against the Putin government led Russia to turn off the natural gas pipelines that had previously heated German homes and shielded European residents from the real costs of renewable power dependency. This must have come as a shock to readers of mainstream American news publications, which a few years earlier assured readers that Germany's dependence on Russia was exaggerated.

As energy prices climbed throughout Europe, clips of the German delegation to the United Nations famously laughing during a 2018 Trump speech circulated within right-wing media outlets. Trump warned against Germany's dependence on Russia for such a critical resource as natural gas to smirks and mockery from German delegates. "Reliance on a single foreign supplier can leave a nation vulnerable to extortion and intimidation," he said. "Germany will become totally dependent on Russian energy if it does not immediately change course."[19]

At the time, the collective eye roll from fact checkers at American media outlets had been hard to miss. Quick to reject Trump's claims, they fixated on the phrase "totally dependent" to dismiss Trump's legitimate (some might say prophetic) concerns. CNBC wrote, "Natural gas is just one of the fuels that powers Germany's industry, households, power plants and vehicles. While natural gas plays a significant role in fueling Germany—especially in heating German homes—it's hardly the dominant fuel source."[20] PBS made a similar point, claiming Germans had moved to diversify their sources and supply. "Germany's energy comes from a diverse mix of oil, coal and renewables. Less than one fifth of the country's power is powered by natural gas; at the moment, just 9 percent of the country's power is generated by Russian gas," PBS reported in 2018.[21]

No doubt Donald Trump is a man who speaks in superlatives—the best, the greatest, the most! But debunking his use of superlatives, as the media loved to do, is not debunking the point of the statement. And in this case, Trump was absolutely right. Germany's dependence on Russia for natural gas made the country vulnerable. As prices doubled, then doubled again after Russia shut down the Nord Stream 2 pipeline, one German executive warned, "I fear a gradual deindustrialization of the German economy."[22]

Despite the desire of European nations to stick to their climate goals, after Russia's invasion the limitations of renewable energy were laid bare. Even the true believers had to question precisely where this agenda was taking the world.

The State Battleground

Meanwhile, as 2022 went on, state elected officials were getting a taste of where ESG might lead here at home. An unlikely but promising battlefield had begun to form. As inflation raged and gas prices hit historic highs in the early summer, Fox News personality Tucker Carlson introduced a new kind of warrior in the battle against ESG. Though not the first state treasurer to recognize the ESG threat to our capital markets, Marlo Oaks is representative of many others who would join the ranks of a growing movement to push back.

The statewide office of treasurer doesn't generally spark a lot of political controversy. Treasurer races tend to be sleepy affairs for a job many voters don't completely understand. America's fifty state treasurers manage the investment funds, issue state debt, and move cash to and from state entities. It's a job focused on money and has traditionally been more technical than political.

On this night, Carlson introduced Utah state treasurer Marlo Oaks, who had served less than a year in his new role. But Oaks had a lot to say about ESG. "Today's inflation really starts with ESG," Oaks told Carlson. He noted that gas prices were high because there simply wasn't enough supply to meet demand. "The reason that we don't have enough supply in this country, one reason why, is that we don't have enough capital going into oil and gas projects."

In 2015, he said, there were fifty-nine private institutional investment funds that raised $46.6 billion for oil and gas projects from investors globally. Six years later, in 2021, only $4.6 billion was raised in eleven funds for oil and gas projects from these same kinds of institutional investors. This represented a drop of more than 90 percent at a time of improving economics for oil and gas. "The only explanation that makes sense is ESG," he concluded, blaming an active drive to cut off capital to the fossil fuel industry.[23]

When the former institutional investment manager threw his hat in the ring to fill a midterm vacancy for the office of Utah state treasurer in May 2021, he never imagined he would be stepping into ground zero of the war on capitalism. What is usually a low-profile, mundane, nonpolitical office, the Utah treasurer role had become the unwitting center of a global initiative.

Having spent his career in investment management, Oaks knew about sustainable investing. But it wasn't until he took office that he learned how the concept had morphed into something much more duplicitous and aggressive. Sustainable investing had evolved into a tool that converts financial institutions into political ones.

Foundational principles of fiduciary responsibility and shareholder primacy were being upended in favor of ideological policy objectives. As a new state treasurer, Oaks realized he was in a unique position to do something about it.

"People told me ESG is too far engrained in the system," he said. But Oaks knew enough investors in the market to doubt the inevitably of this transformation. He knew them to be independent thinkers. "ESG felt like a European system designed to force compliance," he said. "I knew it was not universally accepted and I knew the states would have to stand up against it." Oaks believed the threats in the private sector were real. People's livelihoods were threatened. For him, the pushback had to happen now. "We cannot wait for this to spread. It is like cancer. It must be eradicated or it will kill the patient."

State treasurers play a pivotal role in the success or failure of capitalism in their states. And the Democratic Party knows it. In a road map from ahead of the 2022 election cycle, the Democratic Treasurers Association laid out the agenda for leveraging state investment and retirement funds to help promote and pay for leftist policy objectives:

> *State Treasurers have the power to exert force nationally because they oversee trillions of dollars and have a direct line to Wall Street, Main Street, and into corporate boardrooms. State Treasurers' power will endure no matter which party controls Congress and the White House. No matter what happens in November, they will have the ability to ensure that climate risk is addressed, racial inequity and gender bias is confronted, and to protect workers and small businesses.*

In a list of reasons America needs Democrats in state treasurer roles, the very first bullet point (and presumably their highest priority) was to "instigate shareholder activism . . . to address climate risk, workplace bias, and other environmental, social, and governance (ESG) issues."[24]

When money is weaponized for power and political agendas, the treasurer's office suddenly takes on new importance. State financial officers are more important than ever. Even the *Washington Post* recognized the need to keep politics out of pension investing when they endorsed Maryland's Republican candidate for comptroller, noting his "reluctance to use the pension fund as an ideological tool."[25]

Never has it been considered the primary job of a state treasurer to confront "gender bias," or "ensure climate risk is addressed," as described by the Democratic Treasurers Association.[26] They have a more important role: they are the gatekeepers to billions of dollars in state, municipal, and pension funds. Their real job is to maximize those investments for taxpayers and plan participants and to raise money through state-issued bonds.

Oaks is the kind of person institutions pay to oversee large portfolios designed to meet critical investment objectives. He could see ESG had evolved into a mechanism that was incompatible with free markets. ESG metrics are a way for global elites to set the goals, essentially dictating what the economy will produce.[27]

ESG standards assume that everyone agrees on the causes, solutions, trade-offs, and timeline of a climate apocalypse. They don't. While many Americans support sustainable investments, their support drops as they become more aware of the trade-offs. A full 71 percent of registered voters tell pollsters they are concerned about the climate. That part isn't controversial. But 35 percent say they would not be willing to spend any of their own money to reduce the impact of climate change. Just 17 percent say it would be worth between $1 and $10 a month to them.[28] How many are ready to give up plastics, meat, cars, or pension value? How many would be willing to live a nineteenth-century lifestyle to reach net-zero carbon emissions by 2050? No one asked them. The climate conversation is a one-way discussion about risks without addressing the costs and sacrifices required to achieve the only discussed solution—abandoning traditional energy.

"Fundamentally, this is completely anti-American," Oaks observed, noting that "the ESG system threatens to substitute our pluralistic institutions like the financial markets where diverse views about the future result in buying and selling of the same security on any given day, for centralized control." As a fiduciary, he recognized that investment managers pursuing political agendas were violating their fiduciary obligation to the state.

BlackRock, the largest investment management company in the world, created a stewardship group that engages with companies to adopt political ESG policies. "When a manager changes their investment style they are often fired for 'style drift.' We hire managers whom we can trust will manage our assets in the way we are required to by law as fiduciaries," Oaks explained. "BlackRock changed and has adopted an agenda that goes beyond a traditional fiduciary mandate."

Oaks quickly banished BlackRock from the state's investment portfolio on the basis that the firm was pursuing a dual mandate, elevating political goals to the same level as investment returns.

Oaks was an unlikely warrior in this battle. Though his wife, Elaine, had long been engaged in local politics, he didn't consider it his "thing." During the 2008 recession, Oaks had very successfully minimized market losses for Farmers Insurance Group in Los Angeles before going on to work as director of investments for Utah's Intermountain Healthcare and later Crewe Capital. When the unexpected vacancy for state treasurer popped up in the summer of 2021, Elaine urged her husband to consider applying. His background easily qualified him to manage the state's $27 billion in investment funds, which included a short-term portfolio in which more than 750 municipal entities across the state invest.

Prior to 2021, the march toward sustainable investing had seemed benign. When the administration changed, Oaks noted it was like a light switch was flipped. The largest banks in the United States signed on to net-zero climate pledges in 2021. Shareholder activists became more aggressive in submitting political ESG proposals for shareholder votes. And the largest investment managers, using their sustainability or stewardship groups, engaged with more companies to change them from the inside.

It was just a way to support sustainable growth and fund the transition to cleaner energy. There had been little pushback. But as Europe's access to cheap fossil fuels came under threat, the consequences of abandoning reliable energy came into focus. Was it better to save the world from theoretical climate destruction in the distant future or to heat homes through the approaching winter?

Sustainable investing was the tip of the iceberg. The reality of the Great Reset of the world economy was not just about promoting a policy agenda. It was a threat to American pluralism. Taken to its logical end, the ESG movement's inevitable, and perhaps intended, result would be one common, progressive global agenda with which all businesses must comply or be canceled. The primary pretexts for this transition are climate change and social justice. But the real result would likely be political tyranny. "ESG is a pernicious strategy," wrote former vice president Mike Pence, "because it allows the left to accomplish what it could never hope to achieve at the ballot box or through competition in the free market."[29]

It's a transition that is being facilitated on two fronts: first in the private sector, where compliance is made to appear voluntary and popular, and within the federal bureaucracy, where every federal agency is being galvanized to coerce participation. The private sector offers the carrot. Then the public sector comes in with the stick. Asset management firms pressure and puppeteer public companies on the stock market while credit rating agencies exert pressure against the bond markets. On the government side, regulatory frameworks are written and enforced by unelected bureaucrats while major policy is driven by political ideologues representing the interests of global elites. None of these actors ever has to answer to a voter.

CHAPTER 2

Farewell Free Markets, Hello Stakeholder Capitalism

Corporate America has a long history of donating to political campaigns, even if most try to remain publicly neutral. America's motto of *E Pluribus Unum*—"Out of many, one"—has been one of its greatest strengths. The Supreme Court has affirmed that corporations can take political positions—and they have.[1] This type of participation in elections is free speech. But what's begun to happen over the last few years doesn't look like free speech at all.

Never before have corporations been expected—even compelled—to become the political vehicle for one universal ideology. In the past, they may have donated to politicians, hired lobbyists, and tried to influence policies. But now public companies have become the target of organizations that want to compel change using the corporation as the vessel. The corporations have become quasi-political entities themselves—and not always by choice.

Once again, it's not the progressive elected officials stepping in to control business. It doesn't have to be. Progressive politicians have an incredibly powerful middleman: asset managers. These are the folks we hire to grow our wealth. They make investment decisions for our pensions, our retirement funds, and for government and institutional investments. They have one goal: to maximize the value of an investment portfolio. At least, that's how it used to work. Not so much anymore. Politics is increasingly displacing profit as the top priority.

The biggest activist managers are passive. The portfolio of companies in which they invest is set by the index composition of companies. Instead, what they do is create separate Stewardship or Sustainability groups that engage with the companies in which they invest and tell them how to behave. As a result, profits take a backseat to politics.

Selling American voters on sacrificing their pension returns to pay for climate change would be a heavy lift if it had to be done legislatively. Penalizing them for driving cars, cooling their homes, consuming meat, working in disfavored (but crucial) industries, or funding police is likewise a tough sell. Politicians could lose elections over that. The left could lose power. Not to mention that controlling market behaviors to this extent is incompatible with American capitalism.

Instead of abandoning capitalism, the left has tried a different strategy. They simply take over the institutions. They redefine capitalism to mean the opposite of what it is. Free markets are out. Stakeholder capitalism is in. Since Americans rejected the mammoth spending of the Build Back Better plan, the social reengineering of the Green New Deal, and the global fiscal obligations of the Paris Climate Accords, the left has gotten more creative—and more deceptive.

The story of what's happening behind the doors of America's boardrooms can be hard to sniff out. Few want to risk offending their largest shareholders by disclosing what's happening—not on the record anyway. Now it's not enough to acknowledge that the climate is changing or to encourage investing in clean energy. Corporations are under intense pressure from asset managers to shun fossil fuels and fund selective kinds of renewable energy.

Likewise, it's not enough to have a socioeconomically and ideologically diverse board of directors. Companies must define diversity the way the left defines it—by skin color, gender identity, or certain nationalities that comprise Democratic voting blocs. (Asian

Americans, for example, are considered by *White Fragility* author Robin DiAngelo to be "white-adjacent.")[2] Companies that depart from the enforced orthodoxy will suffer consequences.

What's crazy is that you probably already know this is happening, but it likely just seems to be activists providing healthy "accountability" for big business. Instead, it's more like a shakedown.

Corporate intimidation by shareholder activists with support from the largest asset managers like Vanguard, State Street, and, of course, BlackRock creates leverages against management and boards to adopt policies that harm shareholder value. Corporations adopt these counterproductive policies because they could lose control of their board otherwise.

Using Stewardship or Sustainability groups, large asset managers, acting as a company's largest shareholder, pressure corporations to adopt the leftist agenda of ESG.

"They could single-handedly end our company if they wanted to," a senior executive at a multibillion-dollar retailer told me on the condition of anonymity. Though his company caters to a more conservative market, they've had to be extremely progressive when it comes to ESG and climate disclosures.

"If [our largest shareholder] says you guys better clean up your act and be more diverse, we will write an ESG report," he told me. "We'll show you all the touchy-feely things we do to make the world greener and our organization more diverse. For example—we are releasing this many pounds of CO_2, using this much water, here is our strategy to get to net zero by 2050."

He told me these initiatives require a lot of expense and staff time from his company that would almost certainly be better spent innovating. He shrugs and tells me, "they say we should do it, so we do it. We never say that in our public messaging. We claim it's because it's good for the climate. The real reason we do this stuff is because our largest shareholder says so."

This kind of intimidation is not what the public thinks of when they hear about sustainable investing. The whole sales pitch is that it's voluntary and popular. The idea of allowing investors to put their money where their values are sounds like the epitome of free market capitalism. Those who prioritize decarbonization can support companies and funds that share their goal. Corporate disclosures are pitched as a tool to help investors make informed decisions to align their investments with their values. The free market determines the flow of capital. It all sounds very American.

But it's not.

The market is no longer free when multimillion-dollar companies are told they cannot provide capital to certain industries. "Woke capitalists" have rigged the game. Leveraging other people's investment dollars in large companies that have the ability to vote the shares of passive investors, they decide the role fossil fuels will play in our economy. They set the targets companies are told to reach—currently the push to reach "net zero greenhouse gas emissions by 2050."[3] Americans never voted for that.

The rules are being made, not by any democratic process, but by whomever has the most money. They have the power to decide who fails and who succeeds, who grows and who gets cut off—regardless of what the market wants.

Theoretically, someone who owns stock in a company like Exxon-Mobil gets to vote for members of the company's governing board. They get to vote on proposed shareholder resolutions that bind the company to pursue specific objectives—presumably objectives that maximize profits and manage risk.

But most people don't buy individual stocks. They buy index funds that are invested in hundreds of different companies. It would be all but impossible for individual investors to vote all of those shares. Consequently, a shareholder whose retirement accounts are managed by BlackRock must depend on BlackRock's Investment Stewardship group to vote their shares. It is assumed those votes are cast in the best interest of the shareholder. But what happened at ExxonMobil raises serious questions about the willingness of woke asset managers to vote the interests of their clients.

Three of the largest fund managers in America—BlackRock, Vanguard, and State Street—manage a combined total of $15 trillion in assets, an amount that is more than three-quarters the size of the whole United States economy. They exert an immeasurable amount of influence over the companies in which they hold shares.

BlackRock alone has an ownership stake of at least 5 percent in 97.5 percent of S&P 500 companies.[4] Each of those companies must know BlackRock can make or break them if they don't demonstrate support for leftist policy goals.

Even more problematic is the common ownership of so many competitors in a single market. Capitalism is by definition pluralistic— many different competitors trying different approaches and innovating in different ways. But when "institutional investors own 80 percent of all stock in the S&P 500," it's not unusual for one firm like BlackRock to be the largest shareholder in most of an industry's largest firms.[5] This gives asset managers unprecedented control of the market. They are also the largest shareholders of each other's stock (with the exception of Vanguard, since they don't have publicly traded stock).

BlackRock has been particularly outspoken in its left-wing politics. Displacing the working men and women who nominally set policy in this country through elected representatives is a point of pride for them.

Ironically, when the Supreme Court ruled in the 2010 *Citizens United v. Federal Election Commission* case that limiting "independent political spending" from corporations was a violation of First Amendment free speech rights, the left was aghast. The Brennan Center for Justice, a progressive think tank, called it a "blow to democracy."[6] In a report five years after the ruling, they bemoaned the fact that "a tiny sliver of Americans now wield more power than at any time since Watergate."[7] A Salon headline almost a decade later still claimed the case "broke American democracy."[8]

These headlines seem ironic at present given the extent to which an even tinier "sliver" of woke capitalists now control our system from within, virtually forgoing the whole democratic election process to wield their power behind the scenes.

Now, instead of thousands of companies underwriting political campaigns, we have a few big players directing that spending to a uniform policy agenda. And the penalties for straying from the popular dogma are growing. Few on the left seem concerned that large investment managers are now leveraging raw market power to force compliance from companies beholden to their goodwill.

Legislating from the Boardroom

The activist takeover has had concrete, deleterious effects on the market. It's tempting to blame bad progressive policy for economic crises, but far more influential is the corporate activism that the rhetoric from progressives inspires.

In a baffling June 2022 letter to American oil producers, President Biden demanded that companies like ExxonMobil "provide the secretary with an explanation of any reduction in your refining capacity since 2020."[9] This is a question asked by *Joe Biden*, who in 2019 promised, "I guarantee you. We're going to end fossil fuel," and yet now seemed oblivious to the conditions created by his own words.[10]

Before Biden's green regime came to power, ExxonMobil had announced in 2018 an aggressive plan to triple daily production in the Permian Basin of Texas and New Mexico and invest $2 billion in terminal and transportation expansion, a move the company said was made possible by "changes in the U.S. corporate tax rate," that is, the Trump tax cuts.[11] Had they stuck to that plan, the pain Americans were experiencing at the pumps in the lead-up to the midterm elections might not have been so acute.

But by June 2021, all of that had changed. Powerful shareholders had listened to Biden's rhetoric. Not only had the pandemic lockdowns of the previous year wreaked havoc on demand, but Exxon itself had undergone a transformation, courtesy of shareholders—or at least courtesy of their proxies. Three of the company's twelve board seats were now occupied by activist environmentalists determined to refocus the company on the long-term investment into renewable energy.[12]

It was no coincidence that the company subsequently announced a plan focused on reducing greenhouse gas emissions, not meeting the demand for its product. The new five-year plan released in 2020, which included "input from shareholders," was a step toward a fundamental rethinking of the company's business model. Exxon agreed to cut future capital spending by billions of dollars, but activists still weren't happy, calling the move "small but meaningful."[13]

Likewise, in June 2021, Chevron shareholders voted to cut emissions, defying the company's board. Royal Dutch Shell, on the same day, was forced by a Dutch court to expedite cuts to emissions, while days earlier, ConocoPhillips investors defied that company's board to force reductions in emissions.[14]

What happened between 2018 and 2020 to cause Exxon and other producers to cut production was driven by climate activists in the boardroom, with support from large fund managers like BlackRock, State Street, and Vanguard. The president of the United States railing against fossil fuels was just the tip of the iceberg. His words also had a chilling effect as they sent a message that regulatory risk was a serious issue. This uncertainty further chilled investment in the sector.

What's happening in America's corporate boardrooms seldom shows up in our news feeds, but it could have a more direct impact on our day-to-day lives than what's happening in the United States Capitol at any given time.

In Washington, D.C., the cameras are on. The votes are public. The debate is open and the lobbying is fierce. Power is checked and separated. And accountability is built in every two to six years.

But in America's boardrooms, the shareholders are passive. They vote by proxy. And the proxies, in many cases, are the fund managers, not the actual shareholders. That's exactly how ExxonMobil Corporation found itself debating whether to cut several major global oil projects in the fall of 2021, just months before Russian sanctions would create an insatiable worldwide demand for Exxon's products.[15]

A hedge fund called Engine No. 1 was behind the successful activist campaign to elect environmentalists to Exxon's board in May 2021. Though Engine No. 1 didn't control enough shares to get their candidates elected, large hedge funds and proxy advisory firms did. With support from large fund managers, the tiny activist fund shocked company management by installing two board members whose primary objective was not shareholder value, but transitioning the company away from fossil fuels.[16] They captured that third seat shortly thereafter.[17]

How did Engine No. 1 attract enough votes to install board members committed to making oil and gas investments less profitable? Likely from the proxy votes of state investment funds, pensions, and commercial index funds. Fund managers can vote those proxies however they like. And they did.

Individual investors can only vote their shares if they own company shares. If they own companies through a fund, the fund manager or fund company votes those shares on behalf of the investors. That's why the fiduciary concept is so important. Progressive activists have taken notice.

Under the guise of "empowering shareholders to change corporations for good," nonprofit advocacy group As You Sow documents on its website hundreds of shareholder resolutions being run in corporate boardrooms across the country. Through shareholder resolutions, they seek to "drive companies toward a sustainable future."[18]

What they really drive companies toward is a market that looks more like China's than America's—with a uniform progressive agenda. The number of political shareholder resolutions being run through corporate boardrooms has proliferated dramatically in the last three years. A *Proxy Preview 2022* report indicates a record 529 ESG-related shareholder resolutions were filed with publicly traded companies in 2022—a 20 percent increase over 2021's record year, according to Capital Research Center.[19]

These resolutions frequently call for the kind of disclosures one might request in a lawsuit in order to quantify damages. Not only do they demand data that is time-consuming and intrusive to collect, they want cherry-picked statistics that will help them build political narratives harmful to the company's customers and shareholders.

For example, many shareholder resolutions demand companies quantify their damage to the environment. They demand corporations disclose the effectiveness of their diversity, equity, and inclusion (DEI) programs. They require "quantitative metrics" including data by gender, race, and ethnicity—a tactic often used to gain representation for specific classes of voters that traditionally skew left, like African Americans and those who identify as LGBTQ.[20] These requests are typically one-sided, designed to inflict damage on the industry and harm on the investor.

I couldn't find one resolution that called for energy companies to quantify their positive contributions to economic growth, technological innovation, or prosperity. None called for quantifying political or ideological diversity within the company. These are cherry-picked requests designed for political use. The authors of these resolutions aren't looking to evaluate the trade-offs of energy production or to improve the quality of management to maximize profitability.

Most shareholder resolutions are unequivocally political. One that repeatedly shows up calls for a company to publish an annual report "analyzing the congruence of its political lobbying, and electioneering expenditures" against its publicly stated company values. In other words, they must commit in writing to support only certain kinds of candidates and causes.

Let's repeat that one more time: if a company decides to support a candidate who opposes "company values"—values shaped by ESG standards—that company could be subject to boycotts and harassment. Donors to California's 2008 Prop 8 gay marriage measure were subjected to harassment and intimidation, blacklisting, angry protests, and vandalism. It's not a great leap to assume that ultimately, many companies would shy away from conservative causes, even as they are incentivized to fund leftist movements.

Some resolutions demand disclosure of a company's plan to support racial justice. Presumably they aren't talking about helping Asian kids get into Harvard or Cuban immigrants into Florida. This is about the kind of racial justice that benefits left-wing voting blocs.

Other resolutions dictate how companies can use plastics or consumer packaging. Others demand compliance with greenhouse gas reduction targets as established in the Paris Climate Accords, an agreement unilaterally undertaken by the executive branch with no input from lawmakers. The American people have never had a say. One resolution called for Uber to produce a "third-party audit analyzing the adverse impact of Uber's policies and practices on the civil rights of company stakeholders." I didn't see any resolutions asking companies to disclose whether forced labor in China was part of the supply chain that produced their solar panels, despite the prevalence of that problem.[21] Coincidentally, monitoring the civil rights of marginalized Uyghurs in China produces neither profits nor votes.

Nonetheless, the disclosures that activists demand provide data that is easily weaponized against financial entities who disclose it. Disfavored industries like mining, utilities, or energy production have especially become targets of activist political groups. As of February 2022, there had been more than 1,800 climate-related lawsuits filed, 75 percent of which are in the U.S.[22]

This is what got the attention of Utah's new treasurer soon after he took office. Utah has multibillion-dollar investment funds, not even counting the state's retirement fund. And like most passive investors, Utah relies on managers who rely on proxy advisory firms to recommend how to vote Utah's shares in the boardroom. A police officer may own shares of a plastics manufacturer through her state retirement plan, but her shares may be used to vote for a resolution that will make the company less profitable and reduce the return on her investment. Essentially, her own money is being used against her.

"Unlike George Soros, who uses $10 trillion of his own money," Oaks told me, BlackRock CEO "Larry Fink uses $10 trillion of other people's money." Indeed, BlackRock used its proxy voting power to oppose the election of eight hundred company directors in 2021.[23] Companies have a strong incentive to stay on BlackRock's good side or else risk a hostile takeover of their board.

Those shareholder resolutions are one more end run around the democratic process. They pass because the real shareholders aren't there to oppose them. And the fund managers in whom shareholders have entrusted their vote are following the advice given to them by proxy advisory firms who do not have fiduciary accountability to recommend what's in the best economic interest of the ultimate fund beneficiaries.

It's not just those on the right who are calling this out as a problem. Charlie Munger, the billionaire partner of Warren Buffett and vice chairman of Berkshire Hathaway, warned that the power shift to corporate decision makers will "change the world" for the worse. "'We have a new bunch of emperors, and they're the people who vote the shares in the index funds,' Mr. Munger, 98 years old, said at the annual meeting of Daily Journal Corp., a publishing company he has chaired since the 1970s. 'I think the world of Larry Fink, but I'm not sure I want him to be my emperor,' he said of the BlackRock CEO."[24]

Large asset managers are one more necessary and crucial institution that has been hijacked by the left. They deny that their climate and social justice agendas compromise profits by citing the need to consider "long-term value." But their view of what hampers long-term value is quite selective.

As we'll see, stakeholder capitalism's single-minded focus on long-term value prioritizes the threats of climate change and social injustice while ignoring threats from a nuclear-armed China or Russia, oil and gas shortages, a border overrun by drug cartels and deadly fentanyl, the possible loss of the dollar's status as the world reserve currency, runaway inflation, and a $31 trillion national debt. These items don't seem to factor into this concept of long-term value to nearly the same extent. The things stakeholder capitalism ignores puts the lie to its claim that it really is just about facing future threats.

Coincidentally, calculating the long-term risk stemming from these policy shifts for an ethereal threat is also a lot less lucrative than addressing more tangible issues. The solutions to the China threat, the border threat, the currency threat, and the debt bomb involve financial sacrifice, whereas the threat of climate change and social injustice demand substantial, immediate "investments."

Shareholder resolutions push companies to invest in DEI initiatives that largely employ Democrats and silence conservative voices while trying to indoctrinate the workforce. They push investments in renewable energy infrastructure that has been subsidized by government and underwritten by elites. They penalize companies that sympathize with the views of political adversaries. States like Texas, West Virginia, Wyoming, or Utah, which believe domestic oil and gas production are important to national security and economic stability, are penalized. Which is precisely the point.

"I believe the decarbonizing of the global economy is going to create the greatest investment opportunity of our lifetime," Fink wrote in his 2022 letter to CEOs. "It will also leave behind the companies that don't adapt, regardless of what industry they are in."[25]

There will be winners. And there will be losers. In capitalism, they are decided by the markets as people vote with their wallets. But in this new counterfeit version of capitalism, men like Larry Fink get to pick the winners and losers.

Stakeholder Capitalism

Once again, all of this is happening because there's no way voters would approve of such anti-market activism if they saw it at the ballot box. Stakeholder capitalism, oriented by ESGs, is very different from free market capitalism.

Whereas free markets presume that individuals and entities will pursue their own rational self-interest (profit), stakeholder capitalism presumes the opposite—that companies "exist to serve multiple stakeholders" and that they prioritize "long-term value creation."[26] Conveniently, long-term value, as promoted by globalist organizations like the World Economic Forum, requires adhering to left-wing political objectives on climate change and social justice under the unprovable faith-based assumption that long-term gains will be better than they might have been without climate-related restrictions. According to consulting firm McKinsey & Company, one of the ways long-term value is created is by "minimizing regulatory and legal interventions."[27] In other words, companies who comply will not be sued or regulated into oblivion by the B Team's leftist allies. It's the stick that identifies as a carrot.

ESG scores are just the metrics by which supposed long-term value is judged. And they're conveniently aligned with leftist political objectives. Today it may be okay to invest in environmentally destructive mining operations in China, but not clean natural gas from Oklahoma. Tomorrow the standards may require the boycott of different industries, states, or nations, depending on the political objectives of the people who make the rules.

In this new utopia of stakeholder capitalism, markets are not free, they are manipulated. Compliance is not voluntary—it is forced. Capital does not flow—it is diverted. BlackRock CEO Larry Fink famously boasted in 2017 of his ability to force change on the American economy. "Behaviors are going to have to change and this is one thing we are asking companies, you have to force behaviors and at BlackRock, we are forcing behaviors."[28]

Fink preaches as gospel truth the highly speculative notion that only total decarbonization by 2050 can save mankind. "Every company and every industry will be transformed by the transition to a net-zero world," Fink preaches. "The question is, will you lead, or will you be led?"[29]

Fink's vision is a puppet master democracy in which "free" markets can be led by elites like himself. It is one where the world can only be saved by quietly replacing the most prosperous economic system in the history of the world with one that has a spectacular record of failure. Replacing investors and capital markets in the role of pricing and allocating capital with political ideologues more closely resembles a command economy than a free market. The historic record is quite unimpeachable as to where each of these systems leads. A centrally planned system, in which the elites with the most money (like BlackRock) direct the flow of capital and the rewarding of privilege, has no record of creating long-term value.

Nonetheless, Fink disingenuously attempts to frame the hijacking of our capitalist institutions as a feature rather than a bug. Following increased scrutiny of ESG policies in the wake of Russian oil sanctions, Fink wrote a 2022 letter to CEOs defending the system his policies are designed to break. Titling his letter "The Power of Capitalism," Fink wrote, "Stakeholder capitalism is not about politics. It is not a social or ideological agenda. It is not 'woke.' *It is capitalism*, driven by mutually beneficial relationships between you and the employees, customers, suppliers, and communities your company relies on to *prosper*. This is the power of capitalism."[30] Therein, Fink, in typical condescension, redefines "beneficial" in elitist, leftist terms. When activists and society are elevated to the same level as shareholders, they serve a political agenda, not the company's traditional stakeholders.

A capitalism that subjugates prosperity to ideology is not capitalism. And a democracy that substitutes the judgment of elite oligarchs for the will of the people is not democracy. Oaks, who was up for election to finish out his predecessor's full term in November 2022, sees the threat as an existential one for America. "The American system really has two parents—capitalism and democracy," he told voters during his 2022 election campaign. "And ESG is trying to castrate capitalism and neuter democracy."

CHAPTER 3

The Progressive Catch-22

I n addition to the first prong of pressure from large asset management firms on public companies, there is a second prong of pressure applied to the bond markets, which are often dominated by government entities managing state and local tax and pension revenues. As pernicious as this practice is, it also gives rise to a potent weapon Americans can wield to fight back: state governments.

A clever way that the ESG schemers insulate themselves from criticism is by portraying any sort of governmental pushback as authoritarian interference with the free market. Never mind that stakeholder capitalism is profoundly anticompetitive in nature; the left claims that any attempt to take on powerful asset managers is government obstructing markets. It's a catch-22 for American business.

If they comply with the demands of the woke agenda, they risk undermining their future growth and profitability. If they don't, they find themselves at odds with their largest shareholders—or at least, with the asset managers that control large chunks of those shares. If they turn to government for relief, it's authoritarian overreach. If they appeal to the markets, it doesn't matter because the middlemen who control the index funds are in the driver's seat. Now the credit scoring agencies have also joined the fray, working to promote arbitrary ESG standards.

Who is left to take on the fight? One group is uniquely empowered with constitutional authority to wage this war. State elected officials—financial officers, governors, and legislatures—are given tremendous power in our federalist system, even if that power is limited to a small geographic area. To protect investors, these are among the asset owners and managers who hold the key to restoring fiduciary standards over arbitrary ESG scores.

State and local governments depend on good credit ratings to attract favorable interest rates on public bonds. For those coveted ratings, they rely on credit rating agencies. Traditionally, these entities had a single purpose: to assess the ability of a company or government entity to repay its debt. A better credit rating translated to lower borrowing costs.

ESG threatens to turn this equation on its head, potentially driving market participants (the asset owners and investment managers) to provide the lowest rates to the most politically compliant entities and punishing those whose politics do not align with the Current Thing.

With very little initial pushback, credit rating agencies have begun to jump on the ESG bandwagon. Standard & Poor's, Moody's, and Fitch Ratings have each begun to integrate ESG metrics into their methodologies for credit and bond rating analysis. These changes will likely mislead investors with information that is unreliable and inherently political. More importantly, the new standards could penalize states, municipal entities, and companies with the wrong policies in the form of higher borrowing costs.

For example, in January 2021, S&P placed several issuers tied to the oil and gas industry on CreditWatch, revising the industry risk from intermediate to moderately high based on the assumption that greenhouse gas emissions and not meeting the government emission standards posed a financial threat to the industry. The rating also considered "challenges and uncertainties engendered by the energy transition."[1] This is quite remarkable given the nearly $5 trillion in subsidies over the past twenty years on renewables that has resulted in only 5 percent share of global energy produced from those sources.[2]

Remember, credit rating organizations are supposed to provide investors with information that will help them assess risk and make profitable investments. They're not there to advise investors on which investments will help them support progressive-defined environmentalist goals. Those goals, as we've seen, are often highly controversial, focusing on long-term damage that is far more hypothetical than immediate risks.

But the huge, ESG-motivated focus on climate change has blinded these agencies to just the sort of immediate issues—say, an impending war and acute energy shortages—that should have led them to give entirely different scores for the oil and gas industry.

We saw this play out in 2021, when, according to ESG factors, the oil and gas industry was becoming riskier. But according to geopolitical factors, market demand for its products was about to explode. The well-telegraphed Russian invasion of Ukraine and subsequent sanctions had a much more predictable and immediate impact on the energy industry than "growth of renewables" was likely to have.

A baseline assumption that all climate change goals are justified, no matter the cost, also ends up obscuring the true financial risks involved in implementing environmental goals. For instance, an honest accounting of risk from the climate agenda would consider just how much the goal of net-zero emissions will cost the global economy. (The answer: a hell of a lot.)

Americans have never had an honest accounting of what this goal will cost us, nor have we made a collective decision to pursue it through any democratic means. The one serious effort to push it through any democratic process resulted in defeat—the Green New Deal.

A study by McKinsey found that the transition from fossil fuels to a net-zero economy would require an investment of $275 trillion, or about $9.2 trillion per year. "The increase is approximately equivalent, in 2020, to half of global corporate profits, one-quarter of total tax revenue and 7 [percent] of household spending," the report suggested.

The McKinsey study also shed light on the potential political challenges. "We find that the transition would be universal, significant and front-loaded, with uneven effects on sectors, geographies and communities, even as it creates growth opportunities," the study concluded.[3] Presumably, energy-producing states would be among those unevenly impacted. And that's just the fiscal price tag. The cost is much higher if one considers the potential damage to free market capitalism as we know it.

The cost will be paid, not just through our taxes, but through our pensions and investments. When we allow fiduciaries to make investment decisions on the basis of politics, we give them permission to fail. Spending $5 trillion for 5 percent is a strikingly bad return on investment; this is what happens when government tries to create winners and losers. The markets are better at allocating capital. The climate activists demand we must transition. But to what?

Our investments no longer have to be profitable. They just have to be woke.

State Pushback

If there is hope to be found in this story, it is the promise of states in general and treasurers/comptrollers (they use different titles in different states) in particular to defend the interests of taxpayers and investors. That is where the power lies to fight ESG. States are just getting started.

In late March 2022, S&P Global released a subscriber-only report that rated states on a set of ESG criteria that assigned a value between 1 and 5, with the lowest value being the best score. No state scored a 1. Many, including some of the best-managed states in the nation, received moderately negative scores.

When S&P sought comment from state and local governments on the integration of ESG into its global ratings, the state of Utah pushed back—and it pushed back hard. Utah is one of five states that have never been downgraded from the best and strongest AAA credit rating. They have the best bond rating in the nation. Through a combination of prudent spending, young and growing demographics, a well-diversified economy, and careful debt management, the state had a sterling reputation. But state treasurer Marlo Oaks realized none of that would matter if ESG factors figured prominently in future ratings.

His state is a producer of oil, clean natural gas, rare earth metals, and critical minerals. It is a desert state that relies on water storage behind large dams to supply drinking water to its residents. The state's politics are conservative. A majority of residents belong to a traditionally conservative organized religion. These are all factors that have traditionally drawn people to the state. But by ESG standards, they could lead to a lower ESG score, thereby making borrowing more expensive. Meanwhile, states that have been more financially profligate but politically compliant would theoretically receive better ESG ratings simply because their politics align with the globalist agenda.

In a letter signed by every statewide elected official, the Speaker of the House, president of the Senate, and the state's entire federal congressional delegation, Utah categorically objected to the ESG scheme and demanded that S&P withdraw those credit indicators and cease to publish a separate ESG rating for Utah, writing, "We view this newfound focus on ESG as politicizing the ratings process."

Oaks maintains that if any ESG factors are financially material, such as the impact of Utah's drought, that factor belongs in the traditional credit rating. There is no reason to create and publish a separate ESG score that combines financially material items and blatantly political and financially immaterial factors into a new rating. Such a score can adversely impact an organization's ability to borrow money.

The letter made a compelling case to keep financial and political

Credland

Christopher W.

Mon Aug 14 2023

The puppeteers : the people who contro
the people who control America / Jason

31815221823168

p10736815

assessments separate, citing the damage done during the 2008 financial crisis when credit rating agencies got their financial assessments wrong.

> *S&P should have already learned the costly lesson that undue influence over its credit ratings can lead to disaster—both for the company and the nation. The failure of credit rating agencies, including S&P, to accurately assess mortgage-backed securities and related credit default swaps in the lead-up to the financial crisis of 2007–2008 contributed to the proliferation of these products and the resulting catastrophic collapse of the financial system and the global economy along with it. Indeed, S&P admitted in its $1.375 billion state Attorney General and Department of Justice settlement that it succumbed to conflicts of interest in rating these products by prioritizing business relationships with issuers over accuracy in its models and ratings. Many Americans suffered because of S&P's failures. These failures should have resulted in S&P's greater commitment to sound financial practices rather than extraneous political impulsions.[4]*

Likewise, other states joined the fray. Idaho followed with a similar letter, signed by its governor, state officials, and members of its congressional delegation. "Idaho is solvent and should not be penalized by you or any other entity for its sovereign decisions," officials wrote, demanding that the ratings be taken down.[5]

In West Virginia, state treasurer Riley Moore accused S&P of using "politically subjective metrics to try and paint our state in a negative light." Moore pointed out the potentially costly impact ESG ratings could have for his taxpayers. He wrote, "despite our state's excellent financial position, our taxpayers could now be punished with higher borrowing costs simply because S&P doesn't like our state's industries and demographic profile."[6]

The pushback against S&P is just part of a broader initiative by states to defend against the political encroachment of a weaponized financial sector that threatens to undermine their sovereignty by creating a way to penalize them for noncompliance with a political agenda. In other words, states could see their costs rise simply for having the wrong politics.

Moore was one of the first state financial officers to take on ESG. In January 2022 he banished BlackRock, the world's largest asset manager, from managing state investments. Citing BlackRock's rejection of its fiduciary responsibility to serve the best interests of the investor, in this case West Virginia, Moore issued a press release expressing his concerns. He wasn't willing to use taxpayer dollars to subsidize an agenda hostile to his state's economic interests. Given BlackRock's embrace of "net zero" investment strategies punitive to producers of fossil fuels, Moore said BlackRock's corporate policies directly threaten the lives and livelihoods of America's largest coal-producing state.[7]

Even as BlackRock pushes other entities to adopt net-zero climate goals, the company itself invests heavily in the world's largest producer and consumer of coal and coal-generated electricity—China.[8] Moore warned that BlackRock's investments in China were subject to blatant government interference and market controls by the Chinese Communist Party (CCP). "Any company that thinks Communist China is a better investment than West Virginia energy or American capitalism clearly has a bad strategy," said Moore. "We will continue to give our state's business to people who aren't simultaneously trying to destroy our economy."[9]

BlackRock's share of West Virginia's $8 billion portfolio may be a drop in the bucket for a conglomerate that at one point managed $10 trillion. But a coalition of states could have a powerful effect on the market. As of this writing, twenty-four states have expressed support for the fight.[10] Large treasury portfolios in Florida, Arizona, Louisiana, Utah, and Arkansas have joined West Virginia in moving investments from BlackRock. South Carolina divested its college savings funds. Texas, Kentucky, and Oklahoma are signaling their own possible divestment in the future.[11] Sadly, progressive states have not stopped to think what the implications might be for them should the day come when the rules are set by their political adversaries. That is a situation even red-state treasurers hope to avoid. The goal is to get politics out of the capital markets so they can function as they were intended.

It's not just the state financial officers who are raising the stakes for proponents of ESG. Texas governor Greg Abbott signed into law a bill prohibiting the state from investing in businesses that boycott the oil and gas industry—a commitment they must make to receive the best ESG ratings. A second targets companies that restrict capital flowing to the firearms industry, prohibiting state and local governments from working with such companies. Given the size and status of oil-rich Texas, this is a significant blow to the movement.[12]

Idaho's legislature passed a bill bringing proxy voting under the treasurer's office. Florida's governor, Ron DeSantis, has acted to strip proxy voting authority from outside fund managers.[13]

Former Arizona attorney general Mark Brnovich opened an investigation of ESG as an antitrust violation. In a March 2022 *Wall Street Journal* editorial, Brnovich explained, "The biggest antitrust violation in history may be in plain sight. Wall Street banks and money managers are bragging about their coordinated efforts to choke off investment in energy."[14]

Now states, too, are coordinating. When Biden's Securities and Exchange Commission proposed a new rule to enhance and standardize climate-related disclosures, twenty-three state financial offices signed on to a letter objecting.[15] Nineteen red states have launched an investigation of the involvement of six banks in the United Nations' "Net Zero Banking Alliance."[16]

That the very same progressive Americans who fretted during the Trump administration about "saving our democracy" are sold on this concept of stakeholder capitalism is a testament to the power of climate alarmism and identity politics. These pretexts have been indispensable in the left's success at weaponizing public and private institutions. No power grab is unjustified in the face of possible planetary extinction; no retaliation is too harsh in the throes of honorary victimhood.

As the always colorful columnist Jonah Goldberg once noted, "If you honestly believe that climate change will end all life on Earth (it won't) or lead to some dystopian hell where we use the skulls of our former friends and neighbors to collect water droplets from cacti, what policies wouldn't you endorse to stop it?"[17]

These emotionally provocative challenges of climate change and social injustice are real and difficult. But the idea that we are better off letting powerful elites dictate the solutions, rather than innovation, is simply absurd. American markets have a long and successful history of innovating their way out of intractable problems.

While many of us in recent elections were worried about who would represent us in Congress, the more consequential vote might just have been those sleeper races for state treasurer. Back in Utah, Oaks won his election. He is now focused on defending economic freedom, ensuring his state remains fiscally strong, and finding as many allies as he can to fight against anticapitalist counterfeit democracy. With him and so many other state officers laser-focused on this issue, the ESG puppet masters may have met their match.

Meanwhile, the Biden administration is hard at work deploying the B Team of federal agencies to ensure the integration of ESG into the financial system. The revolving door between the bureaucracy and the woke-industrial complex will ensure that voluntary policies from the private sector soon become mandatory regulations without ever having to pass through a legislative body. Once that happens, they won't need to raise taxes to fund their agenda. Our retirement accounts will do it for them.

CHAPTER 4

The End of the World Justifies Any Sacrifice

There's no money left in the federal piggy bank. But the party of Joe Biden and Kamala Harris has an agenda that demands trillions be spent annually, under the pretext of paying for government solutions to climate change and social injustice. Republican lawmakers are never going to sign on to this agenda, of course. To solve this pesky problem caused by democracy, our globalist puppet masters have gotten more inventive. They seek to tap into the wealth of America's vaunted financial sector. If they succeed, the businesses, investments, and retirement accounts on which many Americans depend may never recover.

The federal government says it will do anything to pay for climate change. What that actually means is that it *can do* anything, *thanks to* climate change. Existential threats are great for government. They give it license to justify any sacrifice from taxpayers.

The administration's vision for funding its political wish list includes a combination of new regulations, aggressive enforcement actions, and low-profile slush funds. Printing money and raising taxes aren't the only way to pay for an incomprehensibly costly agenda. Other methods of siphoning money out of the economy are preferable because they don't require the left to win every election.

In early 2022, calling for "the highest sustained tax burden in the nation's history," President Joe Biden released an eye-popping budget proposal that would spend $73 trillion over ten years.[1] He kept his promise to raise taxes, signing the ironically named Inflation Reduction Act in August 2022. Though the bill does nothing to reduce inflation, according to the Congressional Budget Office, it sucks $737 billion out of the U.S. economy.[2] That came on the heels of a $1.9 trillion American Rescue Plan, and a $1.2 trillion infrastructure bill.[3] All of that is above and beyond the $30 trillion the United States currently owes and the $160 trillion–plus in unfunded liabilities (promises we've made, but haven't funded).[4] Given that tax revenues are projected to be just over $4 trillion a year, it's safe to say that the federal government is broke. Anything more that Congress spends must be borrowed. And interest rates on that borrowed money increased steadily following COVID-related government spending sprees written by Nancy Pelosi's Democratic House leadership under both President Trump and President Biden.

The only way to pay the astronomical price tag of Democrats' ambitious and wasteful Build Back Better climate agenda is either for Congress to borrow more or for Democrats to raise taxes beyond what any voter is likely to tolerate. The party that succeeded in generating that kind of tax revenue in the short term would surely lose the next election—or many elections.

But in the minds of Democrats, there is another way. There is plenty of money in America. It just doesn't belong to the government. It's sitting in our retirement funds. Or it's being generated by profitable corporations and financial institutions, where it is largely used to innovate, create jobs, and invest in growth.

Left to their own devices, American innovators would likely use that money to create solutions to the very problems that keep Democrats up at night. But then government and its political allies wouldn't get their cut.

Since the Biden administration can't access all of that money through taxes, they are trying to tap into it through regulation. They prefer that partisan politicians and bureaucrats—rather than innovators, investors, and scientists—dictate where the money flows. You'll invest in their recommended funds by default, even if it reduces what you can live on in retirement. You'll comply with their irrational climate targets, or you'll be fined and forced to donate to the charities of their choice.

Conveniently, their plans direct the flow of capital to their own donors, investments, and political acolytes and away from any entity with a nonconforming point of view. Pluralism is out. According to the administration, America will solve what they contend is a "climate crisis" their way or not at all.

We are led to believe that the only way to ensure a future for our children is to adopt an extreme leftist agenda. In reality, we don't have consensus on whether perpetual climate changes are an immediate crisis. But if they are, we don't know the likelihood that human intervention could improve, much less stop them. And even if that is possible, we should question whether the government is truly the more trustworthy vehicle to address the problem, over the innovators who have the better track record of problem solving. But we're not supposed to acknowledge these inconvenient truths. We're merely expected to take it on faith that expensive and repressive climate "solutions" administered by leftists will fix everything.

That's why this administration is obsessed with regulating financial institutions and investments. Regulatory institutions we once counted on to protect us from shysters and con artists now perpetuate their own shakedowns to enforce political conformity.

It's hard to find a federal agency that isn't currently writing expansive rules and regulations to govern the financial sector. President Biden calls it a "whole of government approach" to regulation.[5] But this time, the rules aren't about protecting your investments. They're about tapping into them to feed a woke-industrial complex that keeps Democrats in power.

Paying for Net Zero by 2050

At the end of 2021, Americans had socked away an astronomical $39.4 trillion into retirement funds—an average approaching $150,000 for every adult between the ages of thirty-two and sixty-one.[6] It's enough to pay off the historically high national debt with a few trillion to spare—a trade-off few of us would willingly agree to make. Still, America's entire retirement fund would only be enough to pay for about 14 percent of the total cost of reaching "net zero" emissions by 2050, based on projections from McKinsey.[7] The high cost of small gains is exemplified by a statistic from Goldman Sachs economist Jeff Currie. After a decade in which a jaw-dropping $3.8 trillion was invested in renewable energy projects, fossil fuel consumption as a percentage of total energy use dropped by just 1 percent. From 82 percent of total consumption in 2011, fossil fuels were still 81 percent of the total $3.8 trillion later.[8]

No one in America has voted to sacrifice retirement returns to pay for the Green New Deal agenda. But they'll be doing it anyway. The government entities that were created to protect consumers and safeguard their investments are no longer in the business of putting consumers first. They're in the business of putting politics first. And with the help of the Biden administration, they'll have that in writing.

It's a staggering amount. And an ambitious goal. The 2050 timeline is presented as a fait accompli. President Biden even signed an executive order committing to that timeline. In December 2021, he pledged "a carbon pollution-free electricity sector by 2035 and net-zero emissions economy-wide by no later than 2050."[9]

Why 2050? You won't believe the answer to that question. It's because "a group of women" (described as "lawyers, diplomats, financiers, and activists") in Scotland "sat around a kitchen table" in 2013 debating how to measure global compliance with the heavy sacrifices their agenda would require.[10] They came up with "net zero"—a term that represented the balance between greenhouse gas inputs and outputs. It wasn't a scientific term or goal. There were no scientists involved in the discussion. It was pure marketing.

Two years later, the goal showed up in the Paris Climate Accords. Later, the UN adopted it. Today many countries and corporations are working on plans to reach net zero by 2050. It's a milestone set by environmental activists. There is no scientific consensus that this date has any particular significance.

The government-funded scientists at the UN Intergovernmental Panel on Climate Change (IPCC) do not even agree with the 2050 date. Their reports predictably legitimize the government position that investments in renewable energy are urgent and profitable. For them, 2050 is too late. Incidentally, the IPCC has a long record of relying on flawed modeling and exaggerated climate change predictions.[11]

Despite the lack of scientific foundation for the 2050 deadline, or any real reckoning of what trade-offs will be required to meet it, 2050 has become a top priority for the B Team. Any debate that climate change could be manageable or that the cure for climate change could be worse than the disease is not allowed.

The McKinsey study highlighted the political challenges of getting public support for net-zero emissions goals on that timeline. Remember, the study described the impact as "universal, significant and front-loaded, with uneven effects on sectors, geographies and communities, even as it creates growth opportunities."[12] In other words, everyone will feel the pain long before any real benefits (if any) can be felt, some will feel it much more deeply than others, and a few people are going to get stinking rich. Part of the formula for making that happen begins in the retirement funds of working Americans and retirees.

Diverting Retirement Funds

My great-uncle Joe was a character. He regularly wore a wide-brim straw hat, had a beer in one hand (if not both), and a belly about the size of a basketball. He was usually a bit crusty on the outside. But he had a heart of gold, with a soft spot for his country and his family. My great-aunt Louise, whom we called "Weezie," always looked out for her Joe, including during a tough battle he had with emphysema.

Like many Americans of their generation, they lived modestly and came to depend on the pensions they earned while working. Back then, pensions offered a defined benefit—they got the same amount whether the markets did well or not. The risk was on the taxpayers, not the pensioners. They didn't have to worry about what stocks were doing.

Home was in Yarnell, Arizona, for the cooler months, and when it warmed up, they stayed in a one-room cabin at the West Fork Cabin Camp in Ennis, Montana. It was tight living. I know. In my midteens I spent a month with them in the summer, sleeping in the bed right next to theirs. By the time I came along, Joe and Weezie were well into retirement. During the time we lived in Scottsdale, Arizona, my parents would put me and my younger brother, Alex, on a Greyhound bus in Phoenix. It had a stop in Yarnell. They would come on and talk to the bus driver to remind him that there were two young kids in the back of the bus who would need to be told when to get off. Despite how scary that sounds, it worked like a charm every time!

We would go spend weekends from time to time with Uncle Joe and Weezie. One year I was invited to join them for the summer. Uncle Joe taught me how to fly-fish that summer in Montana, and I always enjoyed hearing his old stories, no matter how embellished they might have been. He gave me a pocketknife, a tool kit for home, and made me some waders by gluing some shag carpet to the bottom of my shoes. Old-school waders worked!

Uncle Joe had a productive career, serving in the United States Navy and later working for an electricity company—the bulk of his career. When he retired, he counted on the money coming in from his military and employee pensions. Their income was fixed, but with decent returns, it was enough to live on.

Though Joe passed away a number of years ago, I can only imagine how irate he would be if, after a lifetime of work, his pension had been worth a fraction of its potential value because some puppeteer decided their social agenda was more important than his quality of life. Gone are the days when governments and employers shouldered the risks of the market. Most of us have a 401(k) that has a fluctuating value based on the quality of our investments and the health of the economy. That's a risk we all have to bear. It's unfair to ask anyone else to bear it. But where there is risk, there must be choice. We shouldn't have to depend on some shadowy puppeteer to decide for us whether their climate goals matter more than our financial stability at the most vulnerable time of our lives.

We all have an Uncle Joe or Aunt Weezie in our family—someone who is completely dependent on their 401(k) or pension to pay for a twenty-five- or thirty-year retirement period. Many of us will be in that situation ourselves—only we can expect a lot less from Social Security given that even the government projects the Social Security trust fund will be depleted by 2035 without major tax hikes from Congress.[13] After that, the program would have to operate at 80 percent of the previous program cost—and that's the best-case scenario. Americans will need good returns on their retirement investments to survive financially.

But that's exactly what is at risk for the next generation of retirees if the Biden administration passes the financial rules currently under consideration. They're hoping you don't notice that return on investment is going to have to take a backseat to environmental and social activism. Stakeholder capitalism means they don't have to seek good returns as long as the funds are flowing in a politically favored direction.

That's the idea behind a new Department of Labor (DOL) regulation fundamentally changing the rules of retirement accounts. In 2020, the Trump DOL passed a final rule strengthening investor protections in the Employee Retirement Income Security Act (ERISA). That rule reiterated that plan managers have a fiduciary obligation to act solely in the interest of plan participants. "This rule will ensure that retirement plan fiduciaries are focused on the financial interests of plan participants and beneficiaries, rather than on other, non-pecuniary goals or policy objectives," said U.S. secretary of labor Eugene Scalia at the time.[14]

It's a concept that should not be the least bit controversial. But the rule prevented plan sponsors from defaulting investments into ESG funds. Participants could still choose sustainable investing, but it couldn't be chosen for them. This enraged Democrats.

Just a few months later, the Biden administration proposed to rewrite that rule, which was many months in the making, with the justification that they need to "remove barriers to considering environmental, social, governance factors."[15] That's totally misleading.

What they really want is tyranny. To force participation in these funds—to divert investment to their favored industries at the unwitting expense of plan participants compels compliance through the allocation of capital. They're sending a message familiar to tyrants everywhere: behave and you will receive your portion. According to an exposé by a former BlackRock global chief investment officer for sustainable investing, Tariq Fancy, those now-underperforming funds have higher fees with little offsetting environmental impact.[16]

Of course, if you google "ESG funds," no doubt you'll find all kinds of links from environmental nonprofits and other interested parties claiming that ESG is just as profitable as other investments, if not more so. But think about it. These funds are not supposed to prioritize profitability—they advertise that they are about "long-term value." They must put the climate first. If world geopolitical crises drive up the price of oil, the ESG funds aren't going to be moving their investments to oil to make a profit. In 2021, under that exact scenario, ESG funds underperformed their non-ESG counterparts.[17] The industry struggled even more in the first half of 2022 as demand for fossil fuels, rising interest rates, and high inflation hit the economy hard and interest in ESG stocks flagged.[18]

The *Wall Street Journal* describes how plan participants get shortchanged in this process: "Retirement plan sponsors won't merely be allowed to prioritize climate and social factors in how they invest. They could be sued if they don't. Workers won't get much say because plans won't be required 'to solicit preferences' on ESG."[19]

As we know, those sustainable investments with good ESG scores also generate higher fees for administration allies like BlackRock. Fees for socially responsible exchange-traded funds (ETFs) are 43 percent higher than standard ETFs. According to the *Journal*, that translates to $2 million annually per $1 billion fund.[20]

Taking BlackRock to task over its failure to prioritize returns for investors over political considerations, former Arizona attorney general Mark Brnovich joined with eighteen other state attorneys general to demand answers. In a letter to BlackRock CEO Larry Fink, they wrote, "Rather than being a spectator betting on the game, BlackRock appears to have put on a quarterback jersey and actively taken the field."[21] The letter noted that BlackRock had engaged with over 2,300 companies about the climate, taking voting action against 53 of them, and putting another 191 companies on watch.

Given the billions of dollars in state and local investment funds these nineteen states represent, the letter was significant. In an interview with Fox News' Neil Cavuto, Brnovich explained how Black-Rock's ESG emphasis bifurcates the economy. "They're basically trying to starve industries they don't like, that aren't woke enough, or that aren't green enough out of existence for their radical green agenda," he said.[22]

In Utah, state officers submitted a letter to the DOL outlining strong objections to the Biden/Harris administration's new fiduciary rule. Signing that letter were state officers from twenty-three other states. Of the letter, Oaks remarked, "Politics needs to be handled by elected officials. Investment managers and activist shareholders are not accountable to voters. Using hard-earned retirement money to further political agendas is costly to participants and undermines our political process. This should not be a partisan political issue."[23]

But it is. The DOL rule is a transparent attempt to legislate through bureaucrats what has repeatedly failed to gain traction in Congress. The old fiduciary standard of serving the best interest of the client would be subjugated to a new standard. Your pension fund doesn't need to turn a profit so long as it's invested in companies whose board members come in a wide enough variety of skin colors and sexual orientations. The rule assumes your interests are best served by investing in woke companies rather than profitable ones, by strong virtue signals rather than strong profits.

Right now, that means the administration hopes to use your retirement fund to help pay for their climate change agenda. But as the political winds shift, ESG standards (and leftist priorities—but I repeat myself) could likewise change. For example, the outbreak of war in Ukraine quickly caused European banks to reconsider their ESG-driven punitive measures against defense companies. With war raging on European Union borders, the strategy of labeling weapons and weapon systems as "unsustainable" investments and limiting their access to capital seemed a bit shortsighted.[24] Though the Biden administration appears unmoved on its commitment to destroy the oil and gas industry, they could plausibly use ESG criteria to go after any industry they see posing a political threat, regardless of public opinion on the matter.

Uncle Joe and Weezie loved the great outdoors, as I do, and cared about the world we live in. We all want a better future. We understand that what we throw into the air, or what we release into the water, has an impact on our quality of life. While no energy source is perfect, climate activists have worked to malign some of the most promising clean energy solutions. Nuclear doesn't have a high cost to the environment, although it has been mischaracterized as dangerous. Natural gas burns much cleaner than other energy sources, but is disparaged because it is a fossil fuel.

The decision to starve the oil and gas industries of capital and feed it to less efficient forms of energy (energy that also exacts high environmental costs) is a purely political one. It's not a scientific or market-based one. Our choices drive the markets. What you and I demand in our lives determines what is produced. By starving the oil and gas industry of capital, we limit our market choices and our economic growth. This is a form of tyranny. When elites determine how we must live our lives, we have lost our capitalist system of economic freedom.

Redirecting retirement funds away from fossil fuels and toward the renewable infrastructure into which taxpayers are already involuntarily heavily invested is not guaranteed to end climate change.[25] After all, the mining for and disposal of those solar panels, lithium batteries, and unrecyclable windmill blades have their own impacts on the planet.[26] As anthropologist Jason Hickel observed, "No energy is innocent. The only truly clean energy is less energy."[27] And that goal comes with trade-offs, many of which most Americans hadn't been asked to consider until oil and gas became scarce in 2022. And even then, no one really talks about the costs of abandoning cheap, reliable, and plentiful oil and gas. We only hear of impending catastrophe if we don't invest in leftist energy schemes.

Hidden Trade-offs of Renewable Energy

We have no guarantees that renewable energy fully deployed will have less of an impact on the climate than our current reliance on fossil fuels. What default investments in ESG funds are guaranteed to do is divert wealth from one sector of the economy to another that is more favored by the administration. That's a dangerous precedent to set. Furthermore, it is a complete rejection of our market system in favor of centralized control.

No one talks about the hidden trade-offs of favored energy sources. The increase in material extraction that will be needed to meet world demand for solar and wind power by 2050 is astounding. A 2017 World Bank report tried to quantify the extraction needs to reach a net-zero 2050 goal.[28] Using the World Bank's model, *Foreign Policy* magazine extrapolated that solar and wind utilities would require 34 million metric tons of copper, 40 million tons of lead, 50 million tons of zinc, 162 million tons of aluminum, and a minimum of nearly 5 billion tons of iron. Extraction of neodymium for windmills would need to increase by 35 percent, silver for solar panels would need to increase between 38 and 105 percent, and indium for solar technology would require a 920 percent increase in extraction. Lithium extraction for batteries would need to increase by 2,700 percent over current levels.

And all of that is just for electricity. Vehicles will require 70 percent more neodymium and dysprosium, double the copper, and quadruple the amount of cobalt. To get an idea what that impact might look like, consider silver. To extract the silver needed to reach net zero by 2050, another 130 mines the size of the world's largest— Mexico's Peñasquito silver mine—would be required. *Foreign Policy* points out that mining is problematic for the climate. Scientists blame it for deforestation, the collapse of ecosystems, and loss of biodiversity, even as current global material use exceeds what economists estimate is sustainable by 82 percent.[29]

Obviously, investments in renewable energy will be a veritable gold mine to well-connected companies and investors. It reminds me of my experience during the Obama administration when the president forked over half a billion dollars in loan guarantees to troubled solar company Solyndra.[30] Ostensibly, the money was to help the U.S. transition to renewable energy. But what it really did (and I would argue what it was meant to do) was pay off a loyal political constituency.

That money didn't ultimately do anything to help offset climate change because the company went bankrupt within two years. But Obama fundraising bundler George Kaiser, who was coincidentally among the private investors behind Solyndra, was happy. He ultimately enjoyed hundreds of millions of dollars in tax breaks from Solyndra's bankruptcy. No doubt the many contractors hired to build the plant that would manufacture cylindrical solar panels did pretty well, as well as the people who got to distribute those lucrative contracts. The political payoff didn't end there.

A congressional investigation later learned that just before the 2010 midterm shellacking of Democrats, Solyndra had planned to lay off workers. But in response to pressure from the White House, they held off to avoid further political damage to the party and its candidates.[31] President Barack Obama later told ABC News he had no regrets about the Solyndra deal.[32]

Controlling the flow of capital is critical to maintaining power. Climate change and social justice have become mere pretexts for exerting power and control. This time, instead of having to tax Americans to pay for infrastructure investments, progressives will just redirect your investments to the very companies they would have used your tax dollars to subsidize.

Leaving no doubt that such spending is politically directed, in September 2022, the Biden administration tapped former Clinton campaign manager John Podesta to distribute $370 billion in climate spending authorized in the Inflation Reduction Act.[33] Republican senators refer to the fund as the Climate Slush Fund.[34] Podesta is described by the *New York Times* as "the consummate Washington power broker."[35]

Podesta's slush fund isn't the only one. It isn't even the only climate slush fund. The UN Green Climate Fund (GCF), established more than a decade ago, was ostensibly an effort to "exclusively serve low- and middle-income countries." That's doubtful. Adopted in 2010 at the United Nations Climate Change Conference in Cancún, Mexico, the GCF was to be funded with contributions from developing countries of $100 billion per year. President Obama pledged $3 billion to the fund, of which he was able to deliver $1 billion before leaving office.[36] President Trump, upon announcing his withdrawal from the Paris Climate Accords in June 2017, reneged on the remaining $2 billion commitment. During his speech from the White House Rose Garden, he questioned the GCF, saying, "nobody even knows where the money is going to. Nobody has been able to say, where is it going to?"[37] Though the fund was marketed as a way for rich countries to help poor countries, some suggest it was a way for the poor in rich countries to fund the rich in poor countries.

"This is a direct subsidy to, frankly, to kleptocracies," atmospheric and space physicist Fred Singer said. "We know what happens to that money. It goes into the pockets or bank accounts of the people who run these countries—it's been happening all the time, and I think it will continue to happen."[38]

Climate-related slush funds unfortunately are just the tip of the iceberg. The Obama administration pioneered a whole new way to fill slush funds without having to be dependent on congressional appropriations.

Why Tax When You Can Fine?

To understand why some financial sectors are such a critical component of the Biden administration's climate agenda, we have to go back and look at what happened the last time Democrats controlled the White House and Republicans controlled the purse strings. The creativity of the Obama administration in finding ways to divert the flow of capital from government to pet charities depended on generating lucrative fines from private sector companies. Though the Trump administration ended the practice of diverting fines into government slush funds, President Biden, on his second day in office, began laying the groundwork to restore them. It's important to remember: revenues generated by taxes have to be appropriated by Congress. Revenues from fines do not.

Ironically, it was through the federal government's top law enforcer that President Obama found a way to subvert the Constitution's separation of powers. Instead of Congress directing federal spending, the Department of Justice (DOJ) could direct settlement funds to preferred nongovernment entities through the legal process. Obama's not-so-independent attorney general Eric Holder, who once told the media, "I'm still the president's wingman," developed a scheme to bypass the Republican-controlled Congress and subsidize entities aligned with the president's agenda.[39] It was a path through which money could flow from banks directly to progressive nonprofits without congressional approval. One path went through DOJ, the other the Consumer Financial Protection Bureau (CFPB).

For Biden to deploy the same strategy going forward, he needs aggressive financial regulation that will generate large-scale enforcement actions on par with the housing crisis settlements of the Obama era. His hiring choices for key regulatory agencies set him up for success if that is his goal.

DOJ Slush Funds

Everybody loves a good heist film. Especially if our intrepid, armed heroes divert the funds of the big and powerful to the poor and deserving. But heists in real life? They are rarely that charming and straightforward.

The day he was inaugurated, January 20, 2021, President Joe Biden issued a sweeping executive order calling for review of many Trump-era environmental rules and regulations.[40] Among the many orders slated for review was one issued by Trump's attorney general from 2017 to 2018, Jeff Sessions. Sessions had put an end to the DOJ practice of diverting settlement funds away from the U.S. Treasury and into the coffers of partisan progressive nonprofits.

"When the federal government settles a case against a corporate wrongdoer, any settlement funds should go first to the victims and then to the American people—not to bankroll third-party special interest groups or the political friends of whoever is in power," Sessions said at the time.[41]

DOJ bureaucrats probably think of themselves as the Robin Hood hero, with underhanded slush fund payouts diverting money they confiscate to people they deem deserving. But to any normal person, it looks remarkably like a heist.

Biden's order, coming as it did on his first day in office, sent a strong signal. Should he find himself facing the closed purse strings of a Republican Congress, he, too, could look to the financial industry as a source of unregulated revenue for the nonprofits who serve his party's agenda. Sure enough, in May 2022, the DOJ published an interim rule to resurrect the Obama-era practice.[42]

The original Holder bank shakedown involved negotiating settlements with lenders accused of financial fraud during the housing crisis, and then directing that money to the very interests that promoted those bad loans in the first place. But it was the network of consumer advocacy groups, many of them under the umbrella of left-wing nonprofits like ACORN, that had used millions of dollars of taxpayer money in Department of Housing and Urban Development (HUD) grants to facilitate mortgages for people who could not afford them, including illegal immigrants, under the guise of "financial justice."[43] Only it was the lenders that would pay the price.

In 2014, when Citigroup was charged with financial fraud for lending to people who couldn't pay, the Obama administration signed a $7 billion settlement with the bank. Among the terms of the settlement: Citigroup had to pay $10 million in "community relief." That money went to Democrat-friendly nonprofits from a list provided by the Justice Department. Citigroup also paid "$15 million in legal aid funds" and "$25 million to public or private community development funds."[44]

Incidentally, Congress had tried to slow the flow of funds to entities promoting bad loans by cutting $43 million in funding to "community development, and financial institutions, and housing counseling agencies."[45] But Holder's scheme kept the dollars flowing. The extortion of banks by the B Team to resupply those funds empowers people who were not elected and who cannot be directly held accountable for their actions.

Holder had created in 2012 the Residential Mortgage-Backed Securities Working Group to prosecute institutions responsible for the 2008 mortgage crisis. In creating the working group, Holder explained,

Over the past three years, we have been aggressively investigating the causes of the financial crisis. And we have learned

that much of the conduct that led to the crisis was—as the President has said—unethical, and, in many instances, extremely reckless. We also have learned that behavior that is unethical or reckless may not necessarily be criminal. When we find evidence of criminal wrongdoing, we bring criminal prosecutions. When we don't, we endeavor to use other tools available to us.[46]

Epoch Times reporter Jeff Carlson explained that these "other tools" are "usually civil sanctions and charges that generally result in large fines being paid by firms, often without a statement of true wrongdoing."[47] The working group collected $110 billion in fines, which the *Wall Street Journal* broke down. Some $45 billion went to "consumer relief," which includes "housing-related community groups."[48]

A 2016 congressional committee report estimated that as much as $880 million was "funneled" to outside groups in the previous two years. The report concluded that "[t]hese payments occur entirely outside of the Congressional appropriations and grant oversight process. What is worse, in some cases, DOJ-mandated donations restore funding that Congress specifically cut."[49]

The administration also insisted banks forgive debts to delinquent borrowers in specific Democratic strongholds while offering new loans and building low-income rental housing in those same areas. Where were these communities? Detroit, Cleveland, Atlanta, Oakland, Chicago—the bluest of the blue cities in America.

This was framed as a kind of restitution—but most of the money didn't end up in the hands of the people who were unwittingly given loans they couldn't pay. It went to the nonprofits, who lobbied for more bad loans. As *Investor's Business Daily* described it at the time, "In effect, lenders are bankrolling the same parasites that bled them for the risky loans that caused the mortgage crisis. With new cash, they can ramp back up their shakedown campaign, repeating the cycle of dangerous political lending that wrecked the economy."[50]

It is a repeating cycle. Except the next big shakedown likely won't be as dependent on housing. Democrats have a different trap to set this time, as the next chapter will explain.

Anticipating the very real possibility that Republicans would hold the House majority after 2022, and hence the government purse strings, Biden and Harris put in place this contingency plan to keep the woke-industrial complex of left-wing charities and institutions well fed. The slush fund is also helpful in budget negotiations. In 2012, Democrats disingenuously agreed to cut $80 million in funding to certain left-wing advocacy groups in budget negotiations with Republicans. But, according to a 2022 letter from Republican members of Congress opposing the return of DOJ slush funds, they simply backfilled that $80 million with what the letter called their "forced donation policy."

The strongly worded letter sent by Republican lawmakers to Attorney General Merrick Garland is unlikely to reverse the decision. Only a Republican administration or an act of Congress can do that. Garland's DOJ released an interim rule to restore the practice in May 2022.[51] But in the Republican letter, more than a dozen lawmakers called out the attorney general:

> Serious conflicts of interest arise and public trust is eroded when the DOJ requires defendants to donate to activist groups selected by the DOJ. What is even more alarming is the glaring lack of transparency; more than 11 years after the practice began, Congress and the American people still have no idea where or how the majority of funds directed to third parties, which amounted to hundreds of millions of dollars, was spent.[52]

As the DOJ presses forward, they would need to aggressively regulate banks and other deep-pocketed institutions in order to generate funds. That job will largely fall to two agencies: the Consumer Financial Protection Bureau and the Securities and Exchange Commission. The CFPB has the advantage of offering a slush fund of its own, zero disclosure or accountability, and a virtually unlimited budget.

The Misnomer of the Consumer Financial Protection Bureau

Before the CFPB became a partisan weapon used by the left to funnel money to favored charities, it was intended to be something quite different. In 2007, Harvard law professor Elizabeth Warren envisioned it to be an independent agency with a laudable mandate to help consumers understand credit products, protect them from the terms hidden in the fine print, and hold institutions accountable for deceptive lending practices.[53] The new bureaucracy, launched in 2011, was considered by many on the left to be one of the Obama administration's signature accomplishments, and was supposed to even the playing field between consumers and financial institutions.[54]

What it did instead was allow the left to pick winners and losers, tilting the field to the left, unhindered by interference from the public or their elected representatives. Congress can't touch it. Former CFPB enforcement attorney Ronald Rubin explained, "In 2010, the Democratic House of Representatives, filibuster-proof Senate, and president did not intend to create a regulatory agency independent from politics, just an agency independent from Republicans."[55]

From his firsthand experience, Rubin identified three ways Democrats weaponized the agency against their political opponents from the start. First, they made sure the director was a partisan Democrat who could not be easily removed by a subsequent president. Second, they funded the agency through the profits of the Federal Reserve rather than through congressional appropriations, ensuring there would be no oversight, accountability, or budgetary constraints. Finally, according to Rubin, they staffed the agency with Democrats "top to bottom."[56]

Campaign finance data later confirmed that 100 percent of campaign donations by employees of the bureau had gone to Democrats or left-leaning independents, making it the most partisan agency in the federal government.[57] Rubin described in a *National Review* piece how he, a Jewish liberal arts graduate from Manhattan who should have been the stereotypical leftist, slipped through the hiring process.

"It was too risky for interviewers to discuss politics, so mistakes were possible. I was one of them," he wrote. But two months later, he wouldn't have been so lucky. "As screening techniques improved, Republicans were more easily identified and rejected," he recalled. "Clear verbal and non-verbal signals quickly emerged. The most common, 'I don't think he believes in the mission' was code for 'he might not be a Democrat.'"[58]

As implemented by President Obama in his landmark Dodd-Frank Act, the agency was inherently political—not focused so much on consumers as on politics. The agency even writes its own budget.[59] Only a filibuster-proof majority could rein it in. It had a fully autonomous CFPB director. That changed with a 2020 Supreme Court ruling finding the agency's structure unconstitutional.[60] But that ruling merely enabled a president to appoint the director. It didn't remove any of the troubling antidemocratic structural barriers that let the agency run unchecked.

What may be of greatest value to Democrats, however, is the CFPB's Civil Penalty Fund. This is the receptacle of all civil penalties the agency collects. In 2021, now-senator Warren boasted on her campaign website that the agency had "already returned $12.4 billion to over 31 million people cheated by financial companies." Among the companies she cites are some of the most profitable in America: Wells Fargo, Bank of America, Discover Bank, PNC Financial Services Group, and Ally Financial.[61] There is big money being collected from big players.

The money is meant to provide compensation to victims of fraud and abuse. CFPB also reportedly reserves some of that money for "consumer education and financial literacy programs."[62] Both of those capital flows can be directed to politicized nonprofits, including ubiquitous left-aligned "nongovernmental organizations" (NGOs).

Like the donations that banks broker through the DOJ, the fines levied by CFPB do not get returned to the Treasury. The CFPB has the authority to distribute them to nonprofits, but also the independence to keep from disclosing them. In 2015, *Investor's Business Daily* reported that they had obtained a list of sixty charities eligible to receive the funds. Among them were left-wing nonprofits in blue cities, some with board members closely tied to the administration. Specifically, they named the Legal Aid Society of the District of Columbia, the Mississippi Center for Justice, and People's Community Action Corporation of St. Louis.[63]

A large portion of the $5 billion in penalties reportedly went to "community organizers aligned with Democrats," according to reporting by Paul Sperry in the *New York Post*, who quoted a CFPB consultant calling it "a slush fund by another name." But that was before President Trump tapped Mick Mulvaney to serve as the agency's director.[64]

Rohit Chopra, one of the original partisans who helped establish the agency in 2010, was confirmed in September 2021 as Biden's appointee to direct the agency. He has big plans for the agency, which we'll get to in Chapter 6.

As the Biden administration believed itself to be facing the daunting prospect of divided government, slush funds came roaring back. To maximize the fines, Democrats will empower the B Team to pursue aggressive enforcement of expansive and almost impossibly complicated rules. Biden's carefully assembled B Team is designed to ensure economic hardship for us and a regulatory bonanza for him. This team doesn't just consist of your standard-issue government bureaucrat. These policy influencers are hand-picked for their ties to outside puppet masters. They don't represent voters. They represent the shadowy figures who really hope to call the shots in this country. They represent wealthy and powerful elites, many with ties to the World Economic Forum—the people who control the people who control America.

CHAPTER 5

"Most Power, Least Famous"

The Shadow Government Power Players

Running as a moderate in 2020, Joe Biden garnered the votes of independents and disaffected Republicans by appearing to be the sane option among a sea of extreme choices. Just 41 percent of Democrats viewed Biden as somewhat or very liberal in a May 2020 Hill-HarrisX poll.[1] Meanwhile, 38 percent of independents saw him as a moderate. He won independents by a 54 to 42 percent margin, leading CNN's Chris Cillizza to conclude that the independent vote was decisive. "Biden's win among independents made the difference. Period."[2] But once he took office, Biden's economic policies were indistinguishable from those of his leftmost rival, Vermont senator Bernie Sanders.[3]

It's possible Biden's politics suddenly shifted far left after nearly fifty years in elected office. Or maybe he simply delegated responsibilities to the unelected bureaucrats who advise him. Either way, his economic policies have been anything but moderate.

The point here is not really about Biden. The point is that the result of the 2020 election didn't change the underlying B Team. Even the mildest middle-of-the-road Democratic president will be quickly surrounded by lifelong bureaucrats with opinions just left of Marx. But a leftist president will then bring in advisors with a combination of experience in both the bureaucracy and outside globalist entities. And in fact, that's what has happened with Biden. So, who was Biden's Svengali on the economy? Who had the president's ear on the policies that impact inflation?

Former BlackRock global head of sustainable investing Brian Deese served as the thirteenth director of the National Economic Council and as one of Biden's closest advisors.[4] He was chosen for a reason. And it was obviously not any expertise in preventing inflation.

Deese has little experience in the real-world economy. He is a lawyer with an economics degree who spent the bulk of his career in government. His hiring by BlackRock during the years when Trump left Democrats in the political wilderness was predictable.

BlackRock has "a long history of hiring former government employees, giving them large salaries, and returning them to public service."[5] The goodwill in the halls of government that this custom has fostered has empowered BlackRock to "successfully fight designation as a systemically important financial institution" and avoid the regulatory perimeters of the Dodd-Frank financial regulation passed during the Obama administration.[6] This practice, coupled with over $14 million spent on federal lobbying just since 2009, has helped it remain unregulated.[7]

Named by the *New Republic* in 2011 as one of Washington's "most powerful, least famous people," Deese has a long history of economic involvement in governmental affairs.[8] He has been a key player in some of the worst financial policies of Democratic administrations. Prior to his work at BlackRock, Deese served as a senior advisor to President Barack Obama during the last two years of his presidency. Prior to that, he served as deputy director and acting director of the Office of Management and Budget (OMB) as well as deputy director of the National Economic Council, which he now chairs.[9]

During his time in the Obama administration, Deese emerged as "one of the most influential voices" and was known for "spearhead[ing]" the auto industry bailout.[10] He was the first full-time member of Obama's automotive task force and "shaped the intervention" in Detroit.[11]

Once he was promoted to senior advisor to the president, he shaped more important policies. He played a "key role in forging the Paris climate agreement" in December 2015.[12] He also championed the Trans-Pacific Partnership in 2015, calling it the "most progressive trade agreement in history."[13] In 2016, he was selected to oversee the Supreme Court nomination of Judge Merrick Garland to fill the late Antonin Scalia's newly vacant seat.[14]

Earlier in his career, Deese worked as a senior policy analyst for economic policy at the Center for American Progress under former Clinton NEC director Gene Sperling, but left to join Hillary Clinton's presidential campaign as her economic policy director in 2008. After she lost the primaries, he shifted to work in the same role for Obama's campaign.[15]

Biden reportedly selected Deese because of his expertise on climate change, union jobs, and "human stakes" when it comes to economic policy.[16] Deese isn't there to grow the economy, create prosperity, or be responsive to the American people. Deese is there to see that the (small *d*) democratic process doesn't get in the way of the (capital *D*) Democratic climate agenda. Charlie Gasparino calls him "a lunatic in charge of the asylum," who "is fine as a flack or a ghostwriter for the president . . . but he shouldn't be anywhere near setting policy for an economy approaching $25 trillion."[17]

Deese certainly isn't someone you would want to manage your investment portfolio—much less the economic fortunes of the world's most prosperous nation. He has given speeches highlighting solar panels, batteries, and other renewables as "top investment opportunities," but he fails to highlight how related "costs associated with these renewables drive up electricity prices without creating good jobs."[18] However, much of the money that companies invest in items like solar panels goes to China, whose profitability relies heavily on the constant push in the United States for solar power sustainability.[19] This comes despite the fact that China's solar panel production is tied to human rights abuses in Xinjiang.[20]

Incidentally, Deese's former employer is also heavily invested in

China and Chinese economic success. In August 2022, BlackRock introduced a range of mutual funds and other investment vehicles for the Chinese consumer, becoming the first foreign company to do so. Additionally, they had recently recommended that investors "triple their allocations in Chinese assets" in order to "push billions of dollars into China."[21]

In the past, Deese and BlackRock frequently talked about the idea of establishing a measurement of environmental, social, and governance performance (ESG) for investors. Now Build Back Better advocates echo "climate resilient infrastructure" pushed by Deese and BlackRock in years past.[22]

If ESG climate standards were to become mandatory for American companies, asset managers like BlackRock would benefit from their early investments in climate infrastructure.

In fact, back in April 2021, BlackRock raised $5 billion for its Global Energy & Power Infrastructure Fund, "which invested in businesses connected with 'renewable energy.'"[23] The following November, they announced that they'd raised an additional hundreds of millions of dollars for infrastructure investments for countries like France, Germany, and Japan, whose governments prioritize investments in "climate-focused projects such as renewable energy in emerging markets."[24]

Left-wing nonprofits would benefit from corporate disclosures that quantify impact to the climate and provide a basis for damages in a future lawsuit. Democrats would also benefit from mandatory disclosures that help root out ideological foes, identify regulatory targets, and generate significant fines.

Mandatory Disclosure

The puppeteers want mandatory climate disclosures. And their man on the inside is Gary Gensler, chairman of the Securities and Exchange Commission (SEC). Gensler released a proposal in March 2022 mandating sweeping disclosures to "meet investor demand."[25]

Disclosure is a misnomer for what Gensler is demanding. This is not information sitting on a shelf somewhere that can simply be released. In many cases, this is data that has never been collected before. PricewaterhouseCoopers announced in June 2021 that it would hire 100,000 people as part of an ESG compliance push at a cost of $12 billion.[26]

When disclosure is compelled, the SEC is asking companies to create new data that doesn't exist. This provides an advantage to larger companies who won't feel the investment required to produce the data. More importantly, Gensler is compelling companies to take political positions they may not even support. He's asking them to estimate what the weather will be like years into the future and make a plan based on that estimate.

Regulation and innovation are inversely correlated. Common sense tells us that the more bureaucrats' policies divert the flow of capital away from productive investments to fund regulatory compliance, the less innovators can expend developing new solutions to old problems. If we were serious about solving climate change, we would unleash the innovators.

Predictably, the Biden administration has gone all in on bureaucracy. They believe that all we need to solve the climate crisis is a whole lot more government. More regulators, more corporate ESG specialists, more paperwork, more disclosures, and most importantly—more conformity to the "settled science" that suggests renewable energy can replace fossil fuels quickly and (for favored interests) profitably.

To that end, B Team regulators are working overtime to impose a bevy of new regulations that will likely require companies to expend extensive staff hours, data collection, and reporting to keep the government wolves from the door.[27] Even if companies comply with the new regulations, the disclosures may provide a basis for more enforcement action, lawsuits, and political targeting.

This time, it won't just be public companies in the crosshairs. The unintended consequence of the 2002 Sarbanes-Oxley Act, which increased reporting requirements for public companies, was a shift to private equity. Government pensions have invested heavily, providing 35 percent of private equity capital.[28] The SEC's regulatory agenda for 2022 suggests that this time around, the administration seeks to ensure innovators have nowhere to run.

While Deese has the president's ear on economic policy (or vice versa), and the Labor Department pushes to divert retirement capital to industries and stocks favored by the left, Gary Gensler now holds the power at the Securities and Exchange Commission. Like Deese, Gensler has a long history of writing and promoting bad economic policy. Some of the most destructive financial regulation in our lifetimes has Gensler's fingerprints all over it.

For someone who has never been elected to represent anyone, Gensler has exercised an incredible amount of power over the world economy. He is the B Team in action. Invisible. Powerful. Aggressive. Unaccountable. Ambitious. And highly political.

Gensler came into the SEC chairmanship with experience in the public financial sector. During the Obama administration, from 2009 to 2014, Gensler led the Commodity Futures Trading Commission. He reportedly played a "central role in bringing the big banks to heel in the aftermath of the 2008 financial crisis" by "giving new teeth" to the regulating agency he commanded.[29]

Ironically, he also played a part in originally creating the circumstances that allowed 2008 to occur when he served as the undersecretary of the Treasury Department under President Bill Clinton. The early deregulation he pushed, say some economists, contributed to the 2008 financial crisis.[30] After Clinton's presidency ended, he worked briefly as a senior advisor for U.S. senator Paul Sarbanes and was instrumental in writing the Sarbanes-Oxley Act of 2002.[31]

Prior to public service, Gensler worked for Goldman Sachs, where he rose to become a partner in the mergers and acquisition department, among other responsibilities. In between his latest two stints in public service, he served as a professor of the Practice of

Global Economics and Management at the Massachusetts Institute of Technology and senior advisor to the MIT Media Lab's Digital Currency Initiative.[32]

Gensler's partisan loyalties are anything but hidden. He previously served as treasurer of the Maryland Democratic Party for two years and in 2017 was named chairman of the Maryland Financial Consumer Protection Commission.[33] He has worked for multiple Maryland politicians, including Senator Barbara Mikulski and Governor Martin O'Malley.[34] In 2007 he served as senior advisor to Hillary Clinton's presidential campaign and later served on the Obama campaign. In May 2015 he began serving as chief financial officer of Clinton's presidential campaign.[35]

If the corporate pressure from large asset managers for voluntary compliance provides the ESG carrot, Gensler will wield the coercive stick. Gone are the days when the SEC existed to protect investors and markets from fraud. Gensler seems to seek to enforce political conformity to the administration's agenda.

He can amplify the message BlackRock and others have been sending: demonstrate your fealty to social justice and net-zero goals or suffer the consequences. And no greenwashing. Gensler will be there to ensure that companies not only give lip service to specific political views, but also that they put their money where their mouth is.

In his nearly five-hundred-page proposed rule, Gensler wants public companies to disclose their own greenhouse gas emissions and those of the companies upstream and downstream from their supply chains. The invasive and expensive mandates will compel all public companies to adhere to progressive climate change theories and goals. Companies will be required to research and disclose their impact on the climate, their cost to move away from fossil fuels, and the risks extreme weather events will have on their finances and operations. They will also be required to create a transition plan to manage climate risk, set goals, and report progress.[36]

During the comment period for the new rule, the conservative nonprofit Heritage Action for America created a comment portal to enable feedback. Heritage warned that the new rule would give an immense advantage to green companies while potentially crippling our ability to produce reliable, affordable energy. "Companies, including small businesses, with low ESG scores could eventually find themselves denied loans, access to banking services, and even removed from major stock exchanges," Heritage Action warned.[37]

This rule is designed to measure a company's alignment with a partisan agenda, not to allow for pluralistic solutions to the problem. "ESG disclosures will pressure companies to side with the Left's political agenda and take positions on policy issues that may have nothing to do with the company's actual business activities," Heritage Action explained, adding that they would simply feed "an army of well-paid consultants, lawyers, accountants, and lobbyists."[38]

Companies will be expected to support the energy infrastructure in which elite asset managers have invested, to donate to the charities favored by Democratic donors, and to promote the goals set by partisan activists.

In a March 21, 2022, statement, Gensler justified the rule, claiming that "investors with $130 trillion in assets under management have requested that companies disclose their climate risks."[39] That would be the likes of BlackRock and other asset managers, including asset owners (like blue-state public pension plans) and others who have signed on to net-zero climate organizations' commitments.

Even more disturbing is Gensler's demand that some companies will be required to disclose the emissions of the "upstream and downstream activities of a registrant's value chain."[40] Making companies responsible for the ESG disclosures of everyone they do business with ratchets up pressure on farmers, foreign manufacturers, and small businesses to comply with the Biden political agenda in order to participate in the economy. Doing so would add significant cost, potentially up and down the supply chain, driving prices up.

And it is not even clear that this information is available, no matter how much it is demanded.

That the Biden administration believes the SEC should be in the business of compelling climate adherence rather than protecting investors is chilling. This is just one of many new rules Gensler hopes to enact. The agency, like so many others, has turned into a political enforcement mechanism of an administration determined to implement an agenda, no matter what Congress or the voters say.

The end result of all these new rules is the opposite of innovation—it's more bureaucracy. Unfortunately, it doesn't end with the SEC.

Biden's revolving door of extreme picks for federal appointments seem to be chosen, not for their qualifications, but for their loyalty to the principle of forced partisan conformity with the climate change and social justice agendas. Biden's pick for deputy secretary of the Treasury, Wally Adeyemo, also served at BlackRock as the chief of staff of its CEO.[41]

Treasury secretary Janet Yellen is open about her use of the office to promote far-left ideological goals. In interviews, she encourages financial institutions to embrace Biden's net-zero prescription for climate change. "I don't think that the ESG movement and the emphasis on climate change is creating the problems that we have. If anything, the problem is that we haven't moved as rapidly as we should have," Yellen told CNBC's Andrew Ross Sorkin.[42]

Ignoring the many advantages of fossil fuels that wind and solar energy cannot provide, Yellen repeated the partisan line that America just needed to divert more capital to renewable infrastructure, and we could have avoided the energy crisis over the Russian invasion of Ukraine. Until renewables can replicate plastics, power jet airplanes, or provide a substitute for fertilizer, this is simply not true.

Likewise, Biden's failed nominee for the Federal Reserve Board, Sarah Bloom Raskin, was similarly open about her hope to "integrate climate-based risks and costs into the financial regulatory apparatus."[43]

Senate Minority Leader Mitch McConnell explained his concerns, saying that Raskin

> has spent recent years pressuring the Fed to stop being a neutral regulator and instead become an ideological left-wing activist body. Ms. Raskin has argued openly that unelected Fed governors should use their powers to declare ideological war on fossil fuels and affordable American energy. Ms. Raskin wants our banking system to start picking winners and losers in ways that would stick American families with higher gas prices, higher electricity bills, and more dependence on China. And she wants to implement this agenda from inside one of the least directly accountable institutions in our government, so that voters have no recourse.[44]

Following the Senate's refusal to confirm Raskin, Pennsylvania senator Pat Toomey remarked, "The Senate's bipartisan rejection of Sarah Bloom Raskin's nomination sends a powerful message to the Fed, and to all financial regulators, that it is not their job to allocate capital or stray from their mission to pursue extraneous or politically charged campaigns." He warned, "The Biden administration should nominate in her place an individual who will focus exclusively on implementing the Fed's statutory mandates of stable prices, full employment, and supervision of bank holding companies."[45] As the next chapter will show, Biden didn't.

The solution to climate change will not come from government bureaucrats spending taxpayer dollars to fetter the goose that lays the golden eggs in our economy. We won't solve it by pursuing just one prescribed path to improvement—such as reaching net zero by 2050. Or by handcuffing innovators with ESG ratings that stifle investment in promising energy technologies.

The solutions will come from a strong, diverse, and innovative private sector that is free to invest in and explore life-changing technologies—perhaps even in disfavored industries—without aggressive interference from an army of government regulators or a cabal of righteous bankers. Without large Republican majorities in the House and Senate, it's easy to believe we've lost the tools to win this fight. But that simply isn't true.

The Constitution vests vast powers in state governments. We need strong leadership at the state level to push back against federal overreach. The parallel regulatory institutions in state government must claw back some of the power and authority that has been stripped away. States can regulate environmental quality. They can reject ESG ratings. They can promote cheap and efficient energy exploration and production. They can withhold investment from politicized actors.

But that's just one battlefront. Climate change is an important pretext for empowering big government and its leftist puppet masters. But another threat arises from the pretext of social justice, which is being used to justify unprecedented interventions in markets and schools by regulators and left-aligned nonprofit institutions. These interventions help stack influential institutions with loyal political constituencies and weaponize them against political opposition. Federal agencies weaponize equity. Nonprofits weaponize federal aid. Teachers unions weaponize curriculum. And without an elected representative among them, they drive public policy in the United States.

PART II

Social Justice

CHAPTER 6

Government Needs More Racism

While the pretext of climate change creates an urgency to direct public and private spending to partisan priorities, the pretext of social injustice engenders an excuse to use the regulatory stick against recalcitrant companies, industries, and even schools. Allegations of racism underlie efforts to redirect corporate profits, stack institutions with political loyalists, and control local school curriculums. To achieve this, the puppeteers need racism. They need inequality—and lots of it. Let's look at how that works in the corporate world.

We've seen how money flows from taxpayers to left-aligned nonprofits. Nonprofits have figured it out, too. With this in mind, the nonprofits, acting as de facto regulators, bring suit against deep-pocketed financial institutions, housing developers, and real estate firms. The B Team helps ensure victory by rigging the rules to ensure guilty verdicts. And voila—a revenue stream is born.

By writing and interpreting regulations that favor civil rights over civil liberties, the B Team and its nonprofit allies can depict just about any company as racist. The resulting settlements can then be used to fund the parts of the leftist agenda that Congress won't pay for.

What happened to Seattle-based real estate brokerage Redfin is a harbinger of a future in which a president can partially fund the party's agenda without the approval of Congress. Redfin, by leftist standards, is one of the good guys. CEO Glenn Kelman is an outspoken social justice advocate, assigning agents to unconscious-bias training and hosting a "Race and Real Estate" symposium in 2018—long before the George Floyd riots made such events fashionable.[1] In a June 2020 blog post, Redfin shared its research on how the racist 1930-era housing policy of "redlining," which unfairly excluded Black families from home ownership, had created a "legacy of inequality."

Lenders in the era of racial segregation used color-coded maps of neighborhoods, refusing to give loans to the "red" neighborhoods, where people of color were most likely to live. Redfin's blog post provided an in-depth analysis of home equity values to conclude that "Black homeowners are nearly five times more likely to own in a formerly redlined neighborhood than in a greenlined neighborhood, resulting in diminished home equity and overall economic inequality for Black families."[2] It sure sounded like Redfin was on board with the social justice agenda.

Unfortunately for the company, *redlining* is one of those terms, like *democracy* and *capitalism*, that has been redefined since the days of segregation. It is no longer defined as the deliberate attempt to exclude people of color from home ownership. Under the B Team's definition of the term, just about anyone can be guilty of the practice—even Redfin. Practically speaking, there need only be evidence that a policy has a "disparate impact" on certain Democratic voting blocs in deep blue neighborhoods.

Six months after Redfin's blog post, the company was accused of redlining. But it wasn't the regulators who came after them. It was a powerful nonprofit—one funded with federal dollars, outspoken in its left-wing activism, but acting independent of the government.

The Washington, D.C.–based National Fair Housing Alliance (NFHA), which brought suit, is a partisan nonprofit nominally dedicated to ending housing discrimination.[3] The agenda, however, is much broader than that. Left-leaning housing nonprofits in general play a critical part in keeping money flowing to the leftist agenda in both directions.

The NFHA in particular receives federal funds from appropriations, grants, and potentially from CFPB fines (if such data were to be made public). This money is labeled in the budget as fair housing enforcement. They are one of countless housing nonprofits acting as a pseudo-enforcement agency for civil rights. They can bring suit, collect a settlement, and redistribute the proceeds to other nonprofits and to the inner-city Democratic voting blocs they serve. Between 2009 and 2018, NFHA received more than $16 million in federal grants from HUD, an agency they later sued for departing from leftist orthodoxy during the Trump administration.[4]

Like so many woke nonprofits, NFHA is not shy about projecting partisanship. The agency has been outspoken about issues only tangentially related to its housing mission, including opposition to Trump Supreme Court nominee Amy Coney Barrett, support for the Build Back Better spending boondoggle, and opposition to President Trump's immigration policies.[5] They can also receive private funding, as in 2016, when NFHA received a $475,000 donation from George Soros's Open Society Foundations.[6]

So how did a company as woke as Redfin get in the crosshairs of social justice warriors at NFHA? Apparently, Redfin wasn't losing enough money on real estate transactions. Their business model offers a full suite of real estate services for a flat rate. Sometimes they make money; occasionally they lose money. But in every market, they set a minimum home price to qualify for services to ensure they can stay in business. As Kelman explains, "we don't know how to sell the lowest-priced homes while paying our agents and other staff a living wage, with health insurance and other benefits."[7]

Give Kelman credit for his skillful use of cherished leftist values to defend himself. On the one hand, progressives want every company to pay a living wage and provide health insurance, paid maternity, and other perks; on the other, they sue their own allies for protecting the bottom line that would enable them to offer those benefits.

The company says their flat-rate business model means they know they lose money on some transactions, but the minimum price qualification keeps them in the black. "Every year, by design, we lose money selling low-priced homes," read a company statement. "The only issue in this case is whether we should lose more."[8]

NFHA, in its lawsuit, described the situation differently. "Redfin's policies and practices amount to separate and unequal treatment of communities based on the racial composition of the area," said the alliance in its seventy-six-page complaint, filed in Seattle federal court. "In short, Redfin's policies and practices constitute real estate redlining in a digital age."[9]

There is no evidence that Redfin applies unequal treatment "based on the racial composition of the area." The minimum price is not subjective. It is what it is regardless of a buyer's race, gender, or sexual orientation. If their policy really did exclude people on the basis of race, they would rightly deserve to be singled out. But their policy is obviously race neutral.

Redfin explains the dilemma: "We recognize that systemic racism affects who can pay for a broker, a book, or an airline ticket, but using price to determine which homes we can sell is not only legally permitted, it is the only fair way to make that determination."[10]

NFHA says fairness has nothing to do with it. This is about the staggering amounts of money that can be collected by government-funded nonprofits, who can then keep the money or distribute it to favored constituencies to help keep Democrats in power. The fiction that corporate America is racist and deliberately discriminatory must be maintained to keep the cash flowing.

Inventing Reasons to Fund Housing Agencies

A vast amount of COVID relief funding was directed at housing agencies, which may seem strange once you start to think about it. After all, was it really impoverished renters who needed relief funds? Was there really an urgent problem with selected minorities specifically being targeted by race during the pandemic? No. In fact, the federal government, through the Centers for Disease Control and Prevention (CDC), implemented a legally questionable eviction moratorium that ultimately forced landlords to go nearly a year without rental income to ensure that disadvantaged (and sometimes not-so-disadvantaged) renters could stay put.[11]

Yet COVID relief bills showered housing agencies with money. The Department of Housing and Urban Development (HUD) received millions of dollars specifically to chase discrimination cases and do so-called outreach. The American Rescue Plan allocated three rounds of funding for fair housing enforcement—$13.6 million in November 2021, and another $5.7 million a month later. That's in addition to CARES Act funds of 2.5 million. NFHA, the agency suing Redfin, received $350,000 from the first round of relief funding.[12]

House Democrats didn't even appear to question the expenditures. Both lending and housing discrimination fall under the jurisdiction of the powerful House Financial Services Committee. By no coincidence, this committee is chaired by California representative Maxine Waters, whose long congressional career has been dedicated to redistributive policies that aggressively regulate economic activity and generously subsidize historically marginalized groups.[13]

Waters was a freshman congresswoman from South Los Angeles during the Rodney King race riots of 1992, in which fifty-three people were killed and thousands more injured. Though "her own district office was burned to the ground," Waters defended the riots as "a spontaneous reaction to inequality and injustice."[14] She likewise defended the violence at Black Lives Matters rallies in 2020. "We got to stay on the street," she famously told Minnesota protesters following the death of Daunte Wright at the hands of the police. "And we've got to get more active, we've got to get more confrontational. We've got to make sure that they know that we mean business."[15]

For Waters, the belief in systemic victimhood is almost a religious one. Speaking of the children detained at the U.S. border during the Trump administration, she told protesters on Capitol Hill in 2018, "God is on our side. On the side of the children. On the side of what's right. On the side of what's honorable. On the side of understanding that if we can't protect the children, we can't protect anybody."[16]

Waters's desire to "protect the children" waned pretty quickly once Florida governor Ron DeSantis got behind legislation to protect kids in kindergarten through third grade from radical gender ideology. Asked about the bill by MSNBC's Jonathan Capehart, Waters responded, "You know, what we're experiencing now with this anti-gay movement is beyond the pale." Waters wasn't concerned about the children. Only the Democratic voting bloc of gay voters. "I have been involved with support for the gay community, for the LGBTQ community for years, and I continue to do it," she said.[17]

Waters has a particular talent for getting funds to flow where she wants them, making her a perfect fit to manage the Democrats' housing operation. The biography published on her congressional website boasts of how she sees her legacy as a member of Congress. "She has used her skill to shape public policy and deliver the goods: $10 billion in Section 108 loan guarantees to cities for economic and infrastructure development, housing and small business expansion."[18]

Not only has her district benefited, but so has her daughter, who earns a living wage doing "slate mailer management" and voter cultivation for Waters's campaign. Karen Waters and her public relations firm, Progressive Connections, have been paid in excess of $1.1 million since 2004.[19]

Representative Waters has long promised to support reparations for slavery.[20] A recent study calculating unpaid hours worked by slaves and settlements for massacres and discrimination estimated that America's 41 million Black people are owed $6.2 quadrillion in reparations. That breaks down to $151 million each, at a cost of $18.96 million per taxpayer.[21]

Unable to get a reparations bill through a democratically elected

Congress, Waters and other Democrats seem to have settled for playing Robin Hood between big corporations and inner-city (often swing-state) constituencies. To be successful, they need two things: to prove systemic racism and to justify seismic lawsuits.

The key to both is stacking the deck in the government's favor. Hence redefining terms so we now live under the disparate impact standard, with which Redfin is now very familiar. Replacing the disparate treatment standard, in which intent to discriminate was required, the disparate impact standard only requires plaintiffs and regulators to prove that a policy was more harmful to one group than another, regardless of intent.

Conveniently, most of the criteria used to screen out risk or incompetence also happen to disproportionately impact Democratic voting blocs. I would argue this unfortunate reality has little to do with the color of their skin, the nature of their gender identity, or the history of their oppression; instead it speaks to the modern failure of progressive poverty programs that trap inner-city neighborhoods in failing schools, government dependency, and chronic victimhood. Nevertheless, the narrative requires that "white supremacy" and racial discrimination exist; therefore, the B Team has found a way to deliver them. Any policy that affects more Black people than white people is officially declared racist under the disparate impact standard.

A New Standard: Disparate Impact

The problem with disparate impact, according to Columbia University's Richard Hanania, is that it "criminalizes everything." He calls this and other civil rights laws "the skeleton key of the left" because it unlocks a rationale to target anyone they want.[22] It's a concept that is used very selectively by the left, primarily against policies that place a disproportionate burden on inner-city victims of government dependency.

What if the standard were used more broadly? Let's stop and think for a minute what "disparate impact" looks like when applied to leftist policy priorities like abortion, climate change, blue-state tax offsets, student loan forgiveness, or defunding police.

In 2014, 36 percent of all abortions were performed on Black women, even though they make up just 13 percent of the female population.[23] But we don't see leftist nonprofits suing Planned Parenthood for discrimination. Planned Parenthood isn't required to actively seek out white or Asian women the way Redfin is expected to actively solicit the business of Black families.

In Alabama, Birmingham adoption lawyer Sam McLure went so far as to file a lawsuit on behalf of preborn Black babies, citing Planned Parenthood founder Margaret Sanger's explicit acknowledgment that the organization was created to prevent Black births. Clinics were and are "disproportionately located in communities of color," McLure argued, which still has repercussions for Black families today.

Fully 60 percent of abortions in the state of Alabama are Black babies, despite a population that is just 27 percent Black. "It's a disparate impact," said McLure. "It's in my opinion a targeted impact. That's part of the logic is that that is a fact." Though this is not a Civil Rights Act case under the Title VII statute, McLure sued under the Ninth and Tenth Amendments.[24] Given the leftist response to the Supreme Court's decision in *Dobbs v. Jackson Women's Health*, nobody is losing any sleep over abortion's disparate impact on Black populations.

Likewise, climate change mitigations that will be required if politicians adopt the net-zero-by-2050 approach will have a disparate impact on poor communities. And in densely populated blue cities where segregated neighborhoods are still prevalent, anything that disproportionately affects poor people also disproportionately affects people of color. Climate alarmists love to talk about how they believe climate change will impact the poor fifty or one hundred years from now, but they seldom write about what mitigations will do right now. This, despite that those fifty- and hundred-year projections rely on a lot less certainty than the immediate consequences of decarbonization schemes.

It's not hard to see how abandoning the most efficient and cost-effective forms of energy would hurt low-income communities. Those families aren't investing in solar panels, electric cars, or carbon credits. When government creates a renewable fuel standard, food and gasoline costs rise. This disproportionately hurts the poor and people of color. Since activists sought successfully to shut down the Atlantic Coast Pipeline, consumers in Virginia and North Carolina—states with disproportionately high Black populations—now must pay $377 million more annually for energy.[25]

We don't see the administration targeting these disparate impacts. In fact, they don't even research them. U.S. climate research dollars appear to be overwhelmingly directed at research that aligns with—rather than challenges—federal climate policies.[26] There are many papers and articles exploring the disparate impact of a warming climate, but very few that consider the similar disparities of climate mitigations.

Another high-priority policy is the state and local tax (SALT) deduction cap, which then-speaker Pelosi fruitlessly spent vast amounts of political capital to repeal. Wealthy and upper-middle-class coastal elites are desperate to restore the federal deduction that was capped at $10,000 in the Trump tax cuts of 2017. That deduction allowed them to write off from their federal taxes the astronomical state and local taxes they paid—the taxes progressive policies demand. With that deduction now capped at $10,000, wealthy and upper-middle-class progressive voters are forced to bear a higher share of the burden from policies they voted to pay for.[27]

Keeping the SALT deduction overwhelmingly benefits high earners, but because most would-be beneficiaries are part of Democratic voting blocs in blue states, no one questions the disparate impact. The left-leaning Tax Policy Center estimates that over 95 percent of the benefit would accrue to the highest 20 percent of tax filers.[28] Nobody in the Democratic Party seems curious about the racial or gender makeup of that group.

Though the truth about student loan debt is buried in a sea of news spin, loan forgiveness has a strong disparate impact on poor people and communities of color, who have to fund the debt forgiveness whether they went to college or not. The left-wing Brookings Institution acknowledged that the highest-income 40 percent of American households owe more than 60 percent of student loan debt. And because of income-driven repayment plans used by lower income borrowers, the bulk of payments come from those same high-income households. Brookings noted that to forgive the debt "will exacerbate the long-term trend of economic inequality between those who have gone to college or graduate school and those who have not."[29] Again, Democrats aren't asking about the racial makeup of the people whose loans will be forgiven versus the racial makeup of the people paying for the loans who didn't themselves go to college.

Who was most disparately impacted by efforts to defund the police? Both CDC and FBI data confirm that the rise in black homicide victims from 2019 to 2020 was nearly double that of white victims.[30] Moreover, government surveillance practices favored by leftists also disproportionately affect poor and minority communities.[31] The list goes on and on.

Indeed, most policies have a disparate impact. Capitalism has a disparate impact. The benefits of work are disparate. Human nature itself is designed to be disparate—men and women are each born with innate talents and capacities that enable them to specialize and stand out in disparate ways. Those don't seem to be evenly distributed among the population, or even among racial subgroups.

So where did the idea that disparate impact is illegal, immoral, unnatural, or disqualifying originate? The short answer is bureaucrats.

How Bureaucrats Use Civil Rights
to Attack Civil Liberties

Anyone who lived through two years of Dr. Anthony Fauci's COVID policies can likely appreciate what happens when unaccountable, unelected bureaucrats take the wheel of government. Particularly when those bureaucrats are beholden to outside puppet masters—be they from pharmaceutical interests, foreign powers, or globalist institutions like the World Economic Forum. The history of enforcement of the Civil Rights Act is yet another such cautionary tale.

The problematic new definition of racism began with bureaucrats at the Equal Employment Opportunity Commission (EEOC) who were enthusiastic about the passage of the Civil Rights Act of 1964 (CRA) and its Title VII provisions over employment practices. Career regulators who are paid to find discrimination for a living, and who had likely spent little time in the real economy, took upon themselves the authority to interpret the congressional intent of the law they were charged with enforcing. They dramatically lowered the bar that allegations would need to clear to result in a guilty finding, resulting in a rich stream of fines and a long list of successful actions.

The CRA itself was a historic victory for America and an important step forward for a nation still grappling with the legacy of slavery. Passed by Congress and signed by President Lyndon Johnson, the law was a clear reflection of the will of a democratic majority, despite some vehement opposition by southern Democrats.[32] But nowhere does the CRA refer to a disparate impact standard. In fact, lawmakers at the time specifically called for minimal interference in the internal affairs of employers.[33]

Today's EEOC would vociferously reject that history of legislative intent. Civil rights law has become their bread and butter, generating 67,448 charges of workplace discrimination in 2020 and collecting $535.4 million in fines from businesses, most of which is used for victim compensation.[34] And that's just the EEOC. The disparate impact standard is now used extensively in lending and housing actions as well.

Within a few years of the CRA becoming law, EEOC bureaucrats invented the disparate impact standard out of thin air. Instead of enforcing equal treatment under the law, they began to require equal results.

Ultimately, EEOC was fining companies for advertising job qualifications that might exclude certain races or genders. Given that talents and abilities are not evenly distributed among races, this is a problematic interpretation. University of San Diego law professor Gail Heriot did some research on real-world applications of group disparities.[35] Heriot is a congressional appointee to the U.S. Commission on Civil Rights. Among her many findings:

> **African Americans** *are statistically overrepresented in many professional athletics, particularly the NFL.*[36]
>
> **Chinese Americans** *and* **Korean Americans** *score higher on standardized math tests and other measures of mathematical ability than most other national origin groups. They are also more likely to hold a B.S., B.Eng., M.S., or Ph.D. in one of the hard sciences or engineering.*[37]
>
> **Native Americans** *are less likely to have access to high-speed internet service.*[38] *They are hence less likely to learn of jobs that are posted only on the internet and less likely to be able to comply with requirements that job applications be submitted through the employer's website.*

Such realities have made the EEOC an extremely powerful organization—and one that operates with little oversight. Under these policies, EEOC has made screening for the right job candidate difficult. Screening out applicants based on their criminal record has become downright impossible. Heriot blames the rise in EEOC actions for the dramatic shift in American companies away from small personnel offices to much larger, more resource-intensive human resource departments to help protect employers from selectively enforced civil rights actions.

Unfortunately, in 1972, Congress granted EEOC even greater latitude to bring lawsuits against employers.[39] Today the agency enjoys the presumption that all hiring qualifications can be found illegal.

The EEOC can independently decide which employment practices to target and which groups to protect.

"If everything is potentially illegal, and government does not have the resources to go after everything," Hanania opined on his Substack page, "then the government basically has arbitrary power to do whatever it wants under civil rights law."[40] Indeed, for many on the left, civil rights trump civil liberties. Free speech, religious liberty, privacy, and even private property are not compatible with an agenda that seeks to criminalize thoughtcrime, villainize merit, and penalize profit.

The Democrats have put the cart before the horse. Actually, to move the cart, they're trying to invent the horse. They want to justify censorship, punish religious beliefs about gender and marriage, end meritocracy, and ensure greater government control of private industry. To do that, Democrats need to convince the world that systemic racism is ubiquitous, white supremacy is our greatest threat, and opposing views are racist. Using the disparate impact standard accomplishes all those things, even if it means companies like Redfin have to be branded as racists.

Recognizing the abuse of civil rights actions at HUD, the Trump administration began the long federal rules process to prevent the inevitable shakedown. Not until October 24, 2020, was a new rule promulgated.[41] The day it was to go into effect, the U.S. District Court for the District of Massachusetts entered a preliminary injunction staying the rule and preventing its enforcement. It was never enforced.[42]

Unfortunately, since Justice Anthony Kennedy had sided with liberals in a 2015 Supreme Court decision upholding disparate impact, the rule could not go so far as to do away with the standard.[43] But the Trump rule did at least impose commonsense limits as outlined in Kennedy's decision. The Trump administration rule would have given defendants a chance to produce evidence justifying the policy showing a valid interest. It required plaintiffs to propose an alternative policy approach to meet that valid interest, and that plaintiffs maintain the burden of proof.[44]

The rule was predictably panned by mainstream media as a weakening of civil rights protections and a gutting of discrimination rules. The Biden administration, upon taking office, moved to immediately reinstate the 2013 rule restoring the disparate impact standard and ensuring a heavy flow of dollars into the coffers of leftist nonprofits and voting blocs.[45]

With regard to lending discrimination lawsuits against banks, regulators know businesses have little recourse but to pay up. "Banks are apt to settle to clear a pathway," said a former senior counsel in the CFPB, Richard Horn. "If they're looking to get approval from their banking regulator for a particular activity— a merger or something else—it's not good to have pending fair-lending allegations."[46]

For former chair Waters, the ends justify the means. She openly admitted in a 2019 House Financial Services Committee letter to then–HUD Secretary Ben Carson that adopting that standard is the only way Democrats will win discrimination suits in modern America. In a letter to HUD defending the misleading interpretation of civil rights law, Waters led a group of House lawmakers, writing, "The disparate impact standard is the most important tool for enforcing the Fair Housing Act in today's rapidly evolving housing market." They weren't wrong. If they had to prove racist intent, few enforcement actions would prevail.

The letter continued, "The disparate impact standard holds actors accountable for the discriminatory impacts of their actions regardless of whether the discrimination was intentional. Without the disparate impact standard, a plaintiff would essentially have to prove malicious intent as plain as a 'No Blacks Allowed' sign in order to get relief."[47] And there it is. "In order to get relief." That's the linchpin of the whole scheme, as we're about to see.

CHAPTER 7

Inventing Discrimination to Redirect Capital

While there are undoubtedly many true believers in the fair housing and fair lending missions of the federal swamp, their mission is not what moves the funding up the federal priority list. The mission is a pretext for a shakedown. The true mission is to redirect a vast amount of federal money from the control of elected representatives to the control of the left's puppet institutions. This flow of dollars from both taxpayers and corporate fines ensures funding for partisan priorities. It also protects the power derived from the network of progressive nonprofits dependent on that funding.

What government really wants is what it always wants—to divert money and power away from the people and toward the permanent government. From there, puppet institutions can use it to reward loyalty, silence opposition, advance progressivism, and protect their power. In this, the housing nonprofit sector has been wildly successful.

This is also where we see the B Team generally seeking to reward and advance progressive constituencies. The B Team may be unelected, but they know on which side their bread is buttered. Democrats give the B Team more money, so their voters must be protected. The B Team is hyperalert to any inequitable treatment they perceive will disadvantage those voters. Sometimes there are genuine people looking to correct injustice, but all too often we see bureaucrats "finding" problems that don't exist in order to justify diverting taxpayer money to the left's agenda.

I know firsthand how little interest the mainstream media has in stories of waste, fraud, and abuse. I made a congressional career of trying to break through the wall, but unfortunately, not even the senseless death of a Border Patrol agent by a weapon from a taxpayer-funded gun-running operation could shake the Beltway media's unflinching loyalty to the swamp.[1] Nevertheless, there have been a few stories that briefly found their way past the media gate-keepers.

A comprehensive telling of the waste, fraud, and abuse in the housing sector alone could fill a book. But a representative sample should suffice. Dollars from the Obama-era Troubled Asset Relief Program (TARP) were used by housing authorities in Nevada to pay for personal expenses and perks to the tune of $8.2 million. Among the improper expenses purloined from TARP's Hardest Hit Fund were a $500 per month car allowance, $100,000 for moving expenses, more than $160,000 for legal fees and a private investigator, and another $40,000 for auditors to "clean up the books."[2] So much for the hardest hit.

Near the end of the Obama administration, the *Washington Post* reported that HUD had been paying $37 million *per month* to subsidize ineligible public housing tenants.[3] In many cases, these were people who simply refused to comply with work or public service requirements tied to the payments. With no consequences, they simply freeloaded from taxpayers.

But the most maddening examples can be found in the housing authorities themselves, on which taxpayers have spent trillions of dollars to alleviate poverty. Because they are set up as state and local entities, HUD makes little effort to scrutinize their spending. The result is high salaries and rich benefits for the people who run those housing authorities, exorbitant travel expenditures, expensive office space, high-end art, and unnecessary consultants.

Even as President Biden excoriated productive businesses like oil companies for making a profit, bureaucrats in his executive branch were enriching their nonprofit partners with little oversight from Democrat-run houses of Congress.

In a 2014 floor speech, when Republicans controlled the Senate, Senator Chuck Grassley (R-IA) detailed the findings of his oversight efforts of housing authorities. "There are a lot of people who make a nice profit from the poverty of others," Grassley reported. "Federal funds end up feathering the nests of local housing authority bureaucrats instead of housing the poor." Grassley described four-day workweeks in Florida, a director who pays himself $280,000 plus thirty vacation days a year in North Carolina, a $7 million administrative office in Tampa, Florida, and hundreds of thousands spent in Atlanta for employees to travel to conferences.

Grassley highlighted one particularly egregious example in Harris County, Texas, in 2013, where the Office of Inspector General (OIG) documented more than $1.7 million in excessive payroll expenses, $190,000 for monuments and statues, $66,000 for employee T-shirts with embossed logos, $27,000 for trophies and awards, and $14,500 spent for a helicopter, chartered bus, and golf cart rentals for a grand opening.

"If the Obama administration is truly serious about income inequality, and not just using it for political purposes," Grassley said, "it would stop shoveling taxpayer money out the door with practically no oversight, no controls, and no limits."[4]

As Trump HUD secretary Ben Carson later learned, Grassley's pleas fell on deaf ears. According to a 2017 OIG report, HUD's accounting was such a mess that the OIG couldn't complete its audit, even after HUD officials corrected $520 billion (with a *b*) in bookkeeping errors.[5] The agency spent $131 million on two failed projects over fourteen years to update its financial management system, only to ultimately cancel on both.[6]

Since then, HUD has received billions of dollars in COVID relief funds. While investigations into waste, fraud, and abuse are just getting started, it's clear that civil rights litigation is a lucrative business. While the benefits of the War on Poverty are questionable, the benefits of working for the woke-industrial complex are clear.

But to keep the funds coming, the B Team has needed to pursue an aggressive regulatory strategy that can generate the kinds of settlements the Obama administration enjoyed during the housing crisis of the late 2000s. Despite the vast amounts of cash the B Team could already access, they wanted more.

Fighting for racial and gender equity provides the perfect pretext to shake down American corporations, both through the courts and the regulatory apparatus. Not only does it have the potential to be lucrative, but it provides a convenient rationale for redirecting federal resources to Democratic voting blocs. That's because the way the administration defines racial and gender equity is narrowly tailored to favor groups heavily aligned with the Democratic Party.

Interestingly, protection from racial and gender discrimination is not the controversial part of this agenda. It's the word *equity* that separates the left from the right. Used in this context, *equity* is a euphemism for substituting equality of opportunity with equality of outcome. Like redefining racism to mean disparate impact, this is an example of the left changing definitions to create a pretext for an otherwise unjustifiable confiscation.

In a video tweeted by Kamala Harris the day before she was elected vice president, Harris memorably explained that "[t]he problem with [equality] is that not everybody's starting from the same place." Instead, she embraced equity, saying, "Equitable treatment means we all end up at the same place."[7]

This idea completely rejects the very American premise of meritocracy. The American Dream has always meant that people who work hard can get ahead. Both great success and great failure are possible here because we don't force everything to be equal. Disadvantages based on skin color or gender may be offset by advantages in talent, work ethic, family stability, or community. Just being born in the United States offers a sizable advantage over being born virtually anywhere else in the world. But the left would have us believe that certain Democratic voting blocs are inherently incapable of succeeding. Talk about racism!

Equity suggests that the only cure for racism is more racism. Since Black people have had historical disadvantages, policies must now be developed to offer benefits based on skin color. Essentially, they argue the only way to equalize outcomes is to treat people unequally. Conveniently, this narrative could also be used to justify an unprecedented weaponization of the federal bureaucracy to help Democrats defy the odds in the 2022 midterms.

Weaponizing Every Federal Agency

Though virtually forgotten by the time the midterms rolled around in November 2022, the White House had announced early on that the Biden/Harris administration would be "putting equity at the center of the agenda with a whole of government approach to embed racial justice across federal agencies, policies, and programs."[8] More than ninety federal agencies had announced strategies to remake their missions around racial and gender equity.[9]

Perhaps the most alarming of these efforts was the attempt to use equity as a pretext for federal election interference. In his March 2021 Executive Order on Promoting Access to Voting, Biden directed the head of each of the six hundred federal agencies to develop a plan to "protect and promote the exercise of the right to vote," to "expand access to voter registration and accurate election information," and to "combat misinformation."[10] I had to read it twice. Elections are administered by states. Federal employees are hired to administer federal programs, not to help the ruling party get out the vote to specific groups that tend to vote for the ruling party.

Federal employees are explicitly prohibited by law from participating in political activities. Passed in 1939, the Hatch Act is intended to "ensure that federal programs are administered in a nonpartisan fashion, to protect federal employees from political coercion in the workplace, and to ensure that federal employees are advanced based on merit and not based on political affiliation."[11] But Democrats make a distinction between aligning for votes and helping collect ballots. They consider the latter to be apolitical, despite their transparent efforts to target ballot collection to demographics most likely to vote Democratic.

Biden's order explicitly directed federal agencies to target Black and Native American communities, as well as federal employees. It called for the assistance of nonprofit "civil rights and disability rights" groups, many of whom primarily advocate for voting blocs that help Democrats.[12] Coincidentally, in 2020, Biden received 87 percent of the Black vote and 66 percent of the Hispanic/Latino vote.[13] The Native American vote is much harder to isolate, but between 60 and 90 percent of the Native American vote in precincts on the Navajo Nation went to Biden in 2020.[14] Felon partisan preferences are also hard to track. But a 2014 academic study found that in New York State, there are six Democrats for every one Republican among felons. Other states in the study were closer to five to one, but they cite a study saying 73 percent of convicts who turn out for presidential elections would vote Democratic.[15] There are no data on federal employee voting patterns, but a 2016 study found 95 percent of political contributions by federal employees went to Hillary Clinton over Donald Trump.[16]

Using the pretext of racial and gender equality, Biden and Harris can mobilize every federal agency to get out the vote for specific groups that just happen to be most likely to support Biden and Harris. Such a move weaponizes the whole of federal government in pursuit of partisan objectives and partisan candidates. Did this effort contribute to the surprising results of the 2022 midterms? Time will tell.

Biden's order gave agencies two hundred days to submit plans to his domestic policy advisor, Susan Rice. But as of this writing, none have been made public. Both House Republicans and government watchdogs sought access to those agency plans leading up to the midterms, but the Biden/Harris administration refused to produce them. In a lawsuit filed to enforce its Freedom of Information Act (FOIA) request, the Foundation for Government Accountability called the order an "unconstitutional taxpayer-funded 'get out the vote' effort designed to benefit the president's political party."[17] Two weeks before the midterms, the DOJ claimed executive privilege. It is evidently none of the public's business how the Biden administration is using taxpayer dollars to fund progressive election interference.

Researchers Tarren Bragdon and Stewart Whitson say they couldn't help but notice similarities between the president's executive order and a December 2020 policy brief by the progressive nonprofit Demos that suggested turning the bureaucracy into "voter registration agencies."

In a *Wall Street Journal* editorial, important questions were raised about the effort. "Promoting voter registration and participation—i.e., mobilizing voters—is an inherently political act for a partisan president. The resulting efforts can be directed at groups expected to vote for the president's party and may take the form of pressure to support the party or its policies."[18]

One of the agencies that went all in on the voter registration effort was the Department of Housing and Urban Development. In guidance distributed to housing authority directors, the agency provided instructions for public housing agencies to become official voter registration agencies under the National Voter Registration Act of 1993.

Under HUD guidance, housing agencies can permit the use of public spaces for candidate forums, voting drop boxes, and voting sites, as long as they don't "suggest that benefits are in any way tied to a participant's voting activity." That guidance to more than three thousand executive directors covered more than 1.2 million housing units.[19] Nevertheless, these activities represent a striking change in procedure.

Months before the midterms, the Heritage Foundation's election expert Hans von Spakovsky expressed concerns to the Daily Signal.

"If an individual is dealing with government—whether for Social Security, Medicaid, or veterans' benefits—when a government clerk tells them to register to vote, the typical reaction for someone getting government benefits is: 'I better vote for the party in power, or my benefits will be denied.'"[20]

Even before Biden was elected, state and local housing authorities were already engaging in get-out-the-vote efforts to partisan advantage—and have continued since. One nonprofit to which federal funds have flowed is Columbia Housing of South Carolina. During the municipal election of 2021, under the direction of board chairman Ernest Cromartie III, the agency redirected resources to a get-out-the-vote operation within public housing using "daily robocalls and text messages." Cromartie had donated to one of the mayoral candidates in that race. Four other board members or their spouses had donated to the same candidate, totaling thousands of dollars. Then they used the housing authority's credibility and resources to maximize votes from public housing recipients.

How likely is it that the demographic in public housing skewed in favor of the candidate the board supported? That candidate defended the efforts, claiming such get-out-the-vote efforts by the housing agency were common.[21]

Race is also the focus of the DOJ's Combatting Redlining Initiative. When launched in October 2021, the program was touted by Attorney General Merrick Garland as an effort to make "far more robust use of our fair lending authorities." The new assistant attorney general for civil rights, Kristen Clarke, added: "[R]edlining is not a problem from a bygone era but a practice that remains pervasive in the lending industry today."[22]

Targeting Politically Noncompliant Businesses

In addition to the DOJ initiative, the SEC is attempting to remake its mission to serve the interest of equity. This will involve adding a whole new level of mandatory disclosures. At the time of this writing, Gensler has yet to release his anticipated human capital management (HCM) disclosure rule, but he has signaled that his agency will demand intrusive data collection from American companies in an effort to compel compliance with the administration's political and social justice agenda.[23]

In a June 2021 speech, Gensler described some of the metrics he would like to force companies to disclose. In addition to ESG metrics, Gensler would have companies gather and make public complete workforce demographics, turnover statistics, compensation, benefits packages, and training.[24] Though these disclosures will be marketed as a way to increase diversity, they're really intended to ratchet up pressure on companies to conform with a unified agenda. Activists could then target companies based on their disclosures as part of a lawsuit, a public pressure campaign, or to demand retaliation against the company from other companies up or down the supply chain.

Does anyone really believe Gensler will concern himself with the lack of ideological diversity at public universities, the lack of underprivileged rural Americans in corporate boardrooms, or the overrepresentation of Black NBA players? Of course not. If, as a result of Biden's forced compliance to political ideology, employers begin to discriminate against those who hold unapproved views, will Gensler's diversity and inclusion values extend to the unvaxxed, the climate deniers, or the detransitioned trans kids who have the temerity to speak out? No. Gensler's HCM disclosures will help the agency identify targets for enforcement actions. They may allow government to police the unconscious bias trainings companies offer, the salaries they pay, or the length of paid maternity leave they allow.

Other federal agencies have also geared up to prioritize racial and gender grievances ahead of their traditional missions. Biden's appointees to various agencies reflect those priorities. Many have little experience with the missions of the agencies they will represent. They are chosen for their experience with diversity, equity, and inclusion.

Starting at the top, we have a deeply unpopular Vice President Kamala Harris, whose "word salad" press conferences have become consistently embarrassing for the administration.[25] Considering President Biden's apparent mental decline, by the time this book gets into the hands of readers, she may already be the president of the United States.

Among her most noteworthy professional accomplishments is the aggressive prosecution of the five biggest banks in the United States during her time as California attorney general. Harris was instrumental in reeling in a $20 billion settlement for victims of mortgage abuse. Never mind that more than 70 percent of that amount was used to remove people from their homes or cancel unrecoverable debt.[26] Most of California's $410 million share of that settlement was redirected by Governor Jerry Brown to pay off state housing bonds.[27]

Nonetheless, Harris has bona fides in two important priorities for the Biden administration: her history of taking on banks, and her presumed credibility on issues of race and gender by virtue of her own race and gender.

Heading up the all-important student financial assistance programs for the administration is Richard Cordray, the original CFPB director.[28] Cordray was responsible for reinstating the disparate impact standard that weaponized the agency against lenders during the Obama administration. Former enforcement attorney Ronald Rubin, who was hired by Cordray, has written extensive accounts of the agency's abuses of power under Cordray. He described a culture of discrimination within the very agency charged with rooting it out. He described the targeting of specific entities, the withholding of exculpatory information, the stonewalling of Congress, and the calculation of fines based on the maximum the agency thought a target could afford to pay.[29]

Cordray played dirty. He rigged the game. He violated the very principles he was hired to enforce. That makes him perfect for what the Biden/Harris administration has in mind. He delivered big fines for the administration. Now he sets his sights on student loan servicing companies and for-profit colleges.

Over at HUD, Biden's stalled nominee for HUD assistant secretary is former CFPB acting director David Uejio.[30] His nomination has been held up by Senator Pat Toomey over concerns about his anti-police rhetoric and lack of experience in housing. But he isn't there to be an expert on housing. Uejio was among the loyal partisans hired at CFPB's inception to pursue aggressive regulation of banks. Among his top priorities when he took over CFPB from Cordray was the promotion of racial equity.[31] His move to HUD likely has more to do with his ability to extract settlements from banks than with any skills he has in managing effective federal housing programs. With Uejio now moving to HUD, the CFPB has a new director.

That assignment is a critical one. The expansion of that agency is vital to the left's efforts to transform the American economy. Using claims of racial bias, the Democratic Party hopes to nationalize America's credit rating industry. In so doing, they can ensure that compliance with partisan goals becomes a requirement for any American seeking to use credit.

Big Plans for the CFPB

A major fly in the ointment for President Biden came in October 2022. His administration had big plans for the agency. But the Constitution has finally been vindicated. It took more than ten years to accomplish, but a court has now recognized that the agency's funding mechanism was unconstitutional.

That was something we all knew from the start. I wrote in my first book that the CFPB was a new agency designed by the Obama administration to be impervious to interference from voters or their representatives. Until President Trump was elected, the agency was unlimited, unaccountable, and unchecked. It could easily be used to enforce an agenda that bypasses Congress, checks and balances, and oversight.

Instead of receiving its funding from Congress, the CFPB was funded by the Federal Reserve. Democrats described it as an attempt to make the agency independent from politics. Republicans saw it as a deliberate effort to sidestep government oversight by representatives of the people, making the agency both powerful and untouchable. Congress could not leverage its most potent weapon—the power of the purse.

During a July 2011 Oversight Committee hearing, I questioned Elizabeth Warren about the nascent agency's lack of accountability and obligation for transparency—a responsibility the CFPB continues to evade more than a decade later. At that time, Warren was serving as a Special Advisor to the Secretary of the Treasury for the CFPB. It would be another two years before Massachusetts voters would elect her to the United States Senate.

I knew the agency's design was a problem. But I did not fully appreciate at the time what would happen once similar patterns metastasized across agencies and even outside the federal government to insulate weaponized institutions from public pushback.

Though President Trump succeeded in temporarily clipping the agency's wings to some degree, the Biden/Harris administration had again unleashed it. Following the October 2022 ruling by the Fifth Circuit Court of Appeals that the agency's funding mechanism "violates the Appropriations Clause and the Constitution's underlying structural separation of powers," Democrats are expected to appeal.[32] Meanwhile, the agency continues its work, and the Biden/Harris administration continues its pattern of evading accountability.

For the important job at CFPB, Biden selected Rohit Chopra. A veteran of the original partisan CFPB, Chopra left in 2015 to serve as an advisor to the secretary of education before being nominated in 2018 to the Federal Trade Commission (FTC). While Trump CFPB director Kathy Kraninger believed in taking a preventative approach that relied on education rather than heavy-handed enforcement actions, Chopra was likely selected because he is the opposite of that.

"His track record at the FTC and CFPB demonstrates a commitment to regulatory activism," said Quyen Truong, a former assistant director and deputy general counsel at the CFPB.[33] In his Senate confirmation hearing, Chopra's aggressive regulatory agenda was a red flag for Republican senators concerned about the health of the American economy.

Pennsylvania senator Pat Toomey expressed grave concerns about Chopra's "'shoot first, aim second' approach to the facts by posting online inaccurate allegations about several credit unions" without checking his facts. CFPB was forced to retract those allegations.

"Based on Commissioner Chopra's record, I'm concerned he'd return the CFPB to the hyperactive, lawbreaking, antibusiness, unaccountable agency it was under Obama administration," Toomey said at the hearing. Toomey described Chopra's work at the FTC: "In one FTC case, three of his fellow commissioners publicly rebuked his dissent in a case for its 'disregard of facts and the law,' making 'misleading claims,' and relying on 'false assertions.'"[34]

As expected, Chopra hit the ground running with an update to the CFPB's examination manual to return to the disparate impact standard. Chopra won't be limiting his disparate impact enforcement to lending. With a bias to find discrimination, he'll be going after "all consumer finance markets, including credit, servicing, collections, consumer reporting, payments, remittances, and deposits."

The *Wall Street Journal* reported that Chopra would go after overdraft fees in the hopes of eliminating a practice that he sees as discriminatory. Chopra has already defined redlining more expansively, going after companies whose marketing has the wrong number of white people. The *Journal* speculates, "Now it might go after companies if their social media ads are disproportionately clicked on by white people."[35]

Chopra was instrumental in an October 2021 settlement with Trustmark National Bank over allegations of redlining and lending discrimination in the heavily Democratic city of Memphis. Though Tennessee's 2020 electoral votes went overwhelmingly to Donald

Trump, Memphis's Shelby County went for Biden with 64 percent of the vote.[36]

The Trustmark lawsuit settlement calls for a $5 million payment to the CFPB and the Office of the Comptroller of the Currency. Another $3.85 million in loan subsidies goes to Black and Hispanic voters in Shelby County. Trustmark will pay another $400,000 to "developing community partnerships" (undoubtedly with partisan left-wing nonprofits) to majority-minority neighborhoods to increase access to residential mortgage credit, and $200,000 to market, advertise, and provide help with credit repair.

"Trustmark purposely excluded and discriminated against Black and Hispanic communities," Chopra explained in a news release announcing the settlement. "The federal government will be working to rid the market of racist business practices, including those by discriminatory algorithms."[37]

Yep, that's right. The Biden/Harris administration will argue that algorithms—formulas used to detect credit risk based on objective criteria—are also racist. In fact, the whole idea of predicting credit risk seems offensive to equity agenda adherents. Fortunately, with the court's ruling that the agency's off-the-books funding mechanism is unconstitutional, the agency's future is unclear. At a minimum, Democrats may be forced to support structural changes if they want to preserve the agency. These may include congressional budget controls, inspector general oversight, and government audits that Republicans have proposed and Democrats have categorically rejected prior to the ruling.[38] Until the CFPB exhausts any appeals to the court ruling, it is unknown whether CFPB orders against American companies can be enforced.

Credit Scores Nationalized

The idea that merit-based credit scoring must be replaced by a "fairer" system that distorts the risk assessments in favor of Democratic voting blocs is a priority for the new CFPB, for Chairman

Waters, and for the Biden/Harris administration. Once partisans control the scores that dictate access to credit, they can insert any number of political criteria.

Just as ESG scores for corporations compel compliance with a leftist agenda, some activist groups propose individual ESG scores that could shake up the ratings. Instead of this new credit rating reflecting a client's ability to repay a loan, it would reflect a borrower's worthiness to access credit based on criteria politicians set.

Though the administration isn't talking explicitly about using ESG metrics to calculate individual credit scores, there are other activist groups signaling how that might be done. The Impact Investor, through its website describing all things ESG, describes what factors one might consider when calculating a personal ESG score.

"The purpose behind each person being assigned an individual ESG score is to help reward actions that will help move the world towards sustainability," the website explains. "While there are not currently any downsides to having an ESG score, regardless of how high or how low, there will come a time where too low of a score can result in denials for loans or services similar to the way credit scores currently function."

What are some of the factors Impact Investor suggests ESG-conscious consumers consider? "Buying a gun, alcohol, or even clothing," they suggest. "Not only will your purchases matter, but who you purchase from and how they do business. Your political affiliations also factor into your personal ESG score. Aside from the politics in governance, the party you support and even the person you vote for will make your score go up or down based on that person's actions, policies, and voting habits.

"The type of car you drive, how often, and even how many people are in the car when you drive will also come into play when deciding your score."[39]

Though none of these criteria have thus far been proposed by federal agencies, they give a general idea where credit ratings could go once partisans gain monopoly control of the rating process.

For her part, Waters has also proposed legislation to nationalize credit reporting, creating a single government monopoly over the practice. "Good credit is a gateway to wealth," she argued in a 2021 Financial Services Committee hearing. "Yet, for far too long, our credit reporting system has kept people of color and low-income persons from access to capital to start a small business; access to mortgage loans to become homeowners; and access to credit to meet financial emergencies."[40] Generally, low credit scores are responsible for those challenges, but Waters shows little interest in considering the root causes of low credit scores in inner-city Democratic voting blocs.

Waters wants to fix the problem of racial disparity in credit scores by fixing the credit scores. Race is not one of the factors credit rating agencies evaluate. Waters's real objection is not to racial discrimination, but to discrimination against people who aren't a good credit risk.

Nonetheless, Waters is not alone is calling for nationalized credit ratings that would enable the government to control who can get credit and who can't. Left-leaning think tank Demos is also calling for such a move—and the Biden/Harris administration is heeding the call. As part of its plan to invest in communities through housing, the Biden campaign criticized credit rating agencies for containing errors and contributing to racial disparities.[41]

Multinational law firm Paul, Weiss released a client memorandum in February 2021 that detailed the "coming transformation of the CFPB in the Biden administration." It is important in this instance to go back and remember that "in June 2020, the Supreme Court in *Seila Law* struck down the for-cause removal protection that applied to the director" of the CFPB.

This, in essence, converted the organization from an independent agency into an executive agency much more under the influence of the president. The Biden administration is the first presidential administration in which CFPB will serve as part of the president's administration, so financiers advise for people to keep an eye on Biden seeking to utilize the office for his own political agenda.

The memo signaled several changes to expect. CFPB director Chopra was expected to "strongly scrutinize the credit reporting industry," as just recently he stated that "[i]t is critical that bad actors not be allowed to weaponize the credit reporting system against consumers." Chopra is expected to go along with Biden's proposal to create a public credit reporting agency within CFPB, "which would use rental history, utility bills, and other non-traditional sources of data to evaluate credit."[42]

Between aggressive regulation, targeted shakedowns of deep-pocketed industries, antiracist racism to favor Democratic voting blocs, the weaponization of federal agencies in partisan elections, and the nationalization of credit ratings, the Biden/Harris administration's agenda indicates they will choose preservation of power over prosperity every day of the week.

The disparate impact standard makes all this possible. The left continues to elevate civil rights above constitutionally guaranteed civil liberties. But they have a problem. Civil rights, as Democrats choose to interpret them, are not enshrined in the Constitution. Free speech and other natural rights are. It would take a constitutional amendment to overturn them. But bad interpretations of civil rights policy are simply a matter of law. And elections have consequences. In this case, if Americans want to turn the tide on abusive interpretations of discrimination, it must be Congress, not the B Team, that holds the trump card. That is easier said than done in a world where narratives are set by leftist journalists and progressive activists, amplified by content-moderated social media feeds, and taught to vulnerable kids through partisan curriculum. But pushback against the infiltration of leftist political narratives into our institutions—and particularly our schools—is picking up steam.

CHAPTER 8

Unions

The Education B Team

Stay-at-home mother January Littlejohn was the volunteer of the year in her daughter's Leon County, Florida, middle school. She knew every teacher and was deeply involved in her daughter's education. She thought she knew everything that was going on at school. When her thirteen-year-old daughter, following the social transition of three of her close friends, began to question her own gender identity, Littlejohn, a licensed mental health counselor herself, was concerned. There had been no prior evidence of gender confusion.

She and her husband got their daughter a counselor and did a deep dive researching the topic. They didn't reject her and, in fact, consented to her use of a nickname at school. Hoping to help, they confided in her daughter's teacher, expressing their concerns that this newfound interest seemed to be driven more by social factors than any history of gender confusion.

Unbeknownst to the Littlejohns, the school district had a written policy for handling such situations—one that bestowed extraordinary rights to the child and the school but cut the parents out of the process. As the fruits of their daughter's gender exploration began to manifest in anxiety, depression, and social withdrawal, the Littlejohns grew more alarmed.

Little did they know, their daughter had been guided into a full transition at school by teachers and staff. At a meeting with school officials and mental health staff, she had signed a six-page document changing her name, designating a restroom preference, even choosing which gender to room with on school field trips. This minor child, not old enough to vote, drink, or enter into a contract, was granted sole authority to decide whether her parents could be notified of this monumental life decision.

The "Gender Nonconforming Student Support Plan" was a tool authorized in the Leon County Schools "Lesbian, Gay, Bisexual, Transgender, Gender Nonconforming and Questioning Support Guide." That guidance explicitly called for parents not to be informed when their children announce a transgender identity. To justify this position, the guide claims, "Outing the student can be very dangerous to the student's health and well-being. Outing students to their parents can literally make them homeless." It calls for children to be able to choose a restroom without parent notification.[1]

Littlejohn was outraged. In a speech to the Florida Family Policy Council, she described the impact of the policy on her family, which she said sent a dangerous message that parents are the enemy, that school personnel can do a better job protecting children than their parents can, and that minor children have a legally protected right to keep from their parents any steps taken by the district to promote a gender change. Schools are grossly unqualified to be making decisions that could lead children toward experimental medications and irreversible surgeries with lifetime consequences, Littlejohn suggested.[2]

Littlejohn's experience is unfortunately not unique. The social media account Libs of TikTok has virtually become a household name by simply retweeting TikTok videos of radical leftist teachers bragging about indoctrinating their students, often with gender ideology. Though some are isolated incidents, we will see that the new reality is that victim narratives of the social justice movement are being deliberately injected into the curriculum with the full support of national teachers unions.

The primary focus of the two largest national unions—the National Education Association (NEA) and the American Federation of Teachers (AFT)—is no longer teachers. It's politics. In 2021, NEA spent $66 million on political activities and lobbying, compared to just $32 million on representational activities. The NEA spent twice as much on political activities as representational activities that year, according to an analysis from the Government Accountability Institute.[3] The unions function more like left-wing super PACs than labor unions. And with the help of Democratic politicians, their efforts to influence kids with partisan messaging have become more aggressive.

In fact, undercover investigations by independent journalists at Project Veritas suggest leftists in school leadership positions are going so far as to screen out applicants they deem too likely to be conservative. Residents of Greenwich, Connecticut, were shocked after Project Veritas released video of a school administrator admitting to discriminatory hiring practices. Jeremy Boland confessed on tape that he doesn't hire Catholics, conservatives, or even people over the age of thirty. But instead of denouncing this illegal discrimination, the Connecticut Education Association did damage control, sending a memo to teachers with suggestions for avoiding getting caught on hidden camera. Instructing teachers not to speak to journalists who have not been vetted, and to keep meetings closed, the union advised teachers not to drive traffic to the Project Veritas site by searching for the clip.[4]

Schools are no longer just an institution dedicated to educating kids. American public schools have become a political battlefield for social justice warriors who are intent on leveraging power and diverting funds to achieve political goals. The voters don't call the shots. The unions do. In this case, it isn't even the B Team bureaucrats doing the bulk of the damage—although they do plenty. It's the partisan political organizations masquerading as teacher advocates who are subjugating the needs of kids to the demands of politics.

After all, we can still vote for school board members. But unions are outside our control. There remain countless dedicated teachers in the ranks of America's public schools. In fact, the partisan makeup of teachers in America is hardly one-sided. Surveys indicate 57 percent of teachers in America identify as conservative or moderate.[5] But the agenda is set and the resources directed by the people who run the unions—particularly during Democratic administrations. Union leaders are the ones who meet with politicians, set political priorities, lobby for dollars, develop and promote curriculum, and allocate the union dues they collect from hardworking teachers. So, who are they and what do they really believe?

Compromising Education

To get a full picture of where their union priorities lie, we need look no further than the people at the helm. During the pandemic, the biggest teachers union in America, the three-million-member NEA, has had two leaders: Lily Eskelsen García, whose term ended in August 2020, and current president Rebecca Pringle.

Eskelsen García, whose tenure began in 2014, oversaw what she called "an incredible transformation" in which unions expanded their focus from education to what she refers to as "the whole child." In an interview with *Education Week*, she explained, "That child's world is our business. Whether or not that child's parent is facing discrimination . . . is our business."[6] Hence, we see discrimination is a major priority of teachers unions and a justification for deep involvement in the Black Lives Matter political movement.[7] More importantly, it shows that teachers unions see every aspect of a child's life as their bailiwick. Not just education, but politics, sexuality, parental relationships, values, and more.

Eskelsen García described how she responds to the heresy from those within her union suggesting the union's "core business" should be advocating for their members, negotiating contracts, and protecting pensions. "We have expanded internally and externally what it means to say all students will be prepared for lives they deserve to live," she told *Education Week*.

This focus on the whole child represents a dramatic expansion of the union's mission, putting teachers and unions in the political driver's seat and uniquely positioning them to control what kind of political messages, mental health services, and social values students are exposed to.

Under the subsequent leader, Becky Pringle, the union published a "Racial Justice in Education Resource Guide" to inject leftist narratives about "white supremacy culture," implicit bias and microaggressions, and victimhood into classrooms.[8] The *New York Times* gushes that Pringle has pushed the union to take on a "social justice role."[9]

Both Eskelsen García and Pringle have been active in presidential politics, with Eskelsen García providing an early endorsement of Hillary Clinton in 2016 and Pringle endorsing Joe Biden.[10] During the pandemic and race riots of 2020, both women took firm positions that were arguably harmful to children. Eskelsen García, echoing the Black Lives Matter movement, argued against providing basic school security for students, citing "grave concerns" about employing police as school resource officers to protect students from in-school violence.[11] It seemed children's safety took a backseat to political activism.

Pringle, on the other hand, argued that children's safety was so important, she had to proactively fight against schools reopening. Pringle tweeted, it's no secret we want to keep our students and schools safe.[12] To keep children safe from a disease that rarely infects them, Pringle and her union backed closures that arguably widened educational disparities, increased anxiety and loneliness, and increased the prevalence of childhood obesity.[13]

At the American Federation of Teachers, Randi Weingarten has ruled the roost since 2008. After a brief stint teaching, this attorney came up in the ranks as president of New York City's United Federation of Teachers from 1998 to 2008.[14] Weingarten has been laser-focused on increasing federal involvement in public schools and promoting politically charged curricula. This federal interference amplifies the control of the B Team while minimizing the input of parents and their community leaders.

During her tenure, Weingarten has spent extravagantly on political causes, according to research from the Capital Research Center's Influence Watch project. Political contributions from AFT grew more than fivefold, from $3.7 million in 2008 to $20 million in 2020.[15] Using OpenSecrets to track those contributions, Influence Watch observed 99 percent of those donations funded Democratic campaigns and political causes.[16] Collecting a salary exceeding $560,000 a year, Weingarten's earnings are nine times that of the average teacher she claims to represent.[17]

Weingarten uses the AFT's $300 million budget like a campaign fund to promote left-wing political priorities that may have only a tangential relevance to classroom learning. She has prioritized abortion access, "environmental justice," and gun restrictions, according to reporting by the Freedom Foundation.[18]

Those priorities may not do much for the children, but they've been very good for union leaders. "Weingarten and National Education Association chief Rebecca Pringle probably have more power in the Biden administration than any senator or cabinet member," wrote former New York lieutenant governor Betsy McCaughey in the *New York Post*.[19]

Both Weingarten and her politically active wife have been criticized for their frequent backing of problematic pro-union candidates and leaders in New York City. There, they have backed candidates credibly accused of sexual harassment, sexual assault, fiscal mismanagement, and other misconduct.[20]

Are Union Priorities Teacher Priorities?

Whether the work of these national unions bears any relevance to the things teachers care about is debatable. One thing is for sure— union priorities increasingly bear a strong resemblance to the things politicians care about. In fact, between 2005 and 2021 political and lobbying spending by AFT and NEA increased by $74 million. Among the line items for 2021—a combined $1.475 million to Georgia democrat Stacey Abrams's Fair Fight Action PAC, $30 million to left-wing issue advocacy groups, and $3.5 million to the host organization of the 2020 Democratic National Convention.[21] Between 1990 and 2020, the combined donations of teachers unions to political candidates was $91.8 million, of which $3.8 million went to Republican candidates.

We may not expect teachers unions to align with voters in general—unions don't represent voters—even though they seem to drive a lot of decisions that affect them. But it would seem union priorities ought to bear some resemblance to teacher priorities. And perhaps if you only consider the TikTok set, they do. But education seems to be an "afterthought" for AFT and NEA.[22] Though they are anxious to circumvent the decisions of the people parents elect, they don't seem too interested in how well kids learn basic reading, writing, or arithmetic.

Doing a deep dive into the finances, governance, and political activity of national teachers unions, the Government Accountability Institute (GAI) uncovered details that cast doubt on the stated mission of national teachers unions. In truth, they now function just like any other appendage of the B Team. GAI traced how they use the pretext of social justice to funnel money through elite political networks that enrich their friends and empower their allies. Teachers unions mine data, grow government, and employ an army of progressive liberal arts graduates.

In their groundbreaking report, GAI undertook an analysis of AFT's yearly resolutions to quantify where their priorities lie. As one might expect, a large number of resolutions—fifty-four—focused on education, including "learning, schools, classrooms, teachers or students." But other topics were even more dominant. During the election year of 2020, the topic of elections was mentioned in resolutions 183 times, being mentioned in fourteen of the thirty-four resolutions, or 42 percent of the total. In general, GAI found the context of those references to be expressions of support for then-candidate Joe Biden, to call for election reforms that are believed to favor Democrats, or to criticize President Donald Trump. GAI found references to left-wing narratives about the need to save our democracy, fight violence or authoritarianism, and address leftist narratives about race.[23]

In their report, GAI described the context of election-related language in AFT resolutions, writing:

> When election reforms are discussed, they are framed in terms of increasing minority participation in the election, combatting right-wing corruption, and simplifying the process by which people access the polls and cast their vote. When they discuss the 2020 presidential election itself, AFT attacked what it called the violence, corruption, and incompetence of the Trump administration. They framed the election of any Democrat, and later, Joe Biden, as a rebuke of fiscal austerity and a necessary measure to rescue American democracy from the criminal behavior of the sitting president. Joe Biden was also upheld in 2020 AFT resolutions as a candidate who would solve the COVID-19 pandemic, restore sane foreign policy, and end systemic racism (largely through greater investment in public services).

By the summer of 2021, it was becoming clear that the public was not pleased with Biden's performance on any of those measures. New COVID-19 variants fueled a reenergized pandemic, a foreign policy debacle in Afghanistan was undermining faith in Biden's judgment, and legislative defeats in Congress gave him little for which to take credit. But incompetence in the Oval Office didn't seem to be an issue anymore for AFT.

With no presidential election to influence, GAI noted sharp declines in references to Trump or Biden, even as approval ratings for Biden began dropping precipitously throughout 2021. The topic of elections seemed to have lost its luster in 2021 as well, with only eight mentions across two resolutions that year. Still, GAI found resolutions condemning former president Trump for discrediting the 2020 election and emboldening foreign autocrats. There was even a resolution that summer—seven months before a nuclear power would invade Ukraine—to hold elected officials accountable who refuse to cut defense spending.[24]

Resolutions were arguably being used as a tool to drive public opinion and influence elections. But there's more we can learn from GAI's analysis. The topics that seemed to show up again and again show us what is most important to teachers unions. It's not teachers. It's not children. It's dogma.

Sixteen of thirty-four resolutions in 2020, or 47 percent, addressed issues of race or ethnicity. The trend was repeated in 2021 with 40 percent (eight of twenty) addressing the topic. In their analysis, GAI found, "Specifically, the resolutions addressed issues pressed by Black Lives Matter organizations, social justice, racism, diversity and equity." In addition, sexuality issues got outsize attention from teachers unions, with five resolutions in 2020 and three more in 2021.

The final indignity is the approach unions took to COVID-19. In 2020, when President Trump was at the helm, mentions of COVID-19 dominated AFT's resolutions, with 165 separate mentions across twenty-one of thirty-four resolutions. But by the summer of 2021, with Biden at the helm, it merited just forty-two mentions across a mere seven resolutions. And the context changed dramatically. While the 2020 resolutions called out Trump for failing to manage COVID, Biden is rarely mentioned by 2021. Just two reference Biden, both favorably. Although Biden had the assistance of a vaccine, he presided over more COVID-19 deaths than President Trump did without a vaccine.[25] Yet the AFT had little to say about Biden's milestone relative to their full-throated criticism of Trump.

Looking at the COVID-19-related resolutions, GAI concluded, "the authors of these resolutions explicitly tie reopening plans to widespread access to free, government- or employee-provided personal protection equipment (PPE), increased educational funding by the federal government, abolishing 'whiteness-centered curricula,' and broad renovations of public-school buildings."[26]

Based on this analysis, it's hard to see the national teachers unions as anything other than a partisan political operation. What should be a teacher-driven institution focused on providing a world-class education has become a cudgel for injecting leftist orthodoxy in public institutions. Though we don't elect these people, they have an enormous influence over how our children are taught to see the world. They pull the strings, unimpeded by anything we do on Election Day.

On any given day, the calls to action on AFT's website are more relevant to the partisan agenda of Democrats than the educational agenda of teachers. "Pass the Equality Act," "Protecting the Right to Vote," and "Eliminate Student Debt" were among the calls to action when I visited the union's "Take Action" page.[27] Nothing on science, math, or reading.

The only messaging directed at teachers was a call to fund the AFT Solidarity Strike Fund, which would enable AFT to leverage teachers' jobs to promote the union's political priorities. In fact, I see little evidence that AFT promotes any real policy change in education. What they really want seems to be the same thing the B Team always wants—to grow government. They don't want parents being empowered or elected officials interfering. They'll decide what's best for the kids based on what's best for them.

Propaganda at School

One of the ways they promote political activism is by indoctrinating kids. President Biden, inadvertently saying the quiet part out loud, told teachers that kids are "yours when they're in the classroom." At an April 2022 Teacher of the Year event, the president said, "They're all our children. . . . They're not somebody else's children; they're like yours when they're in the classroom."[28] Indeed, the curriculum and the textbooks being used in many classrooms might never pass muster with parents. Florida officials rejected 41 percent of math textbooks after a 2022 review concluded the books depict "alcohol use, divorce, marijuana, illegal activities, gender bias, racial prejudice, etc."[29]

The matter of who best serves the interest of children has animated many similar conflicts in America's public schools as activist groups seek to influence how politically charged topics are framed. We all saw blue Virginia turn red in 2021 over concerns about controversial race-based curriculum, gender politics, parental rights, and the failure to protect students from sexual abuse in their schools.[30]

A full exploration of the strategies and tactics being used to inject woke politics into public school curricula is beyond the scope of this book. Suffice it to say that a burgeoning industry of political activists are working closely with teachers unions to inject political narratives into our children's classrooms. They pull the strings, and the kids become the puppets.

The topics of race, gender, and equity that drive the progressive political agenda also seem to drive the B Team's educational agenda (as opposed to math, science, or writing). Weingarten insists schools do not teach the controversial principles of Critical Race Theory, which teaches that America's history and free market system are inherently racist and classifies people as victims or oppressors based on their skin color. But her union issued a resolution calling on teachers to celebrate "Black Lives Matter at School (BLMAS) Week" and "teach lessons about related topics."[31]

What are these lessons and where do they come from? The NEA

provides a whole resource guide to use at BLMAS Week, including links to activist sites that provide lesson plans such as "Introduction of Transgender and Nonbinary Identities with I Am Jazz," targeted at pre-K through second-grade students, and "Role Play: What We Don't Learn About the Black Panther Party—but Should."[32] The author of that particular lesson is a group called Rethinking Schools, which frequently attends NEA events to give presentations on activism in the classroom.[33] The group describes itself as "a nonprofit publisher and advocacy organization dedicated to sustaining and strengthening public education through social justice teaching and education activism."[34]

For her part, Weingarten has been an outspoken proponent of controversial curriculum and political censorship. A database featuring lesson plans on politically charged topics of race, equity, and gender was developed during her tenure. Share My Lesson helps teachers indoctrinate kids to take controversial political views as fact, teaching that Columbus Day is actually Indigenous People's Day, introducing principles of Critical Race Theory, all but framing the progressive narrative of the defund-the-police movement.[35]

In addition to teaching kids the narratives of the left, teachers unions have advocated for withholding from them opposing points of view by labeling such views as dangerous misinformation.

The NEA famously sent a letter to social media companies during the height of the 2021 general election season expressing concern about political violence. The concern was a legitimate one, but it was a concern that was conspicuously absent during the destructive 2020 BLM riots. The letter, cherry-picking real examples of parents objecting to school mask mandates, implored media platforms that "this rising tide of violence must be stopped," and implied they must be the ones to stop it (presumably through censorship). But the only violence the NEA cited was "a small but violent group of radicalized adults who falsely believe that graduate level courses about racism are being taught in K–12 public schools because of misinformation spread on social media."[36]

This letter came just on the heels of a letter to the White House from the National School Boards Association (NSBA) comparing engaged parents to domestic terrorists.[37] That letter, later found to have been instigated by Biden administration secretary of education Miguel Cardona, was used as a justification for the administration to invoke the Patriot Act against the left's ideological opponents. Speaking to Fox News, one father who is the executive director at Fight for Schools said, "This looks like a concerted effort between the federal government and outside groups like the NEA and NSBA to interfere with the First Amendment rights of parents." Ian Prior went on to speculate, "it doesn't stretch the imagination to believe that the federal government was also involved in the NEA letter."[38]

Weingarten, too, has joined the fight to "combat misinformation" and "help educators and their students navigate a sea of online disinformation."[39] In 2022 she inked a deal with online "fact-checking" site NewsGuard to provide 1.7 million licenses in schools to filter internet content. Not surprisingly, NewsGuard is a for-profit company with a reputation for disparate treatment of left- and right-wing narratives. According to the Media Research Center (MRC), NewsGuard rates leftist corporate media sites 27 points higher than conservative ones.[40] The MRC sites as an example the ratings difference between information promoting abortion and information opposing it. NewsGuard rates Planned Parenthood a 75/100 rating for credibility. But the pro-life LifeSite News, which provides the counterpoint to abortion arguments, is rated 17.5/100.[41] NewsGuard denies that it is a potent tool for injecting left-wing narratives into schools and censoring or discrediting narratives from the right.[42]

Weingarten's war on free speech didn't end there. Attempting to leverage the $6.3 billion holdings of state and local teacher pension funds in Facebook parent company Meta, Weingarten urged pension fund trustees to support a shareholder resolution aimed at curtailing "misinformation" on the platform. Claiming the mental health of children would be at stake if people could read right-wing narratives on Facebook, the resolution called out "false conspiracy theories like QAnon and catastrophically destructive health disinformation."[43] Given that data now show that lockdowns and school closures were ineffective, masking had little impact on health outcomes, vaccines did little to prevent reinfection in children, outdoor transmission was rare, and natural immunity was real, it seems Weingarten and her political benefactors were the real purveyors of catastrophic health disinformation.[44]

Decisions about curriculum, textbooks, and political narratives in schools should not be driven by unaccountable B Team entities like AFT and NEA. They aren't accountable to parents. They can't be voted out. They don't represent parents or students. Yet they seek to usurp the role of democratic institutions in American public education. Now, with their focus on the whole child, unions have positioned themselves to be political players in a much broader and more lucrative range of public services.

Feeding the Woke-Industrial Complex

To end the biggest strike in thirty years, the Los Angeles Unified School District had to agree, among other things, to fund thirty community schools.[45] Then, in February 2020, the district cut $25 million from school security budgets (school resource officers) and redirected the money to the hiring of more woke staff in jobs that push "restorative justice," "culturally-relevant curriculum," and "ethnic studies."[46] As part of that effort, the district transitioned ten more public schools into community schools for a total of forty district-wide. When the district wanted to reopen schools following the pandemic, the union once again demanded (and got) thirty more community schools as a condition for teachers to return.[47]

That's just the beginning. California governor Gavin Newsom in his 2022 budget pledged to transition one-third of California schools to this union-approved model.[48] At the federal level, President Biden has proposed to increase funding for these schools from $30 million a year to $400 million a year—and his allies in Congress have complied by introducing the Full-Service Community School Expansion Act to commit $3.65 billion to schools that adopt the model.[49]

What is it about this particular model of education that has Democrats opening the taxpayer floodgates? It's not as if they have embraced innovative education models in the charter and private school world. I wish I could say it's the high level of education, the excellence of the teachers, or the academic results. But no one is even talking about that.

Consider what the union promotors of the model have to say about its virtues. The title of AFT's 2016 report praising community schools provides a hint: "Successful and Sustainable Community Schools: The Union as an Essential Ingredient." The report cites the model as "a unique advocacy lever that only the union has access to."[50]

What does that look like? Without even knowing the model, you would do well to guess that it will take power and decision making away from parents and local elected officials and give it to some entity within the B Team. It will redirect the flow of capital or taxpayer dollars to more politicized uses. And it will provide tools to weaken political opponents.

There are two primary differences between traditional public schools and community schools. First, community schools are run by teachers unions. Second, they dramatically expand the scope of education to provide a variety of external services to meet the "social, emotional, physical, mental health, and academic needs of students."[51]

In other words, they provide what they call "wraparound services" that do parents' jobs for them. No longer does a parent have to worry about a student's mental well-being. The unions will carefully select woke counselors to help. The government will take charge of everything from haircuts and grooming services to food pantries, dental and vision care, housing, transportation, social and emotional development programs, laundry—even yoga. And it's all free. For the student. Not for you. Taxpayers get to pay for all of it.[52] But teachers unions get to make the decisions. Parents need not worry about sharing their social, political, or religious values with their children—community schools will teach the values unions believe are important.

"We're trying to build a model around democratic unionism, and democratic running of schools, and real deep coalition work with parents and students that is actually capable of fighting for ongoing funding," said California Teachers Association vice president David Goldberg.[53]

But best of all, this model is profitable for the vendors and unions. Not only do they get to dangle lucrative contracts in front of a broad range of service providers, but they are entitled to the data they collect by monetizing biometric data.

New York City offers a detailed example of how this is done. The local government allocates money to the union, which then exercises the power to choose program providers whose political goals align with the union. The programs collect substantial amounts of biometric data on students and their families, which becomes a new asset they can use to enhance profits and power.

In its report on teachers unions, GAI traced an allocation from New York City's 2022 budget for $1 million to the National Association for the Advancement of Colored People (NAACP), which used the money to fund the Connect ALL Kids program to provide laptops to students. Preloaded on each of those laptops was software from NAACP partner KNeoMedia Limited. KNeoMedia harvests student data to track student progress, openly supporting the use of blockchain technology for the digital tracking of students.[54]

The company's executive director, Frank Lieberman, "has amazing first-hand contacts worldwide in the areas of entertainment, television, technology, pharmaceuticals, and politics," according to his LinkedIn bio.[55] With more than forty years in media and marketing, Lieberman has produced movies and television shows for NBC, CBS, ABC, and PBS and has done marketing for the likes of

Pfizer, Coca-Cola, IBM, and Johnson & Johnson.[56] In touting subsidiary KNeoWorld's partnership with the NAACP in 2018, a press release described how the alliance gives KNeoWorld "an established and very wide-reaching infrastructure across the United States, and the not-for-profit accreditation, to fast-track the sales and the rollout of the KNeoWorld content throughout the US."[57]

Being able to broker these kinds of deals brings a whole new level of power to America's teachers unions. More importantly, it gives them a taxpayer-funded political advantage they can use in their ongoing ideological battle against the political right.

In this case, the biggest political advantage is the ability to politicize the classroom. Theoretically, a political party would have a powerful advantage if it could puppet the next generation of activists. A curriculum designed to teach kids what to think instead of how to think would teach partisan narratives and suppress opposing views. A party or activist group that could control how mental health is delivered, whose values are taught, or how opposing views are perceived could control a counterfeit substitute for democracy. Such a party isn't dependent on winning elections to wield this power over kids. They need to command the loyalty of institutions that benefit from big government.

CHAPTER 9

The Unions Go Global

In the spring of 2022, an ad for Teacher Appreciation Week appeared in a major newspaper, lauding American teachers for reopening schools. Guess who placed it? It was the American Federation of Teachers, in an admirable display of post-pandemic backpedaling, considering this was well after the grim reality of school closure impacts had come into focus. Perhaps hoping the public might forget just how brazenly the unions had leveraged the well-being of kids to negotiate for progressive policy changes, the AFT's ad praised teachers for "working to safely reopen our classrooms and ensuring our kids and families bounce back academically, socially and emotionally." Certainly, many teachers did do that. But AFT did not.

"Despite political interference, disrespect for your professionalism, and a seemingly endless struggle for resources, you rise to the occasion," read the ad's passive-aggressive attack on political opponents.[1] In a classic case of projection, a press release announcing the ad claimed that "extremist politicians" had created difficulty for educators by "waging culture wars and trying to drive wedges between parents and teachers in order to weaken our public schools."[2]

Someone needs to make an "I DID THAT" sticker with Randi Weingarten's picture on it, to apply to every case file where educators and parents were put at odds by school pandemic policies.

As revealed through the inconvenient facts that have surfaced since the official pandemic ended and schools reopened, COVID-19 was a boon for teachers unions. And unions were willing to capitalize on the crisis, even if it meant selling out the kids. They influenced CDC medical guidelines, successfully delayed school reopenings, leveraged the crisis for more funding, and even made some lucrative deals for political cronies.

But at what cost? Predictably, allowing unaccountable interest groups to call the shots on pandemic response didn't pay off for American students, parents, or even teachers. The pandemic's academic and emotional consequences for kids may be generational. Not to mention the fact that the closures exacerbated inequality. In the commonwealth of Virginia, voters took out their frustrations on union-allied school board members. That looks to continue. A movement to "fund students instead of systems" threatens to upend the public education fiefdom that has given unions outsize control for decades.

What many of us didn't realize, however, was just how powerful unions have become. They've gotten so big their ties have become global, not simply domestic, with crony spending connections in China.

The Pandemic Pinnacle of Power

We can only hope the national teachers unions will never again accede to the level of power they wielded during the Biden/Harris administration portion of the pandemic. Who can forget just how influential unions were in shaping CDC guidance on reopening schools?

We weren't supposed to find out. But emails obtained through a Freedom of Information Act request by Americans for Public Trust exposed what it means when CDC says they trust the science. As the CDC was known to be preparing guidelines for reopening schools in February 2021, messages were flying between union officials, the

White House, and the CDC—including Director Rochelle Walensky. Who needs doctors when you can turn to political hacks for medical recommendations?

The *New York Post* published the emails the following May showing how AFT was allowed to help write the scientific guidance that would negatively impact so many American students. AFT senior director for health issues Kelly Trautner wrote to the CDC in one email, "Thank you again for Friday's rich discussion about forthcoming CDC guidance and for your openness to the suggestions made by our president, Randi Weingarten, and the AFT." Trautner then admitted the union was able to review the nonpublic guidance over the weekend and "were able to provide some initial feedback to several staff this morning about possible ways to strengthen the document."[3]

What did it mean to "strengthen the document"? House Oversight Committee Republicans conducted their own investigation—since Chairman Carolyn Maloney (D-NY) apparently wasn't interested. In a report released a year later, they determined that Biden's CDC "overrode routine practice to allow a radical teachers union that donated millions of dollars to Democrat campaigns to bypass scientific norms and rewrite official agency guidance," which "effectively kept thousands of schools shuttered across the country, locking millions of children out of their classrooms."

The report revealed, "The Biden Administration abandoned medical science and replaced it with political science to reward one of their largest donors, harming millions of children in the process. They bypassed the science to put union bosses ahead of children."[4]

Indeed, Federal Election Commission (FEC) filings back up the claim that teachers unions donated millions to Democrats prior to receiving this special treatment. A total of $43 million flowed from teachers unions to "liberal groups and candidates" in the 2020 election cycle alone, according to the report. AFT and NEA, which both endorsed Biden for president, represent a combined 4.7 million members. During this time, we saw teachers unions donating almost exclusively to progressive political campaigns, issuing foreign policy statements on Ukraine, using union funds to support LGBTQ and racial nonprofits, and demanding that governments defund police. Functionally, these institutions appear to be doing the work of political action committees rather than that of teacher advocates.[5]

With Democrats holding the House, the Senate, and the presidency, unions were getting everything they wanted. Having purchased so much political pull, and with a crisis they could not let go to waste, teachers unions flexed their muscle during the waning days of the Omicron outbreak in early 2022. While vaccination numbers rose, case counts dropped, and mandates were lifted, many schools delayed reopening. This was particularly true in left-leaning communities, where teachers unions are most influential.

Despite the federal money that had been showered upon schools to ensure the ability to reopen, many weren't ready. Though these kids were the least likely to contract or spread the disease and the least likely to die from it, they were frequently required to mask— even as the adults around them did not. National teachers unions lobbied hard for continued masking until the schools had reached "no transmission."[6] Earlier in the pandemic, at least one local union was demanding the passage of far-left economic policies in exchange for returning to the classroom.[7]

Throughout the pandemic, unions demanded more federal relief, and Congress, led by Senator Chuck Schumer (D-NY) and House Speaker Nancy Pelosi (D-CA), delivered. Congress had appropriated a $190 billion series of aid packages—the equivalent of nearly $4,000 per public school student—to help schools stay open during the pandemic. That's about six times more than the annual base budget for education, according to CNN.[8] Taxpayers likely expected to see that money spent on personal protective equipment, ventilation systems, or even summer programs. And some of it was. But about $46 billion of that aid in thirteen blue states was redirected to teach Critical Race Theory, according to analysis by One Nation.

California's application for funds called for increasing "educator training and resources" (so far so good) in specific subjects—"Anti-bias strategies," "environmental literacy," "ethnic studies," and "LGBTQ+ cultural competency." That's not very conducive to re-opening schools. Nor to addressing pandemic-related learning loss.[9]

"It turns out President Biden's so-called American Rescue Plan was a multitrillion-dollar progressive shopping list," said One Nation president Steven Law upon the release of the analysis. He called the spending "a massive bait-and-switch for life-saving COVID aid," adding, "Indoctrinating children to judge themselves and one another based on the color of their skin is wrong and has nothing to do with fighting COVID or getting our economy back on track."[10]

Some districts spent their COVID relief money on athletic facilities, bleachers, or hiring bonuses to lure teachers away from other schools. According to data from ProPublica, some of the country's biggest school districts, including New York City and Los Angeles, simply used the money to plug holes in the budget—basically to cover overspending.[11] No doubt those "community schools" were costing a pretty penny.

Where money flows freely, corruption often follows. Education dollars are no exception. No doubt we'll spend the next few years hearing horror stories of misallocated COVID relief funds. It's early yet, but already we have evidence that Randi Weingarten found a way to enrich her well-connected friends.

I didn't set out to tie the leader of a national teachers union to Hunter Biden. But I can't say I was surprised when I looked for cronyism and found his company, Rosemont Seneca, show up.

COVID Crony Spending

This story begins early in the pandemic, with AFT president Randi Weingarten excoriating President Donald Trump for his handling of the pandemic. Weingarten, who transformed the 1.7-million-member union from an advocacy group for teachers into a fundraising apparatus for progressive causes, blamed Trump for a shortage of personal protective equipment (PPE). "We have to try to figure out how to procure this stuff. . . . People are scared shitless," Weingarten said.[12]

Though China had deliberately blocked exports of respirators, gloves, and masks, Weingarten decided she could do a better job sourcing scarce supplies out of a foreign country than the Trump administration could. So, she dipped into the money collected as union fees from her members to purchase $3 million in PPE for school health care workers.[13]

What she did next is a master class in how the woke-industrial complex works. Let's follow the money as it leaves the pockets of teachers to enrich political cronies on its way to being wasted. The expenditures will benefit someone, but it won't be teachers.

As we'll see, Weingarten was closely tied in with the progressive business ecosystem. She may not have had any experience with procurement out of China, but she knew the people who revolve in and out of progressive administrations and who then monetize those connections in deals with progressive institutions.[14] Perhaps it shouldn't surprise us that she turned to two former protégés of Hunter Biden for help.

Alexandra Stanton and Sam Natapoff run Empire Global Ventures (EGV), a boutique Manhattan business development firm.[15] Stanton is a "prominent Democratic donor and fundraiser whose political ties run deep."[16] She has connections to many prominent donors and politicians in the progressive ecosystem.

Stanton and Natapoff, her husband, started EGV in 2011, just after leaving Rosemont Seneca, an investment firm created early in the Obama administration by the son of then-sitting vice president Joe Biden and the stepson of the chairman of the U.S. Senate Committee on Foreign Relations (and later Obama's secretary of state), John Kerry, and their friend Devon Archer. According to *Secret Empires* author Peter Schweizer, the Rosemont Seneca family of investment funds, founded in 2009, was "populated by political loyalists and positioned to strike profitable deals overseas with foreign governments and officials with whom the US government was negotiating."[17]

In 2013, President Barack Obama appointed Stanton to serve on the board of trustees for the John F. Kennedy Center for the Performing Arts, in Washington, D.C. A former senior policy advisor to New York State Senate minority leader David Paterson before he became governor, Stanton had previously been appointed to New York State's economic development agency, the Empire State Development Corporation (ESDC). Sam Natapoff also worked at ESDC following a stint in state government as "Senior Advisor to the Governor of New York for International Commerce."[18]

Stanton had coordinated with Paterson to attend policy meetings on the topic of AFT pension investment.[19] She had been appointed to New York State's economic development agency, the Empire State Development Corporation (ESDC), where she served with her husband, Sam Natapoff. Natapoff was similarly well-connected, having served as the senior advisor to the governor of New York for international commerce.[20]

The ties don't end there. Stanton would likely have known Weingarten's wife, Rabbi Sharon Kleinbaum, through her service on the board of directors for Jewish progressive lobbying group J Street.[21] Kleinbaum is on the board's Rabbinic and Cantorial Cabinet Executive Committee.[22] According to the research from GAI, Stanton had a long-standing affiliation with J Street. In fact, Stanton shows up in Hunter Biden's emails asking in 2010 for Hunter's advice in smoothing over the relationship between Vice President Joe Biden and J Street.[23]

With that background, Stanton and Natapoff formed EGV, boasting on their website that the company "supports its clients entering China by introducing them to influential Chinese business partners, providing access to non-public Chinese deal flow, managing the Chinese governmental registration and permitting process, and supplying privileged sector-specific research on the Chinese market."[24]

That language could have been damning had it been read in the context of Hunter Biden's business dealings in China. The story documenting Hunter Biden's shady business dealing as revealed by emails on his own laptop broke on October 14, 2020.[25] Using the Wayback Machine, GAI discovered a fortunate coincidence for EGV. The language tying them to "non-public Chinese deal flow" conveniently disappeared from the website between September 19 and October 20, 2020.[26] That timely change likely spared Stanton and Natapoff some unpleasant scrutiny, given the revelations in Hunter Biden's emails that document the couple's work with Weingarten on Rosemont Seneca.[27]

Weingarten tasked Stanton and Natapoff with finding an "established importer-exporter" for procurement in China. Among the things EGV ended up procuring for Weingarten from China was a likely counterfeit shipment of N95 masks.[28] There isn't a lot of publicly available information about who EGV used to import the first round of supplies, but according to the Department of Labor's Online Public Disclosure Room, AFT initially paid $1,260,000 to China Energy Construction International Investment (CECII) for COVID-19 medical equipment.[29]

Stanton subsequently cocreated her own COVID supply company, AGS Medical Solutions, which does business as Little Lives PPE.[30] The second AFT payment for COVID "Medical Equipment Services"—over $700,000—would go directly to Stanton's new business just five months after the payment to CECII. Little Lives PPE, with a focus on procuring child-sized masks and face shields, was well positioned to capture new business so long as schools had mask mandates in place.[31]

AFT characterized the arrangement with EGV as a volunteer effort in a May 2020 press release. It stated that EGV, which had no record of procuring medical supplies prior to working with AFT, "volunteered its services" to help the union procure COVID supplies. EGV's magnanimity was rewarded, as a few months later,

Stanton's Little Lives would receive the $700,000 payment. Never had AFT used its budget to procure "medical equipment."[32]

AFT has been outspoken about their calls for the DOJ to investigate and prosecute those who profit from the COVID-19 crisis, even going as far as passing a resolution on the subject.[33] But they've been disinterested in exposing Stanton and Natapoff. Perhaps Weingarten's feigned outrage at those who make a profit is reserved only for those who disagree with her.

This episode perfectly encapsulates the way the B Team does business. They don't have to be transparent. They rarely get held accountable. They prioritize political power and the nurturing of political relationships with powerful people. They measure success not by how well they perform their mission, but by how much they can expand it.

These stories raise a lot of questions about the outsize role of teachers unions in America. Ostensibly labor unions exist to serve their members—to negotiate benefits, support professional development, and fight for school funding at the state and local level. Why was a teachers union brokering deals for medical supplies? Why are they engaging with shady political operatives in China? Why are they diverting money taken from teachers' pockets to line the pockets of Hunter Biden's inner circle? Why would the president of a national teachers union in America need to go to Kyiv, Ukraine, following the 2014 installation of an American- and Biden-friendly regime in that country?[34]

Clearly, the pandemic was a boon for teachers unions. But what about the rest of us? What do we have to show for the lockdowns, the school closures, the mask mandates, the virtual learning, and the overdose of social justice spending?

Blue-State Schools Widen Inequality

Ironically, in hindsight it was the most cautious schools that fared the worst. Far-left communities with large minority populations in deep blue inner cities were the first to close and the last to reopen.[35] The *New York Times* noted that low-income students, who are concentrated in large, Democrat-run cities, fell further behind.[36] They referenced a study of school closures across the nation that concluded that "[p]artisanship was much more associated with district reopening plans than COVID-19 rates."[37]

A study by the Committee to Unleash Prosperity ranked each state based on the percentage of cumulative in-person education. Red states took seven of the top ten rankings while the bottom ten were all blue states.[38]

In the pandemic's aftermath, we now have data suggesting we did a lot of things wrong when it came to our students. Devastating learning losses have erased two decades of progress in math and reading, according to results from the National Assessment of Educational Progress measuring the performance of nine-year-olds.[39] Undoubtedly more data will be coming. But early research suggests virtual learning—or the pretense thereof—was costly.

For example, we now know that in most regions, virtual school was no safer than in-person learning.[40] The CDC has admitted that case rates were no higher in schools where masking was optional than in schools with mandates.[41] Though the long-term impact of our policies will be studied for years to come, we are already grappling with learning gaps, mental health problems, and students who have simply disappeared from the school system.[42] Special needs students seem to have been hit particularly hard.[43]

A Harvard study looking at the consequences of remote learning during the pandemic found that, because of early closures and pandemic disruptions, even students who attended school in person throughout most of the 2020–21 school year had a 20 percent learning loss in math during the pandemic. The loss was 50 percent for students in remote learning environments. The *New York Times* called it a "generational loss."

For Black and Latino students, the learning loss was particularly acute. Thomas Kane, one of the study's authors, told the *Times*,

"This will probably be the largest increase in educational inequity in a generation."[44]

So, let's get this straight. Woke schools spent millions of dollars on race-based curriculum, anti-bias strategies, ethnic studies, and LGBTQ+ cultural competency. But they lost ground on educational equity? How is that possible?

This is going to be painful for progressives to admit. But the reality is that schools in conservative-led communities tended to reopen while those in progressive areas stayed closed longer.[45] Minority students and underprivileged students, who tend to be concentrated in large blue cities, were simply far more likely to go remote. They were also more likely to lack internet, separate study space, and daytime parental support. For them, remote learning was the worst possible option.

But the teachers unions insisted that remote learning was safest. They pushed hard to keep schools closed. In Washington, D.C., where half of the public schools have a student body that is 90 percent African American, the AFT affiliate held a sickout to keep schools from reopening. In San Francisco, where minority students make up 86 percent of the student body, almost six hundred teachers signed an online petition to "shut the whole system down" over inadequate safety measures. Ironically, the San Francisco Unified School District had spent its $100 million in Coronavirus Relief Funds to "maintain core operations." Among other expenses, this meant the hiring of more counselors and school nurses, and paying to retain staff.[46] It was a similar story in Los Angeles, where one parent told the *Los Angeles Times*, "We know that a lot of white parents are calling for the reopening of schools—that is simply not the case with Black parents and other parents of color."[47] The United Teachers Los Angeles union said the push to reopen schools was "rooted in white privilege."[48] The previous summer, that same union had demanded major concessions in exchange for reopening, including $500 billion in federal bailout assistance for schools, the passage of federal Medicare-for-All legislation, "a wealth tax on unrealized capital gains for the state's billionaires," defunding of the Los Angeles Police Department, and a "moratorium on new charter schools."[49]

The AFT affiliate in Chicago had to delete a controversial tweet arguing that the push to reopen schools was "rooted in sexism, racism, and misogyny."[50] How ironic that the school closures themselves exacerbated inequality.

Lessons Learned

The lessons of the pandemic are varied. But there seems to be a wide gulf between what parents have concluded and what the B Team and its puppeteer allies have concluded. Hope lies with the parents, who are pushing major political realignments in states like Virginia.

But for the B Team, the lessons are always the same. They just needed to double down on what had already failed and everything would be fine. In their "Health Care" journal, the AFT identified which lessons they believed were most important to take from this whole pandemic experience. Based on those lessons, they had some demands.

The first lesson, they claimed, was that the pandemic "disproportionately wreaked havoc in marginalized racial and ethnic groups." Similarly, the second lesson blamed "the structural racism embedded within the social fabric of the United States" for that inequality.[51] Predictably, that issue and a report cowritten by the AFT and the NEA only identified lessons that would call for the solutions unions have always advocated. The lesson they chose to take was convenient—they just needed to double down on what they had already been doing.

Among the things they say they have to combat are the "deep structural inequities" that result from COVID:

- **More support personnel.** Recruit "substantially more specialized instructional support personnel (therapists, counselors, speech-language pathologists, school psychologists, behavioral specialists, school nurses, etc.)."[52]

- **More tutors.** "Additional tutoring support, whether virtual or in person, must be prioritized . . . to ensure that our highest-need and most vulnerable students receive a maximum amount of interactive, intensified one-on-one instruction."[53]

- **More staff.** Teacher unions should use collective bargaining agreements to negotiate new staffing positions that will increase learning time for students with "opportunity gaps."[54]

- **More health care workers.** Employ "nurses, counselors and psychologists" to "address trauma and social-emotional learning."[55]

- **More teachers.** Increase staffing to accommodate the expansion of "small-group learning," which became necessary due to social distancing requirements.[56]

- **More union positions and training.** Provide "union-developed and -led professional development so that programs ensure safe environments and a focus on social-emotional learning and addressing trauma."[57]

- **Redirect tax dollars to unions.** Teachers unions need increased federal funds to subsidize their expanded professional development training goals, which includes training all nonteacher school employees with a focus on equity and racial and social justice.[58]

- **More taxpayer-funded union jobs.** AFT and NEA "are eager to collaborate with federal and state governments to develop an apprenticeship program" for recent graduates.[59]

- **More full-service schools.** "Implement community schools districtwide . . . to address several of the racial, social and economic injustices that students and families face."[60]

- **More federal money.** AFT and NEA "support deep federal investments that will dramatically expand the number of community schools."[61]

- **Massive mission expansion.** "Now more than ever, multiple systems—childcare, healthcare, social services and public education itself—must be coordinated and fully funded. Only then will we be surrounding students with the supports they need and deserve and creating conditions for them to thrive."[62]

There is a common thread here. There are no policy changes. Just more government, more unions, and more taxpayer dollars from start to finish.

Fortunately, parents seem to have different takeaways from their pandemic experience. And America is seeing it manifest at the ballot box, in the legislatures, and in the public school systems. Public schools have lost more than a million students in the last two years. Polling in the summer of 2022 offered a preview of things to come. An August NPR/Marist poll found, for the first time in eight years, that Republicans had an advantage on the congressional ballot test. The same poll showed that households with children under eighteen—those most directly impacted by school closures—chose Republicans over Democrats for Congress by a jaw-dropping, nearly *two-to-one margin*: 60 percent to 32 percent.[63]

The wide gap between the priorities of teachers unions and the priorities of parents manifested itself clearly in the Virginia gubernatorial election of 2021.

The Harbinger in Virginia

What happened when parents in Virginia tried to push back against the teachers unions' leftist agenda sets the stage for perhaps the most dangerous pretext of all. The off-year gubernatorial race in the purple-trending-blue state resulted in a shocking upset. Former Virginia governor Terry McAuliffe, whose last campaign appearance before the vote was with Randi Weingarten, lost to Republican Glenn Youngkin in what headlines called a victory for parental rights.[64] McAuliffe had openly proclaimed, "I don't think parents should be telling schools what they should teach."[65]

Parents begged to differ. And they showed up in force. Delivering angry feedback at school community meetings, parents vented their frustration with the injection of controversial social issues and leftist political narratives into classrooms. In Loudoun County, Black parent Shawntel Cooper lambasted the board for using principles of Critical Race Theory in school curriculum. "CRT is racist; it is abusive; it discriminates against one's color," she told the board. "Think twice before you indoctrinate such racist theories. You cannot tell me what is or is not racist. Look at me. I had to come down here today to tell you to your face that we are coming together and we are strong."[66]

What happened next was a harbinger of things to come for outspoken voices on the right. In an unprecedented move, Democrats weaponized the Justice Department against parents. Though the fury in Virginia was purely a local government issue, the attorney general of the United States, Merrick Garland, intervened. In a letter to the FBI and DOJ Criminal Division attorneys, Garland warned of "a disturbing spike in harassment, intimidation, and threats of violence." He then directed the FBI to facilitate discussions to address the threats.[67]

Subsequently, a whistleblower produced a copy of a DOJ internal email from the FBI Counterterrorism Division showing the FBI had created a threat tag to track instances of threats to school administrators, board members, teachers, and staff.[68]

Coincidentally, Garland has a son-in-law in the education curriculum business. In fact, the company Xan Tanner cofounded distributes surveys in more than fifty of the largest one hundred school districts in America. Those surveys are used, according to Senate Republicans, to aid schools in teaching Critical Race Theory under the guise of equity and inclusion. A letter signed by Senators Ted

Cruz (R-TX), Mike Lee (R-UT), and Marsha Blackburn (R-TN) suggested such contracts "may be in jeopardy as parents stand up to school boards and demand that their children not be indoctrinated with critical race theory."[69]

Senator Chuck Grassley, in a December 2021 joint letter to Garland with ten other Republican senators, warned of the chilling effect Garland's actions have on free speech. "All of this is an outrageous tipping of the scales in the marketplace of ideas in favor of school officials, who just happen to be a major constituency of the political party that currently controls the White House and the Department of Justice," the letter explained.

How many parents, knowing the FBI Counterterrorism Division is tracking their public comments, will step up and take a position opposing the Biden/Harris administration? How many are willing to be branded as domestic terrorists?

"By now involving the FBI's Counterterrorism Division in this effort, even if you personally believe that division would never cross a line into silencing criticism of local governments," the senators wrote to Garland, "you have given life to the idea that dissidents are synonymous with terrorists."[70] Indeed, of all the pretexts used by government puppeteers to usurp the power of the people, this is perhaps the most frightening pretext of all.

PART III

National Security

CHAPTER 10

Hunting Hatred to Silence Dissent

The story of the FBI's Patriot Conspiracy investigation reads like a novel conceived in the fever dreams of President Trump's most ardent supporters. To hear the broad outlines of the plot, one might think it was a fantastical modern conspiracy theory. But it's not. The Justice Department preoccupation with hunting potential political targets dates back decades. Here's an example from the playbook:

During a time of deep political polarization, the FBI undertook a secret operation to infiltrate patriot groups, using confidential informants and heavy surveillance. They specifically targeted militant white supremacists, which they associated with the right. Giving operatives license to "engage in provocateur activities," the program was allegedly more than just a surveillance effort. Later accounts would reveal a program with the objective to "infiltrate and incite" white supremacist groups to violence.[1]

That's not a January 6 conspiracy theory. That's a real, documented FBI Major Case Group 1 Undercover Operation that dates back at least thirty years, and possibly much longer. Within the FBI, they called it PATCON. The naming convention follows the FBI's longstanding practice of merging multiple words into a single term to describe the case, such as "OKBOMB" for the Oklahoma

City bombing or COINTELPRO for a Counter-Intelligence Program.

Government incitement to violence and political targeting are unfortunately not new. They are not conspiracy theories. They are not isolated incidents. This is a pattern. It's a means of discrediting and silencing political dissent that is well practiced by the government. This is a strategy that isn't dependent on having a Democrat in the Oval Office or on having congressional majorities. It has happened even under Republican administrations and Republican majorities. It is impervious to voter sentiment. In fact, it seeks to manipulate that sentiment.

The Regrettable History of Inciting Domestic Terrorism

PATCON is part of a story that predates more recent allegations, such as the FBI plot to incite right-wing activists to kidnap Michigan governor Gretchen Whitmer.[2] It predates the Obama-era Fast & Furious scandal, which I investigated, and in which a U.S. law enforcement agency, the Bureau of Alcohol, Tobacco, Firearms and Explosives (ATF), knowingly and willingly facilitated violent gun crimes. In that case, the government allowed approximately two thousand guns to walk out the door in hopes of tracing them in future crimes. In December 2010, two of those guns deliberately sold by our government were found at the murder scene of Border Patrol agent Brian Terry.[3]

More than these few incidents alone constitute credible allegations of one-sided political targeting and incitement of potentially violent hate groups by the FBI. But the pattern actually stretches back decades, to the years preceding the 1995 bombing by a militant extremist of the Alfred P. Murrah Federal Building in Oklahoma City. Once we understand how this has been done historically, then we can better contextualize what FBI whistleblowers and leaked Department of Homeland Security (DHS) documents are telling us today.

Inciting Violence

Born in 1991 as a simple undercover sting operation, PATCON morphed under the Clinton administration into a secretive program for targeting right-wing groups that were allegedly racist, militant, or antigovernment. It remained in the shadows until 2007, when it was mysteriously revealed through a Freedom of Information Act request.[4] Later, an eyewitness would come forward with astounding claims of FBI incitement to violence, evidence suppression, and even witness tampering. But after privately alleging threats from the FBI, that witness would recant and then disappear.

In her 2015 book describing the PATCON investigation, Wendy Painting spoke to a former Aryan Nation member from that time period about the FBI's presence at the group's events. "It was well known that at any Aryan Nation event, in a crowd of 300 people, there'd be at least 30 undercover federal agents in attendance to monitor us, and another third of the crowd were informants. . . . It was rampant, just like cops at a Grateful Dead show trying to sell people LSD."[5]

White supremacy is a corrupt ideology with a long history of violence in this country that has no place among freedom-loving people. Though Americans have a right to terrible opinions, no one objects to law enforcement rooting out violent extremists within a movement that has produced far too many of them. But in this case, government didn't just root out the extremists. According to witnesses, government egged them on.

After having his cover blown by the agency in a 2011 Freedom of Information Act response, FBI asset and former U.S. Marine John Matthews blew the whistle on the PATCON operation. Reaching out to Utah attorney Jesse Trentadue, whose decades-long effort to expose FBI complicity in the Oklahoma City bombing had unearthed Matthews's identity, Matthews outed the secret program, an explanation Trentadue described in subsequent court filings.

"He told me that he had been told by the FBI that the purpose of PATCON was to infiltrate and to monitor the activities of [the] extreme political right consisting of organizations such as the Ku Klux Klan and various Neo-Nazi groups," read Trentadue's sworn declaration to the court, "but that he no longer believed what he had been told by the FBI about the purpose of PATCON." Matthews told Trentadue that, based upon his experience, he now believed that the FBI's real objective in PATCON had been "to infiltrate and to incite these fringe groups to violence."[6]

Over an almost ten-year period, Matthews had infiltrated more than twenty militia, libertarian, gun rights, and racist groups. When he learned that the government had let his name slip out in a response to a FOIA request, Matthews was angry. "All those years, I've been a good boy and kept my mouth shut," Matthews later told *Newsweek*'s Ross Schneiderman. "Then you [the FBI] release my name? What kind of [expletive] is that?"[7]

Matthews described an operation designed "to infiltrate and incite." As Painting reported in her book, Matthews described to Trentadue the FBI providing "the ideas, detailed instructions, and even live C4 explosives and automatic weapons to targeted individuals as a way of entrapping them into terrorist plots, so the FBI could capitalize on foiled and actualized plots."[8]

We could expect such explosive revelations to be front page news. But few people ever heard them. In a tell-all bombshell exposé set to be published by *Newsweek* in 2011, an ailing Matthews hoped to get his story on the record. With the help of Trentadue and journalist Roger Charles, Matthews connected with Schneiderman and then-editor John Solomon, who worked to confirm the details of Matthews's story. But before Schneiderman's seven-thousand-word exposé could be published, *Newsweek* managing editor Tina Brown intervened, according to court records.[9] Far from exposing the FBI's overreach, the new, four-thousand-word version read like a promotional piece designed to gin up public support for the FBI.

Brown "cut away virtually all detail that could directly or indirectly impugn the government for the fallout of its PATCON operations," according to reporting from John Kline. All of Matthews's suspicions about the FBI's infiltration of the Oklahoma City bombing plot were removed.[10] Far from exposing the FBI's overreach, the published story omitted any mention of PATCON and favorably highlighted "the bureau's struggles to combat right-wing extremism."[11]

What is allegedly the original version of the *Newsweek* story has been published at the website of the Libertarian Institute, an outlet that has done extensive reporting on the Oklahoma City bombing case.[12] A review of the two versions, Kline writes, confirmed the "existence of a state-media axis in America" on behalf of the Obama Justice Department.[13]

Following his deep disappointment in the *Newsweek* story, Matthews agreed to testify in court in 2014. Trentadue's 2006 Freedom of Information Act case against the FBI and CIA went to trial in Salt Lake City that summer, eight years after it was filed. Matthews hoped to tell his story without the censorship of the Obama media fan club. But the night before Matthews was set to testify, Charles spoke with Matthews by telephone.

"John Matthews said that he had been told by the FBI to 'stand down.' John Matthews also said that he had been told by the FBI to take a vacation so that he could not be subpoenaed," Charles told the court in a sworn declaration one week later. "He likewise said that the 'Bureau' had made it very clear to him that if he did testify, it could result in the loss of his Veteran's health coverage, and Veteran's disability pension." Matthews shared similar details in a call with Trentadue.

The FBI, of course, denies any witness tampering. Since then, Matthews has publicly denied the story. But Judge Clark Waddoups of the U.S. District Court for the District of Utah in 2015 found the allegations sufficiently troubling that he appointed a special master to investigate and prepare a report.[14]

Seven years later, the court still awaits that report before it will rule in the pending 2006 FOIA matter, in which Trentadue seeks documents and surveillance video related to the 1995 Oklahoma City bombing. In recent reporting from the *Epoch Times*, Judicial

Watch's senior investigator Sean Dunagan, no stranger to FOIA litigation, explained the stakes.

"We're one of the largest FOIA litigants in this country, and we've never been involved in anything that involves that degree of alleged misconduct by the [FBI]," said Dunagan. "It's astounding." But Dunagan finds a silver lining in Trentadue's still-pending FOIA case.

"It's very good for Jesse that his case is not being litigated in D.C. If this case were litigated in D.C., it would have been closed years ago," he said. Because the case stemmed from a wrongful death suit brought by Trentadue in Utah, the FOIA case could be tried in Utah. "Judges in D.C. have a lot more deference to agencies," Dunagan added, "particularly when it comes to classification of law enforcement records."[15]

As a Utah congressman, I met with Trentadue in Salt Lake City in 2012 to hear about his extraordinary battle with the Justice Department. I don't know where this story will lead, to what degree the FBI was involved, or if Trentadue will ever be able to force the Justice Department to produce the videos and documents the court has ordered. But I know this: the DOJ has not been apolitical in its investigative work. Tying conservatives to domestic terrorism is part of a larger effort to justify censorship, surveillance, and political targeting. And the white supremacy narrative is the key to all of it.

The White Supremacy Narrative

More than 2.3 million people (that we know of) crossed the United States southern border in fiscal 2022, including at least ninety-eight people from the terror watch list. Data from U.S. Customs and Border Protection indicates an additional 599,000 "gotaways"—unknown migrants who evaded capture.[16] During the month of September alone, CBP picked up twenty people on the terror watch list. But the secretary of Homeland Security is laser-focused on America's greatest threat: white supremacy.

Never mind seizures of deadly fentanyl from Mexico up 311 percent between March 2020 and March 2022, human traffickers earning up to $14 million a day to smuggle people across the southern border, and billions of dollars in taxpayer-funded border wall parts and pieces deteriorating in the desert sun.[17] Forget the Antifa thugs in Seattle and Portland physically attacking conservative protesters and threatening to "dismember" reporter Andy Ngo, or the Trump-hating leftist who plowed into a Waukesha, Wisconsin, parade and killed six people.[18] Secretary of Homeland Security Alejandro Mayorkas doesn't seem to be counting any of this as domestic terrorism.

The real problem Mayorkas wants to solve is "right-wing" white supremacy. Maybe *solve* is the wrong word. The better term might be *fixate on*. Because a fixation on "right-wing" white supremacy is a pretext for what the Biden/Harris administration really wants—more censorship, more government, and more taxpayer dollars being diverted to the institutions that uphold the leftist power base.

It's just assumed that those two things—conservatism and white supremacy—go together. It's a weird flex considering the Republican Party's singular role in ending slavery. Nonetheless, Secretary Mayorkas, who is responsible for border security, airport security, and cybersecurity, in an April 2022 speech made his singular priority clear: "the greatest terrorism-related threat that we face in the homeland is the threat of domestic violent extremism." Speaking to a New York City audience gathered for Al Sharpton's National Action Network conference, Mayorkas went even further, saying, "the most prominent threat is the threat of White supremacists."[19]

Mayorkas didn't connect the two statements, but in a joint address to Congress a year earlier, President Joe Biden did. He said that "white supremacy is terrorism" and is the "most lethal threat to the homeland today."[20] He repeated that claim in an October 2021 speech celebrating the tenth anniversary of the Martin Luther King, Jr. Memorial, claiming, "According to the United States intelligence community, domestic terrorism *from white supremacists* is the most lethal terrorist threat in the homeland" (emphasis added).[21]

One problem. It simply isn't true. The basis for this claim appears to be a March 2021 intelligence community assessment that does indeed point to an "elevated threat" from domestic violent extremists. But that assessment refers to extremists of all stripes, including Islamic extremists, Antifa, lone-wolf mass shooters, and other domestic terrorists who have no connection to right-wing politics. This is according to former acting DHS secretary Chad Wolf, who called out the error.

"There is no data or supporting assessment to claim white supremacists are the most lethal threat to the homeland," Wolf wrote for the Heritage Foundation. However, Wolf pointed out that "[w]hite supremacists and militias appear to be the only threats the strategy focuses on."[22]

The strategy to which Wolf refers is the administration's National Strategy for Countering Domestic Terrorism, announced by Attorney General Merrick Garland in June 2021. That announcement followed on the heels of Garland's budget request to Congress for a $45 million increase in funding for the FBI for domestic terrorism investigations and a $40 million increase to fund U.S. attorneys to handle the subsequent prosecutions.[23]

Given the rhetoric and calls for funding, Americans might expect to see mass prosecutions of right-wing white supremacists. But when Mayorkas visited Capitol Hill in April 2022, he couldn't name a single case that his agency had referred to DOJ for prosecution. Asked by Florida Republican congressman Greg Steube for a specific example, Mayorkas hedged, promising to provide that data later.[24] Maybe there aren't any. But I would suggest a second, more likely reason the cat seemed to get Mayorkas's tongue. Maybe it wasn't so much that he couldn't name an incident, but that he would be embarrassed to cite one. Viewers might be surprised to know what the left is counting as "right-wing" terror these days.

We don't have to depend on Mayorkas for data. Left-wing think tanks are happy to support the narrative. The nominally bipartisan but clearly left-leaning Center for Strategic and International Studies (CSIS), chaired by leftist billionaire Thomas Pritzker, collects and releases data on domestic terrorism.[25]

Left-wing think tanks, newspapers, and nonprofits are more than happy to uncritically repeat the talking points. When CSIS releases data, damning headlines follow. In a 2020 story citing CSIS data, the British newspaper the *Guardian* reported that the "majority of attacks and plots have come from the far right."[26] The April 2021 headline in the *Washington Post*, which did its own analysis based on the CSIS data, documented "The Rise of Domestic Extremism in America."

The *Post* story claimed domestic terrorism was surging, "driven chiefly by white-supremacist, anti-Muslim and anti-government extremists on the far right." According to the story, right-wing extremist attacks and plots greatly eclipse those from the far left and cause more deaths. The data assigns 267 incidents and 91 deaths to right-wing extremists since 2015 and only 66 incidents and 19 deaths to the far left.[27]

I worked with researchers at GAI to dig into the data and methodology of the CSIS numbers. What we found was troubling. First, the database doesn't actually disclose a complete list of incidents being counted, making definitive independent verification of the data difficult. But there are plenty of red flags that raise questions about this and other studies that promote the same conclusion.

It's hard to miss the bias. The data center where users can access the results from the study includes an exploratory map of "right-wing plots and incidents," yet there is no map of "left-wing plots and incidents" anywhere to be found. CSIS would likely argue there are just too few to be relevant—which is probably true given the way incidents are calculated.

CSIS appears to employ a double standard that enables them to apply a very broad definition of "right-wing" and narrow definitions of "left-wing" and "Islamic" terrorism.

I want to be crystal clear about one thing: when there is violent crime perpetrated by white supremacists in this country, it should be tried and prosecuted to the fullest. Whether the perpetrator is left or right, white or Black, wealthy or disadvantaged, they must be subject to the rule of law—no ifs, ands, or buts about it. We cannot tolerate violence.

But when it comes to what CSIS classifies as "right-wing" violence, the data appear to conflate mere threats with violent incidents. For example, listed as an attack is an October 10, 2020, incident in Fort Myers, Florida, involving anti-abortion protesters who were arrested at South Fort Myers Planned Parenthood. Though the sheriff's office clearly documented that "there was no violence with the protest," this incident was counted in the CSIS database as a "right-wing domestic terrorism incident."[28]

The reason some of the "right-wing" crimes described in this CSIS data would have embarrassed Mayorkas had he used them in a congressional hearing is that they weren't crimes at all. Consider a June 3, 2020, incident in Longmont, Colorado.

A group of about fifty Black Lives Matter (BLM) supporters were protesting in the park when Nicholas Fowler approached the crowd and, while imbibing a bottle of whiskey, shouted, "All lives matter!" After a protester told him to leave, Fowler "pulled out a hatchet and held it up without saying anything." He then used the hatchet to start to cut down a city sign and a tree before "throwing the hatchet and walking away." Certainly this is childish, ineffective, and inappropriate behavior. But by CSIS's methodology, this meets the threshold for right-wing domestic terrorism.[29] Imagine if Mayorkas had cited this example in his congressional testimony?

By contrast, when it comes to defining left-wing groups like Antifa, the CSIS methodology is much more malleable. Because Antifa extremists are using "violence in the context of ideological clashes at demonstrations," CSIS says they do not match "common definitions of terrorism."[30] Too bad that standard couldn't be applied to the Longmont, Colorado, ax wielder, who was also in an ideological clash at a demonstration.

Notably, two high-profile left-wing hate crimes don't show up in the database. The death of officer David Dorn during the BLM protests appears to be missing. The November 2021 terrorist attack in Waukesha, Wisconsin, appears to fall outside the date range of this database. But an incident in which a radical leftist drove into a Christmas parade, killing six people and injuring more than five dozen others, certainly would not fit the narrative CSIS appears to be building.[31]

To make matters worse, attacks by Muslims only count if they are "inspired by groups such as the Taliban, al-Qaida and the Islamic State." Lone-wolf perpetrators who identify with a stereotypically right-wing issue are automatically counted as right-wing extremists. But incidents involving a lone-wolf Muslim or loosely aligned Antifa group ostensibly unconnected to a larger entity are not counted in the data.

In his hearing on Capitol Hill in April 2022, Mayorkas admitted as much, telling Representative Steube that he didn't consider Black Lives Matter to fit the definition of domestic terrorism.[32] I asked Congressman Chris Stewart (R-UT), who is a member of the House Permanent Select Committee on Intelligence (HPSCI), about the data on right-wing domestic terrorism.

"Factually inaccurate, untrue, not backed up at all by the evidence or the statistics," he told me emphatically. "This 'surge' of right-wing violence is simply not true." He said House Republicans have asked Democrats to produce the evidence behind their claims of escalating right-wing violence—to show the examples of actual extremism that they are counting. They never do, Stewart said.

Yet, based on these false numbers, the woke-industrial complex of elected officials, cabinet officials, leftist nonprofits, and media have spun a narrative that is not only false and misleading, but dangerous.

Blowing the Whistle on DOJ Abuse

I was almost finished writing this book when House Judiciary Committee Republicans released their thousand-page report documenting the politicization of the FBI. A string of credible whistleblowers confirmed many of our worst fears. The FBI inflated and manipulated statistics on domestic terror for political purposes.

Multiple FBI sources from a variety of offices confirmed to House Republicans that they had been pressured to find more cases of domestic extremism. One suggested investigators had been told to reclassify cases even if there was "minimal, circumstantial evidence to support the reclassification." One FBI agent anonymously complained to the *Washington Times* about the supply-and-demand problem with white supremacist crimes. The White House in September 2022 held a United We Stand summit to gin up support for "counter[ing] the corrosive effects of hate-fueled violence on our democracy," according to a statement by White House press secretary Karine Jean-Pierre.[33] But current and former FBI agents expressed frustration to the *Washington Times* with the administration's white supremacy obsession.

Reiterating that the demand for white supremacy coming from FBI headquarters vastly outstrips the supply of white supremacy, one agent complained that investigators felt they were "trying to find a crime to fit otherwise First Amendment–protected activities," and complained that there were more agents assigned to investigate such crimes than there were people committing them. Most chilling, the agent described what the FBI seems to look for when hunting hatred: "If they have a Gadsden flag and they own guns and they are mean at school board meetings, that's probably a domestic terrorist," the agent added.[34] While those things don't link someone to white supremacy, they are certainly signs that a voter might be conservative.

The report further confirmed that the FBI had "downplayed serious allegations of wrongdoing leveled against Hunter Biden" after materials from Biden's laptop implicated the son of the president of the United States in various potential crimes. Whistleblowers also complained of the agency abusing its foreign surveillance authorities, targeting a conservative charity under the guise of investigating unrelated alleged crimes, and purging employees who refuse to align themselves with the leadership's political ideology.[35]

While our law enforcement apparatus is obsessing and diverting resources to this fake narrative, real threats abound. That's not to say there is no racially animated crime. I went looking for it. An inexcusable incident in Lakewood, Colorado, in which a deranged gunman killed five people in 2021 was frequently cited. That gunman had documented extremist views on race, but also publicly ridiculed "right wing larpers" for being "pro government."[36] He knew each of his victims and had a history of psychiatric episodes.[37] Another incident in Winthrop, Massachusetts, involved a twenty-eight-year-old man who had written racist diatribes and killed two Black victims. His writings were clearly racist, but not political.[38]

Race-based violence is nothing to be ignored. But it's not a right-left issue. Actual domestic terror incidents perpetrated by Black men with a documented animosity toward white people seldom get the same kind of attention from the racial justice warriors, but they are just as concerning. In April 2022, a Black man named Frank James shot ten commuters on a New York subway, injuring thirteen others. Checking his social media history, journalist Andy Ngo found posts proclaiming, among other things, "O black Jesus, please kill all the whiteys." The Waukesha parade killer had previously tweeted, "the old white ppl 2, KNOKK DEM TF OUT!! PERIOD." Yet another killer, Noah R. Green, approached the barricades at the U.S. Capitol in 2021 and knifed two Capitol Police officers before a third shot him. Green, likewise, had written on social media that the Jew-hating Louis Farrakhan was "my spiritual father."[39]

This is not a political problem. This is a cultural problem that is being weaponized by the left to justify censorship and criminalization of political wrongthink against one side. Consider the protests in Washington, D.C., on January 6, 2021. President Biden himself has tried to tar every Trump supporter in Washington that day with the violent extremist brush. Biden has concluded, "The violent, deadly insurrection on the Capitol nine months ago, it was about white supremacy, in my opinion."[40] The pernicious generalization that antagonism to the election of Joe Biden is simply a manifestation of white supremacy signals a dangerous attempt to criminalize political opposition.

CHAPTER 11

Criminalizing Dissent

The elevation of domestic terror as one of the nation's greatest threats and one of the administration's highest priorities conveniently provided the pretext for expanding federal power, repressing civil liberties, and targeting political opponents. This has been an all-hands-on-deck effort, involving multiple agencies and engaging the full attention of this administration's most able puppet masters. It has been used to justify unprecedented government-directed censorship, some of which has only recently come to light. But it's an effort that has also brought the unelected puppet masters into the light.

On his first full day in office, President Joe Biden began laying the groundwork for a restrictive and invasive domestic terror agenda. Calling for a one-hundred-day comprehensive review of the government's efforts to address domestic terrorism, Biden requested threat assessments to determine how the government can share information to "address threats, prevent radicalization, and disrupt violent extremist networks." The Huffington Post called the review "a stark acknowledgment of the national security threat that officials see as posed by American extremists motivated to violence by radical ideology." Of course, it was always unlikely that this administration's "comprehensive threat assessment" would be . . . comprehensive, and identify threats exacerbated by leftist policies.[1]

Less than five months later, the administration unveiled its new "National Strategy for Countering Domestic Terrorism." The plan identified the two most lethal elements of today's domestic terror threat. It wasn't the known gang members, cartels, and human traffickers flooding across the border to spread the deadly scourge of fentanyl. It wasn't the alarming proliferation of violent crime in America's inner cities or the violent protests that arise whenever a Supreme Court decision or police action displeases the left. No.

According to the Biden administration, the real threats are much more politically convenient, including "(1) racially or ethnically motivated violent extremists who advocate for the superiority of the white race and (2) anti-government or anti-authority violent extremists, such as militia violent extremists."[2]

The White House plan called for leveraging every government agency in "rooting out racism and bigotry." It committed to ensuring domestic terrorists are not employed by the military. It emphasized countering the polarization often fueled by disinformation, misinformation, and dangerous conspiracy theories, which would form the rationale for what would later come to be called Biden's "Ministry of Truth."[3]

But perhaps the most consequential pillar of the plan was its demand for enhanced domestic terrorism analysis and information sharing—aka surveillance and data collection. That included State Department help in tying domestic terrorist groups to foreign entities—a strategy that is also conveniently helpful in providing pretext for domestic surveillance and unmasking.

After all that research and assessment, it turns out that all we needed to deal with the number one national security threat was more leftists in unaccountable positions of power: more government to protect us in the form of more scrutiny of our personal information and more control over the information we share and receive. Note that they aren't calling for more representative democracy. They want more bureaucracy.

The plan doesn't sound so bad when the target is domestic

terrorists. But what happens when the target is a doctor, a scientist, or a teacher trying to defend our best interests? We need only think back to how militant the left was about suppressing information on school closures, lockdown impacts, masking efficacy, alternative COVID treatments, and vaccine risks to see how dangerous this plan could be. Valid questions, legitimate science, and knowledgeable experts were suppressed and punished in order to promote a narrative that was more politically useful to the party in power. These policies potentially criminalize the truth.

Condemning Mainstream Discourse

On February 7, 2022, two weeks before Russia invaded Ukraine—potentially igniting a third world war—the Department of Homeland Security (DHS) issued a National Terrorism Advisory System Bulletin announcing a heightened threat environment.[4] Not because of the coming conflict with a nuclear superpower, the very real likelihood of energy and food shortages, or the possibility of enemies crossing our borders during wartime. No. This important bulletin warned against speech and wrongthink by people who disagree with the administration.

"The United States remains in a heightened threat environment fueled by several factors," the summary read, citing "an online environment filled with false or misleading narratives and conspiracy theories, and other forms of mis- dis- and mal-information (MDM) introduced and/or amplified by foreign and domestic threat actors."

Are we talking about war conspiracies? Attacks on critical infrastructure? The bulletin identified, and sort of lumped together, two groups of people: first, those spreading "false or misleading narratives regarding unsubstantiated widespread election fraud and COVID-19" because "grievances associated with these themes inspired violent extremist attacks during 2021."

The second group consisted of "malign foreign powers" that "have and continue to amplify these false or misleading narratives in efforts to damage the United States." So—the foreign threat that worries them most is the one that allegedly aligns with right-wing political views.[5]

In other words, anyone who questioned the results of elections in 2020 (not 2016, of course) or who has grievances with the way our government addressed COVID-19 is listening to malign foreign actors who are trying to damage America, and thus is connected with terrorism.

This is even more dangerous than it sounds. Tying domestic political foes to foreign enemies is a strategy Biden signaled to when he made his cabinet appointments. Once his team was in place, his administration would take steps to criminalize dissent in America.

Architects of Equity

More than ninety federal agencies have now released what they're calling equity action plans. There seem to be two parts to these plans: first, to ensure federal privileges and benefits are directed to specific groups (who coincidentally tend to be Democratic voting blocs); and to use agency authority to promote "justice" with punitive enforcement measures against certain groups (who conveniently don't tend to vote for progressives in large numbers). There is a carrot and a stick—incentive and penalty—us and them.

For example, the Department of Health and Human Services (DHHS) has committed to increasing outreach to "communities of color" (code for deep blue inner cities where government dependency has led to intergenerational poverty, but everyone still votes for Democrats) and to encourage enrollment in free and low-cost health care.[6] It's a nice carrot for a strong Democratic voting bloc.

Wielding the stick will look like this example from the Environmental Protection Agency. The EPA commits to "reinvigorate civil rights enforcement to ensure that environmental justice is at the heart of the agency's mission." That would be code for using the disparate impact argument to aggressively fine the fossil fuel industry based on a claim that pollution has a greater impact on people of color.

In the spring of 2022, Homeland Security secretary Mayorkas gave Americans a preview of his agency's equity efforts. To "help counter domestic violent extremism to better address the terrorism-related threat to our country posed by white supremacists and other domestic terrorists," he created what many refer to as the "Ministry of Truth." His appointment of Nina Jankowicz to head up the Disinformation Governance Board was announced as a way to "combat misinformation." But it was clearly setting the stage to impose the *administration's version* of truth. As someone who had promoted Russia collusion disinformation and supported the suppression of the truth about the Hunter Biden laptop, Jankowicz was a spectacularly poor choice.[7] Ultimately, she quit amid outcry from proponents of free speech and civil liberties.[8]

But we now know that DHS and FBI were already involved in censorship before the disinformation board was ever announced. Bombshell reporting by the Intercept's Lee Fang published documents validating allegations of regular biweekly meetings between the United States security apparatus and technology companies as recently as August 2022.[9] Exposing a trove of leaked documents, Fang exposed a previously undisclosed government portal allowing agencies to directly flag content they want throttled or suppressed. Among the topics DHS documents suggest the agency planned to throttle were "the origins of the COVID-19 pandemic and the efficacy of COVID-19 vaccines, racial justice, U.S. withdrawal from Afghanistan, and the nature of U.S. support to Ukraine."

A lawsuit filed by then–attorney general Eric Schmitt (R-MO) alleging government censorship by the Biden administration has exposed what Schmitt calls "a vast censorship enterprise" involving dozens of government officials.[10] Hopefully by the time this book is in print, government puppeteers will have been required to testify under oath about these censorship requests. What other political activity was being facilitated through these equity plans?

In a report analyzing twenty-five agency equity plans, the Heritage Foundation established that they "violate federal civil rights laws . . . make the government . . . much less efficient; award contracts to uncompetitive bidders, thereby wasting taxpayer money; impair national defense; and further hamper the drive for excellence—or even adequacy—in the nation's schools."[11]

This is going on across every federal agency. And someone is coordinating it. The Domestic Policy Council is a low-visibility entity that most people probably couldn't name. But for some reason, President Biden appointed as its director someone who had been on the short list to be his vice president. Someone who had very close ties to President Barack Obama as well as former secretary of state Hillary Clinton. Someone whose loyalty and willingness to fall on her sword to ensure the regime's power is tested and proven. You've definitely heard of her.[12]

"The shadow president," according to former Trump acting director of national intelligence Richard Grenell, is former UN ambassador Susan Rice. It's hard to know who really calls the shots in this administration, but if I had to bet money on it, my money would be on Rice. In her position as director of the Domestic Policy Council, she is deeply involved in the government-wide effort to subjugate agency missions to partisan equity messaging.[13]

"Every agency," she said upon taking her position, "will place equity at the core of their public engagement, their policy design and program delivery to ensure that government resources are reaching Americans of color and all marginalized communities—rural, urban, disabled, LGBTQ+, religious minorities and so many others."[14]

Rice is certainly one of the primary architects of this strategy to prioritize identity politics in the delivery of government services. It's a strategy likely to depend on extensive data collection to identify which voters affiliate with which races, religions, gender identities, and "dangerous" ideologies. I'm sure the administration would want us all to know that they would never abuse this data for partisan purposes.

Besides Rice, another key architect of the initiative is National Security Advisor Jake Sullivan. He, Rice, and National Economic Council director (and former BlackRock executive) Brian Deese work together to "align domestic policy, economic policy and national security unlike ever before."[15] No kidding. Deese undoubtedly works on the ESG strategy to compel compliance with leftist climate goals through financial markets. Sullivan's role is likely to involve the national security piece.

Sullivan's proximity to scandal and disastrous policy is a parade of horribles. As Vice President Joe Biden's national security advisor in 2013, Sullivan was on the front lines when Hunter Biden flew with his father to Asia to leverage the family name for money. GAI's Peter Schweizer was able to corroborate emails from Hunter Biden's laptop showing off-the-books meetings between Hunter Biden, his father, and some of Hunter's business partners. Hunter's and his partners' associations with numerous CCP or CCP-linked officials is something that Sullivan could not have missed. Schweizer documented five separate business deals netting $31 million for the Biden family or their businesses on Sullivan's watch.[16]

From there, Sullivan went on to negotiate the disastrous Iran nuclear deal, which was supposed to prevent Iran from getting nuclear weapons but ended up allowing them to keep their weapons intact, their centrifuges spinning, and evade inspections until, at the end of a decade, they could fire it all up.[17]

Sullivan's next stop was the State Department, where he was deputy chief of staff to one Hillary Rodham Clinton. There he sent "top secret" emails—classified emails—to the nongovernment email account hosted on her homebrew server. Escaping prosecution for that crime, he jumped over to Hillary for America—Clinton's presidential campaign organization.[18]

He was also the subject of allegations under investigation by Special Counsel John Durham. Though Durham did not ultimately bring charges against Sullivan, his final report may yet shed light on allegations that the Clinton campaign used federal surveillance data to fabricate evidence that her political opponent was colluding with foreign enemies to threaten the homeland. His role in pushing false Russian collusion narratives may yet catch up to him.[19]

Name a major administration scandal of the last decade and it seems Sullivan will have his finger in it.[20]

Sullivan is now working with Rice to coordinate the rollout of a program in which the Biden/Harris administration will use the very tools the Clinton campaign abused. But it's definitely not going to be political. Right.

Like Rice, Sullivan and Deese have deep ties to the Obama administration. And like other Obama administration holdovers, they prospered greatly during the years when Trump sent their party to the wilderness. Financial disclosures only share ranges, but Deese's assets jumped from the $81,000–$215,000 range when he was at OMB in 2015, to between $2 million and $7 million. His salary jumped from $175,000 at OMB to $2.3 million at BlackRock.

Sullivan also did well for himself, with real estate investments and stock holdings pushing his postgovernment income to between $7.5 million and $27.5 million.

Rice returned to the executive branch much wealthier the second time. ABC News reports her income nearly quadrupled between the time she joined the Obama administration and when she'd joined the Biden/Harris administration. New disclosures show between $36 million and $149 million in assets, with large stock holdings in major companies as well as oil and gas stocks. She earned $620,000 from speaking engagements the year before her return and earned $250,000 from book royalties.[21]

Rice was a curious pick for the position. Though she had experience in the Obama administration, Rice's résumé is all foreign policy. She has served as an assistant secretary in the State Department, as the US ambassador to the United Nations, and as national security advisor to President Obama. Yet she was chosen to head up domestic policy. Some suggest that given her reputation, the president needed a position for which Senate confirmation was not required.[22] There is likely some truth to that.

Rice is best known for openly lying to the American public in appearances on five Sunday news shows following the 2012 attacks on the U.S. consulate in Benghazi, Libya. In those interviews, Rice brazenly spun a story of a spontaneous reaction to an anti-Muslim video in Cairo—a now-proven lie she has said she does not regret.[23] My visit to Libya just a month after the Benghazi attacks there confirmed with certainty that Rice had been lying.

Rice again came under scrutiny when it was revealed in 2017 that she had allegedly abused national security tools reserved for use in terrorism investigations to order the unmasking of Trump campaign and transition team officials. In other words, she accessed the private communications of American citizens. In March of that year, she had told then–HPSCI chair Devin Nunes (R-CA) in a transcribed interview that she knew nothing about unmasking and was surprised to see reports of it.[24]

Whether it was appropriate for Rice to unmask the communications of American citizens depends on the motive—was she investigating legitimate claims that transition officials were tied to foreign terrorists, or was she weaponizing information for partisan advantage? In response to a FOIA request for documents that might answer that question, the National Security Council has told Judicial Watch the documents have been removed to the Obama Library and cannot be produced.[25]

Rice admitted to unmasking Trump transition officials, but claimed the unmasking was not done for any political purpose—not "to spy, expose, anything." She denied ever having leaked anything and claimed she just did "what any official would do."[26] She described unmasking as routine.

But as *National Review*'s Andy McCarthy pointed out at the time, the White House does not do investigations, neither criminal nor intelligence investigations.[27] It has no authority to do so. Had unmasking—capturing surveillance data that happened to intersect with White House political adversaries—been necessary for such national security purposes, Susan Rice would not have been the one to do it.

The questionable claims continued when Rice testified under oath that she had never been told, during her time as President Obama's national security advisor, that the FBI was investigating Donald Trump for collusion with Russia. That lie got blown up when Obama FBI director James Comey later testified to briefing Obama on the FBI's investigation in Rice's presence.[28]

Rice's loyalty (and likely the fact that there seem to be few lines she will not cross) has obviously endeared her to the Democratic ruling class, despite her documented history of breathtaking dishonesty. The left hailed her as a hero. She was even in the mix as a vice presidential contender before earning a key role in the Biden/Harris administration.

So why was Rice, with her formidable foreign policy chops and independent wealth, chosen to head up the relatively obscure Domestic Policy Council? The motivation behind Rice's appointment has never been articulated, but a Brookings Institution analysis from January 2021 lays out a possible and indeed highly plausible explanation.

Rice's appointment to lead the Domestic Policy Council likely solidifies the Biden administration's efforts to "blur" lines between international policy and domestic policy. Brookings speculates she will take on issues that "lie at the intersection of domestic policy and national security" and "assume an outsized role in policymaking beyond purely domestic issues like health care and children's wellness."[29]

Grenell theorized that Rice's appointment signals that "all of our foreign policy will be treated like domestic policy."[30]

Given Rice's penchant for accessing surveillance data on suspicionless Americans who just happen to be political adversaries, we might question whether "domestic terrorists" (as defined by the Biden administration) will now be treated like foreign terrorists—

subject to heavy surveillance, stripped of their rights, and targeted for prosecution. If that were the plan, one can certainly see why she might be chosen to implement it.

Likewise, the man at the helm of the DOJ, Merrick Garland, has enthusiastically signed on to Rice's coordinated equity campaign. In January 2022, Garland's DOJ rolled out a new domestic terrorism unit intended to address the "elevated threat of violent domestic extremism." Critics say it is aimed at silencing or punishing political opponents.[31]

In written remarks before the Senate Appropriations Committee in May 2021, Garland testified that at DOJ, "we are committed to using every appropriate tool at our disposal to deter, disrupt, and punish acts of domestic violent extremism and domestic terrorism." With the rate at which the left is redefining terms in this country, one has to wonder what Garland means by "appropriate tool."

He went on to explain that DOJ is "deepening collaboration with foreign partners to explore any links to the international counterparts of domestic violent extremists."[32] That's important. Once DOJ can tie a right-wing protester to someone overseas, legal surveillance is possible.

Representative Stewart explained to me how it works. "Right now, if you have a citizen and they talk to a person with ties to terrorism, you can get a surveillance warrant to look at that person. But beyond that, they can look at two or three hops. That person's friends and those friends' friends," he said. In other words, they can "accidentally" collect information on someone who is not their target.

Garland also told the Senate that DOJ was "sharing information as appropriate with technology companies to help them address the spread of domestic violent extremist activity online."[33] Certainly, none of the equity plans are likely to lay out strategies for using programs like the secretive PATCON to surveil, infiltrate, or incite violence. But they do appear to involve, at a minimum, the collection of data, the identification of information that reveals political views, the suppression of dissident speech, and the demonization of mainstream conservative views as racist, violent, and authoritarian. How big is the leap between the way we target and surveil foreign terrorists and the way the party in power treats its domestic political opposition?

Fuel for an Ideological Purge

The Biden strategy has a solution to all this domestic terrorism. And it shouldn't surprise us to know that the recommendation is more government—and more partisan government that can bypass the legislative process.

Likewise, the leftist Center for American Progress (CAP) published a policy blueprint to end white supremacist violence. Arguing that "notions of racial superiority, hostility toward immigrants and minorities, and the myth of an embattled white majority" have infiltrated mainstream American discourse, the CAP blueprint includes a call to "leverage executive branch actions"—in other words, bypass the legislative branch and enact everything by fiat. The recommendations in this section are already happening. In a press release applauding Biden's domestic terror plan, CAP claimed that Biden's plan "embraces many of the suggestions" in their policy blueprint.

Indeed, the very first step in the CAP blueprint requires federal departments to develop strategies to target white supremacist crime, allocate resources "commensurate with the threat," work with local governments to ensure they adopt the same priorities, and collaborate with international partners to tie domestic incidents to international groups. Given how much the administration is relying on the federal workforce to direct this effort, it stands to reason they would need loyal partisans in place for the plan to work.

The second step outlined in the CAP blueprint, not surprisingly, is to purge the federal government of people who are "contributing to white supremacist violence."[34] Given how the left defines racism and white supremacy, it's not hard to see how that could turn into an ideological purge. Indeed, that's precisely what FBI whistleblowers tell House Republicans is happening within their agency. The report alleged, "Multiple whistleblowers have disclosed how the FBI leadership is conducting a 'purge' of FBI employees holding conservative views."

In the CAP blueprint, on which the Biden plan is patterned, there was a call for updating federal hiring standards and screening—a potential cover for doing as CFPB has done in screening out anyone whose opinion does not align with those in power. It calls for mandated training, data collection, and reporting of the federal workforce.

The next step, however, is the most dangerous. The plan calls for improving data collection, research, and reporting. It sounds benign if you don't understand the federal government's history with data collection.

CHAPTER 12

Justifying Surveillance

The endgame of the president's domestic terror strategy is enhanced surveillance and censorship. That conclusion is so apparent that even the typically left-leaning American Civil Liberties Union (ACLU) warned against it. Though the Biden-friendly advocacy group characterized the strategy as being "grounded in good intentions," ACLU sounded an alarm that the president's plan would entrench bias and invite "expansion of intrusive and abusive police powers."[1]

The very possibility that government could be tracking which voters support the current administration and which ones would likely oppose it provides an irresistible temptation for the puppet masters hoping to retain their power. The opportunities for abuse are endless. Government could reward and punish—targeting and harassing political opponents while looking the other way in matters involving loyal partisans. It could target specific voters with ostensibly nonpartisan get-out-the-vote activities. Indeed, many allege these things are already happening.

The danger of giving government unfettered control of vast amounts of data and surveillance information is no longer theoretical. We need only look across the Pacific to see how such tools can be abused to maintain corrupt power structures.

A Legitimate Pretext

People at high risk of transmitting a communicable disease can do considerable damage if permitted to freely travel and spread disease while sick. That was the premise for creating health apps around the world that could conduct contact-tracing services. But in the hands of a government bent on protecting its hold on power, such potent tools are easily abused. In China, residents scan their mobile phones to check in at nearly every place they visit. A three-tiered color code determines their travel permissions. For most places, a green code is required. A yellow code indicates someone who has been exposed to an infected person and needs to self-isolate for seven to fourteen days. Both yellow and red codes restrict travel, but a red code indicates a current infection and a possible involuntary quarantine at a centralized isolation center.[2]

One such case of government abuse involved Chinese citizens who were unable to withdraw their own money from local banks. An ongoing bank run in China was threatening the economy in June 2022 and residents were becoming desperate to get their money out of Chinese banks. But when some residents of Henan Province, who spoke with the *Epoch Times*, attempted to drive to the provincial capital to withdraw funds, the health codes on their COVID-19 apps turned red.[3]

For Chinese citizens, a red code is a virtual prison. They can't travel, use public restrooms, shop, or even return home. For some residents who had been unable to access their funds since April, conditions were dire. By May, freezes on bank withdrawals had been in force for a month, with Chinese media reporting nearly one million depositors frozen out of their accounts. The state-run *Sanlian Life Week* reported by June that an astounding 39.7 billion yuan had become inaccessible—the equivalent of $5.91 billion.[4]

At first the Chinese government ignored protest movements led by desperate depositors. But as the weeks dragged on, protesters reported an odd coincidence. Those en route to protests were being deterred by the red code on their app. They weren't sick, and in some cases had left home with negative PCR tests in hand. But without a green code, they couldn't participate in protests or travel to other bank locations.[5]

Since the start of the pandemic, many governments and companies have been working in unison to establish surveillance states. The ACLU might characterize these efforts as "grounded in good intentions." New smartphone apps that track your locations and conduct other "contact tracing" services have been established in "at least 54 of the 65 countries covered by this report." Several examples include:

In the United States, apps like COVIDWISE have partnered with many states to develop "privacy-by-design contact tracing" methods.

The Russian app SOCIAL MONITORING mandated Muscovites to send photos of themselves "to prove they were quarantining," often erroneously punishing those who allegedly did "not comply."

In Turkey, screening and permission are required by HAYAT EVE SIGAR in order to participate in any domestic travel, including things like public transit or airlines.

Chinese app ALIPAY HEALTH CODE is one of dozens of invasive health monitoring apps that collects personal data easily accessible by authorities.

Ecuador's public health platform SALUD EC aggregates "location data, surveillance footage, and personal information" from users of the app.

The Estonian app HOIA conducts its services through a decentralized system that accesses users Bluetooth services to contact trace.

In Bahrain, affected citizens are required to quarantine and wear electronic wristbands that send user data directly to government servers. Anyone who fails to comply faces criminal penalties.[6]

Here in the United States, governments have tapped into telecommunications data to monitor the spread of COVID-19 by going through the mobile advertising industry. The advertising companies "handed over aggregated and anonymized location data to federal, state, and local governments." However, by going through advertising companies instead of mobile service providers, government branches and agencies (like the CDC) "bypassed the minimal privacy-oversight mechanisms built into US law" that are designed to regulate those service providers.[7] In this case, government actors circumvented what little protections already existed and were established to protect U.S. consumers.

Few pretexts for data collection are more justifiable than a global pandemic. Yet—that data is already being abused. Is the trade-off worth it? That should be a question for the people to answer through their elected representatives, not a question for the B Team. The practice of surveillance and data collection can be legitimate and grounded in good intentions, but the trade-off still may not be worth it. Would Chinese citizens prefer to risk getting COVID or lose their ability to petition their government? It's a trade-off they didn't get to consider before their health apps were deployed. Government's track record of protecting data and preventing abuse does not inspire confidence. Particularly when one considers the vast troves of data already in government hands.

What the Government Knows

Long before President Biden released his domestic terror strategy, the United States was already collecting a staggering amount of data. During my chairmanship on the House Oversight Committee, we researched what the government gathered. Even back then, I was astounded by the sheer volume of what they compile. It includes data they collect themselves, data they buy, even data they receive from foreign governments. There is metadata, photographic data, consumer information, health history, social media use, and more.

It's maintained by the usual suspects at the FBI, the CIA, and the IRS. But readers might be surprised to know who else is collecting data and what they're doing with it.

"It could wipe out any form of anonymity that we have in our society," testified Elizabeth Goitein in a July 2022 Judiciary Committee hearing on government data collection practices. A senior director at the left-leaning Brennan Center for Justice, Goitein testified that "the government is exploiting the resulting legal loopholes to obtain Americans' most sensitive information without a warrant, subpoena, or any legal process whatsoever," and called biometric data such as facial recognition technology "one of the scariest technologies out there."[8]

Even several years ago, when I was in Congress, I had concerns about how extensive the government's data collection efforts were. I ran bipartisan legislation curbing warrantless tracking of electronic geolocation information by law enforcement, demanded accountability for government data breaches, and convened a hearing to question the FBI about its unauthorized facial recognition database.[9]

During that hearing, which had strong bipartisan support, I learned that most faces in the FBI's facial recognition database at that time were not even of criminals. In a May 2016 report, the Government Accountability Office (GAO) found the database contained images of over 411 million people, only about 30 million of whom were "criminal and civil mugshots."[10]

A June 2021 GAO report suggested that use of facial recognition has only proliferated. GAO found that twenty federal agencies—many not typically thought of as law enforcement—use the government's facial recognition technology. Among them are the U.S. Fish and Wildlife Service, NASA, and the U.S. Postal Service.[11]

The late Elijah Cummings (D-MD), the ranking member and eventual chair of the House Oversight Committee, had long expressed concerns about the accuracy of this type of data, particularly given the technology's tendency to misidentify people with darker skin tones. "According to these reports, if you're Black, you're more likely to be subjected to this technology, and the technology is more likely to be wrong," Cummings said during the 2017 hearing. "That's a hell of a combination, particularly when you're talking about subjecting somebody to the criminal justice system. We need to let this sink in."[12]

The facial recognition databases have since been used to identify suspects who participated in the January 6, 2021, protest at the U.S. Capitol and to find people who participated in the 2020 Black Lives Matters protests following the murder of George Floyd.[13] But as I allowed previously, use of the technology is hardly limited to Justice Department agencies.

For example, the U.S. Postal Service operates an Internet Covert Operations Program (iCOP), which surveils social media posts. The internal program inside the U.S. Postal Inspection Service (USPIS)—the "primary law enforcement, crime prevention, and security arm of the U.S. Postal Service"—employs federal law enforcement officers who enforce some two hundred laws. Their duty is to achieve the agency's mission of "[protecting] the U.S. Postal Service and its employees, infrastructure, and customers; [enforcing] the laws that defend the nation's mail system from illegal or dangerous use; and [ensuring] public trust in the mail."[14]

The iCOP carries out this enforcement by monitoring potential threats "to postal service employees and its infrastructure" through open-source intelligence gathering. It then often cooperates with federal, state, and local law enforcement agencies to handle potential threats. The entire method employed by the USPIS is unknown, as it refuses to "discuss its protocols, investigative methods, or tools" in the name of "preserving operational effectiveness."[15] However, the organization does occasionally release memos designed to help its enforcement, and from those we can get an idea of the actions they are taking.

The program drew specific attention in April 2021 when Yahoo! News published an article claiming that a memo released by iCOP in March contained details about surveillance of social media posts related to "anti-lockdown and anti-5G protests."[16] The work being done reportedly involves "having analysts trawl through social media sites to look for what the document describes as 'inflammatory' postings and then sharing that information across government agencies."[17]

The report specifically cites protests that took place "internationally and domestically on March 20, 2021," likely a reference to that day's World Wide Rally for Freedom and Democracy, which "protested everything from lockdown measures to 5G."[18] It appears that despite the massive controversy involving National Security Agency (NSA) domestic surveillance on the population following the revelations of Edward Snowden, the government continues to monitor domestic social media users.

More disturbing is that the original mission of iCOP seems to have strayed heavily from its course, and it is running largely unchecked. Testifying before the House Oversight Committee in April 2021, Chief Postal Inspector Gary Barksdale told lawmakers that iCOP began in 2017 to investigate crimes being conducted and illegal content being transported through the mail system. However, following the George Floyd protests of spring and summer 2020, the organization altered its course and began monitoring social media in the name of "the potential threat to Postal Service workers and buildings."

South Carolina Republican representative Nancy Mace said that Chief Inspector Barksdale was "unprepared to the point of incompetence," and that "he couldn't tell me when this [surveillance] program started, how much money is spent on it, or where the authority to spy on Americans came from."[19] This grows even more concerning because of USPIS capability to hack into any encrypted mobile phone or device. Their 2020 report states they employed the method "to extract previously unattainable information from seized mobile devices," but further they also state that they plan to "expand its use of the hacking tools in the future."[20] USPIS has refused as of yet to comment as to whether they have produced any lawfully required Privacy Impact Assessments on the hacked phones to justify their hacking.

In relation to the investigations after January 6 by Congress and law enforcement, iCOP assisted both in tracking down old social media posts and providing tips for companies to investigate. Reporting shows that iCOP, unlike its law enforcement peers, dedicates resources to monitoring fringe websites and social media services to find evidence of more extremist activity; iCOP has identified both givemebass.com and Wimkin as two popular fringe forums that "coordinate militia groups nationwide" and promote threats against politicians.[21] They have also confessed to monitoring certain Parler and Telegram accounts of right-leaning individuals.[22]

Chip Gibbons, the policy director of Defending Rights & Dissent, has stated his concern for iCOP's involvement in the January 6 investigations, stating that "the FBI has jurisdiction over domestic terrorism, whereas the Post Office—I don't even know how they're involved in this."[23] Indeed, it is interesting that the Postal Service inspectors are devoting so much effort to assisting these investigations when their main purpose is devoted to protecting the "Postal Service and the public by facilitating the identification, disruption, and dismantling of individuals and organizations that use the mail or USPS online tools to facilitate black market Internet trade or other illegal activities," as explained in the USPIS 2019 annual report.[24] Why then is an organization devoted to policing mail and mail-related activities involving itself in policing social media and non-mail-related activities?

That's just one example of one government entity. Others are misusing data they've collected or buying data they can't legally collect. In a 2022 San Francisco rape case, then–district attorney Chesa Boudin explained that "the San Francisco police crime lab has been entering sexual assault victims' DNA profiles in[to] a database used to identify suspects in crimes."[25] This practice would come into potential violation of constitutional protections as well as California's own Victims' Bill of Rights.

In February 2021, the Treasury Department's inspector general issued a letter "warning that the IRS's purchase of cell phone GPS location data may be unconstitutional in light of a landmark 2018 Supreme Court decision requiring a warrant for such collection."[26] (See *Carpenter v. United States.*[27]) The report addressed the IRS Criminal Investigation (CI) division's purchase of a one-year web-based subscription license of location information from cell phone users through the contractor Venntel. It further addressed the fact that the IRS had used this practice several times in the past in order to circumvent seeking a warrant, but they should be cautious to pursue such action in the future in light of the *Carpenter* case.[28]

Unfortunately, the IRS's actions are not an exception. The Brennan Center claims that the "FBI, Department of Homeland Security, and Department of Defense" have all been caught "secretly purchasing cell phone location information, as well as other sensitive consumer data."[29] The same is true of the Secret Service.[30] By buying data instead of obtaining it through a subpoena, warrant, or court order, federal agencies are circumventing the safeguards against invasive policing found in the Fourth Amendment, which specifically requires police to obtain a warrant from a judge before conducting a search or seizure.[31]

It is apparently not unusual for federal agencies to purchase data to target certain communities. Leaked documents reveal that at least two branches of DHS—Customs and Border Protection and Immigration and Customs Enforcement—bought cell phone location data.[32] Using those tools to track people who are not citizens of the United States and who are crossing the border illegally is something I have supported.[33] Using it to create an entry and exit system for foreign nationals who travel to the United States is a legitimate use. But my concern is that these same tools developed for use against criminals are available for use against Americans who are under no suspicion of committing crimes.

For instance, data company Mobilewalla used cell phone information collected from the George Floyd protests of 2020 to estimate the demographics of protesters. According to the company, the data was collected to satisfy the curiosity of its own employees about what the data might suggest. But Senator Elizabeth Warren expressed concern that such data could easily be sold to the FBI for law enforcement purposes. "This report shows that an enormous number of Americans—probably without even knowing it—are handing over their full location history to shady location data brokers with zero restrictions on what companies can do with it," Warren said. "In an end-run around the Constitution's limits on government surveillance, these companies can even sell this data to the government, which can use it for law and immigration enforcement."[34]

All these revelations display how concerns toward government data collection should be a bipartisan issue. If the government can purchase data to target religious groups and protesters of one issue, they can do it for every issue, creating a state where the ruling party (whoever it may be at the time) can crush the voice of the minority.

Even five years ago, when I was in Congress, I had concerns about how extensive the government's data collection efforts were. I ran bipartisan legislation curbing warrantless tracking of electronic geolocation information by law enforcement, demanded accountability for government data breaches, and convened a hearing to question the FBI about its unauthorized facial recognition database.[35] In 2018, I applauded Apple CEO Tim Cook's efforts to lobby for federal legislation protecting the fundamental right to privacy.[36]

But those concerns were just the tip of the iceberg. What we see happening in China should be a wake-up call to all Americans. In a recent *New York Times* investigation, we learned just how far government will go to hold on to power. After reviewing and analyzing more than 100,000 Chinese government bidding documents, the *Times* uncovered the scope of an extensive system of cameras using facial recognition databases to track movements. In Fujian Province alone, police believe they were storing 2.5 billion facial images for "controlling and managing people." They are using geolocation tracking to connect the digital footprint to a person's physical location. Using phone trackers, which are used in all thirty-one Chinese provinces, the *Times* found that police in Guangdong could identify which phones had Uyghur-to-Chinese dictionary apps installed in order to identify those who belong to that ethnic minority. The Chinese are collecting DNA, iris scans, and voice prints, which they hope to connect with digital profiles accessible by the government.[37]

Could that happen here in the United States? Consider what has already happened here.

Abuses Are Not Theoretical

Among the ACLU's objections to Biden's domestic terror policy was a belief that law enforcement use of these new tools and authorities would be "rife with racial and religious bias."[38] Those concerns are not unfounded. Even under Democratic presidents, the DOJ has a history of targeted prosecutions.

In 2010, Attorney General Eric Holder defended the use of government sting operations against American Muslims that began following the terrorist attack on September 11, 2001.[39] These were not necessarily politically motivated prosecutions, but they did disproportionately target a religious minority—which was the very concern ACLU expressed regarding the Biden domestic terror plan.

Two decades after 9/11, we now know the government recruited fifteen thousand informants to dig up dirt on American Muslims that would leverage others to become informants. The FBI had to create a custom software program—known as Delta—to track them all. Echoing the allegations in the PATCON story and the Fast & Furious scandal, the Intercept contributing writer Trevor Aaronson reports that informants "played essential parts in supposed terror plots, often providing the weapons, money, and logistical support needed."[40]

Addressing Muslim civil rights activists, Holder called these operations "essential," claiming that "in those terrorism cases where undercover sting operations have been used, there is a lengthy record of convictions." He assured activists that Muslims would be treated fairly in America.[41]

But Aaronson points to an unusual dump of classified information from Holder in 2010 to refute that claim. Based on Holder's disclosures, Aaronson found more than five hundred Muslim terror defendants in the decade following 9/11. Of those, nearly half were targeted through an FBI informant, and forty-nine had encountered an "agent provocateur."[42] Among all of those hundreds of cases, Aaronson said, "I could count on one hand the number of actual terrorists . . . who posed a direct and immediate threat to the United States." The rest were small-time criminals with distant links to terrorists overseas, persons charged with lying to authorities, or immigration violators. Aaronson concluded: "While we have captured a few terrorists since 9/11, we have manufactured many more."[43]

It's not just the DOJ using data to track targeted groups. The U.S. military found a way to circumvent the legal process that allows them to collect location data on American Muslims. They aren't *collecting* data, which would be illegal. They are receiving it—or rather, buying it. Revelations unveiled through public records and interviews with those involved show that there are "two separate, parallel data streams that the U.S. military uses, or has used, to obtain location data." The first relies on the tech company Babel Street, which created a product called Locate X.[44]

This service is used by U.S. Special Operations Command, the "branch of the military tasked with counterterrorism, counterinsurgency, and special reconnaissance," as an aid to overseas special forces operations.

The second stream is through a company called X-Mode, which acquires location data directly from various apps, then sells that data to contractors—notably the U.S. military. The apps sending data to X-Mode in this instance include Muslim Pro, an app with over 98 million downloads, which reminds users when to pray and provides passages and readings of the Quran; and Muslim Mingle, a Muslim-exclusive dating app with over 100,000 downloads. Thus the U.S. military is using data collected from Muslim religious and dating apps to ascertain individual locations for reasons undisclosed.[45]

X-Mode's then-CEO Joshua Anton revealed that the company "tracks 25 million devices inside the United States every month, and 40 million elsewhere," and that its company's tracking technology (SDK) is embedded in "around 400 apps." Other apps that X-Mode uses to track locations include topics such as step counters, dating sites, and weather apps.[46] Many users never even realize they are being tracked through this technology, which is then sold to third-party bidders. Since the story was reported, both Apple and Google have banned X-Mode from their respective app stores. But the company questions whether the data it collects is any different from what Apple and Google themselves are collecting.[47]

With that context in mind, consider what the CIA and FBI do with bulk data collection. The Central Intelligence Agency has been collecting in bulk "some kind of data that can affect Americans' privacy," according to a recently declassified April 2021 letter by Senators Ron Wyden (D-OR) and Martin Heinrich (D-NM), both of whom currently sit on the Senate's Select Committee on Intelligence. The letter was drafted by the senators about a month after receiving a report titled "Deep Dive II," which was "part of a set of studies by a watchdog board scrutinizing intelligence community operations under Executive Order 12333."[48]

The executive order, originally drafted by President Ronald Reagan in 1981 and subsequently amended in 2003, 2004, and 2008, laid out rules for "reasonable and lawful means . . . [used to acquire] the best intelligence possible," and address intelligence collection activities that Congress has left unregulated by statute.[49] The two senators urged Biden appointees Avril Haines (director of national intelligence) and William Burns (CIA director) to declassify all the related activity and "any internal rules about querying the data for information about Americans."[50]

In 2013, Edward Snowden's revelation that the NSA was collecting bulk logs of Americans' phone calls using a disputed interpretation of the Patriot Act led Congress to act and change the existing law. Prior to the change, the *New York Times* reported that the CIA had been "paying AT&T to analyze its vast trove of call records for associates of the agency's overseas terrorism suspects." But in 2015, Congress banned bulk collection of telecommunications metadata under the Patriot Act and limited other types of bulk collection by the FBI under existing laws of the Foreign Intelligence Surveillance Act (FISA). This is where the senators' letter comes in; they claim that under order 12333, "the CIA has secretly conducted its own bulk program . . . entirely outside the statutory framework that Congress and the public believe govern this collection, and without any of the judicial, congressional or even executive branch oversight that comes with FISA collection." This is the fact that the senators claim, "has been kept from the public and from Congress."[51]

Meanwhile, over at the FBI, a declassified court ruling from October 2019 found that the FBI may have violated the rights of "potentially millions of Americans—including its own agents and informants—by improperly searching through information obtained by the NSA's mass surveillance program."

ACLU staff attorney Patrick Toomey said that the revelations from the case "reveal devastating problems with the FBI's backdoor searches, which often resembled fishing expeditions through Americans' personal emails and online messages."[52] The declassified ruling shows that few safeguards have existed to prevent Americans' communications from being searched improperly by the NSA, and subsequently by the FBI.

The extensive data collection exposed by Snowden created a database that the FBI accessed to obtain American communications. In 2017 alone, searches related to U.S. persons by the CIA and NSA combined to account for 7,500. The FBI ran nearly 3.1 million searches through this database. The kicker is that "many of the FBI's searches were not legally justified because they did not involve a predicated criminal investigation or other proper justification for the search, as required by law," according to the FISA court ruling. The Intercept listed some examples of their "abuses," including:

- During a four-day period in March 2017, the FBI searched mass surveillance data for communications related to an FBI facility, suggesting that agents were spying on other agents.
- The FBI regularly used mass surveillance data to investigate potential witnesses and informants who were neither suspected of crimes nor national security concerns.
- In November 2017, the FBI conducted a search of mass surveillance data on a "potential recipient of a FISA order." In other words, the FBI was able to mine mass surveillance data to find out what evidence agents would discover if they went ahead and requested the FISA order.[53]

Many of these cases involve a good-faith effort to catch criminals or prevent violence. The pretext is legitimate, but the practice is a breach of privacy that can restrict the rights of suspicionless Americans. Whether the trade-off of privacy for security is worthwhile in these cases is a question for the people through their elected representatives. But what becomes more dangerous is the potential for a ruling party to weaponize these tools to perpetuate their own power.

Partisan Control of the Surveillance Apparatus

The existence of so much data on so many Americans provides an irresistible temptation for ruling parties who wish to stay in power. There are hundreds of ways to weaponize federal power. A party could conceivably use the taxing apparatus to target and shut down the fundraising of opposition groups. Likewise, they could waive fees for those requesting documents that favor them while denying access to those requesting documents that hurt them. They could apply different standards of justice to crimes committed by allies versus those committed by adversaries. They could surveil political opponents.

All of this has already been done, of course. In 2013, the Obama administration used the IRS to disproportionately target conservative groups, demand information about their donors, and prevent them from engaging in an upcoming midterm election. Despite broad exposure of the plot, no one was ever punished.[54] The Obama EPA denied or refused to respond to twenty FOIA requests from the conservative Competitive Enterprise Institute, while simultaneously granting access to documents requested by the liberal environmental group Earthjustice in seventeen out of nineteen cases.[55] Meanwhile, fees were disproportionately waived for leftist groups.

Obama's Justice Department prosecuted filmmaker and critic Dinesh D'Souza for illegal campaign donations that did an end run around campaign finance law. D'Souza was guilty and paid the price. But legal commentator Alan Dershowitz called the prosecution selective. "If they went after everyone who did this, there would be no room in jails for murderers," he said.[56]

Most appalling was the Obama administration's weaponization of surveillance. Prior to the allegations of surveilling the Trump transition team using a Russia collusion pretext they knew was baseless, the Obama National Security Agency had spied on Israeli president Benjamin Netanyahu, who openly opposed the president's Iran nuclear deal.[57] Swept up in the surveillance were private conversations of another branch of government—members of Congress.[58]

The Biden administration, in its "National Strategy for Countering Domestic Terrorism," has called for "improving employee screening to enhance methods for **identifying domestic terrorists who might pose insider threats.**" It calls for the Office of Personnel Management to "assist investigators in identifying potential domestic terrorism threats" and for the DOJ, DHS, and Department of

Defense (DOD) to pursue efforts to **"ensure domestic terrorists are not employed** within our military or law enforcement ranks and improve screening and vetting processes" (emphasis in original).[59]

One can imagine how such a strategy might be tweaked just a little bit to help a ruling party fill the government and military with partisan loyalists and banish those whose views are not politically aligned.

Congressman Chris Stewart told me he has seen no evidence in his role on the HPSCI that the military has been infiltrated by white supremacists or domestic terrorists: "There is no evidence at all of white supremacy infecting police or military organizations," he said in the conversation. "With more than a million members—there are probably some who apply who hold these views. But they aren't recruited in. They aren't accepted. A true white nationalist is an idiot and not the kind of person who would be successful in military training."

With the surveillance justifications used in the president's domestic terror policy, the threat of partisan weaponization becomes more real. But that worst-case scenario isn't the only problem. As government collects more and more data, they must stay on the cutting edge of cybersecurity to safeguard that information. If there is one thing I learned about the federal bureaucracy during my years on the House Oversight Committee, it's that government is rarely on the cutting edge. They have the track record to prove it. Data breaches are common. During the pandemic, the Government Accountability Office identified 3,200 data breaches in the Department of Health and Human Services between 2015 and 2021, increasing by 843 percent since 2015.[60]

Government Is Not an Innovator

While federal agencies have proven quite innovative when it comes to finding ways around legal restrictions on data gathering, in my experience their methods of securing data are old-school. They don't pay for the best people. They don't maintain the latest technology.

Take, for example, the need for an entry and exit system to monitor foreign nationals in our country. Our government has no idea how many people are living illegally in this country because they have overstayed a tourist visa or a student visa, but Robert Warren at the Center for Migration Studies estimates that visa overstays outnumbered border crossings by a two-to-one margin from 2009 to 2019. For 2017, the DHS tried to estimate the number of visa overstays and came up with an approximation of 702,000 people.[61] An entry/exit program would easily track those numbers.

It's been on the books for a long, long time that we were supposed to have an entry/exit program in this country. The statutory requirement was mandated in 1996 and added a biometric component in 2001. Subsequent legislation has authorized the attorney general to collect data on arrivals and departures of foreign nationals, develop tamper-resistant documents, authorize the program to interface with law enforcement databases, and authorize fees to pay for the project. But despite this legislative effort, the exit system has never come to fruition. At the airport they scan passports. They know who is coming and going. But the federal bureaucracy has never managed to create a way to aggregate that data, citing conflicts over privacy and concerns about accuracy.[62] Other nations like Canada and the European Union manage to do this. We don't.

I can go to my local sub shop, and they can tell me how many times I've ordered a specific sandwich. When I get to my tenth one, I get a free one. But the government can't tell you how many times someone has been in and out of the country. There is a total lack of political will to do things that the B Team doesn't think are important.

When it comes to the collection of private information, we're expected to believe government will take the role of innovator.

In 2013, ID.me (then Troop ID) founder and CEO Blake Hall authored an op-ed in the *Wall Street Journal* in which he listed the reasons he relocated his new start-up to Washington, D.C. In it, he described the government's "ability to spur innovation through access to data and systems" and praised the Obama administration's "forward-leaning stance toward opening up new datasets and APIs." He described this phenomenon as a shift to "government as a platform."

Essentially, it is the shift of accessible and aggregate data from for-profit institutions to any person "at an individual and aggregate level." He believes that public-access data is necessary to "help spur innovation and growth."[63] However, the publicity of our private data could become an issue on multiple fronts—such as with privacy or even national security.

The problem is that there are currently no safeguards in place at state or federal levels that dictate how the data can be stored or used for future purposes. Many states that have contracted with ID.me "have not required ID.me to automatically delete images of unemployment applicants from its database." This means that unless users request deletion, their photos and facial data will not be deleted for three years, "and then only if their ID.me accounts become inactive, [otherwise] the rest will be saved indefinitely."[64] So much for federal innovation.

CHAPTER 13

How to Take On the Puppeteers and Win

This administration's self-indulgent hyperfocus on climate change, racial equity, white supremacy, and domestic surveillance should have proven costly in the 2022 midterms. Voters seemed more concerned about the maladies the administration opted not to address—inflation, energy security, inner-city crime and homelessness, student indoctrination in the classroom, and deadly fentanyl from unrestricted border crossings drowning our communities. Despite many warning signs, Biden's party stayed the course. And was rewarded anyway.

While Republicans saw shifts in the electorate—particularly from minority groups—moving to the right, those changes didn't translate to House victories. Even more disturbing, independent voters broke left in that election cycle, despite their concerns that the country was on the wrong track.

Given the Democrats' overwhelming dominance of so many American institutions, it's easy to feel like the Davids of the right will never defeat the Goliaths of the left. The task before us is not a simple one. But it's also not an impossible one. There are Davids all over America whose slingshots aim true. There is much we can learn from them.

On his final show of 2020, after being diagnosed with terminal lung cancer, Rush Limbaugh said something I think about often:

*We Americans have adapted to our problems. . . . Our free-
dom has allowed our adaptability. If disaster is coming our
way, we don't just sit there and endure it. We come up with
ways to avoid it, to beat it back, to overcome it, but we don't
just sit there and accept it. And, as such, we don't just resign
ourselves to the fact that we're living in the darkest days because we, at least to this point, still have the greatest degree of
freedom of any people on earth. Now, it's under assault and
under attack and we all know this. But I don't believe our
darkest days are ahead of us. I never have. People have been
asking, "You've always told us you'd tell us when it's time to
panic. Is it time?" It's never time to panic, folks. It's never,
ever gonna be time to give up on our country. It will never be
time to give up on the United States. It will never be time to
give up on yourself. Trust me.*

Pushback from the States

The best weapon in our arsenal is the power of states. This is
where lawsuits, like the one filed by now-Senator Eric Schmitt
from Missouri, can expose what the security state tried to keep
hidden. It was through this lawsuit that Americans learned how
the Biden administration controlled the narrative on social media through coercive censorship demands. Documents obtained in
that lawsuit proved Biden's director of digital strategy Rob Flaherty had sent hostile demands to YouTube, Facebook, Twitter,
and Google to censor narratives unfavorable to the administration. In one email to Google, Flaherty demanded reassurance that
Google had "a handle on vaccine hesitancy," and was "working
toward making the problem better." This concern, he assured
them, was "shared at the highest (and I mean highest) levels of
the White House."[1] It's where state treasurers and comptrollers are
hitting back against politicized investment funds. It's where Florida
governor Ron DeSantis showed a better way to manage COVID-19,

and Virginia governor Glenn Youngkin struck a blow to politicized educational curriculum.

Thanks to Schmitt, we know much more about the extent of government censorship on social media.

Lawsuits are not the only way states can push back. It's instructive to consider Youngkin's approach to the pretext of diversity, equity, and inclusion in the commonwealth of Virginia. Youngkin successfully exposed the pretext for what it was by using the left's own proclaimed values against them.

Though values like diversity, equity, and inclusion (DEI) are the pretext upon which progressive self-righteousness is built, there are limits to just how much diversity, equity, and inclusion the left is actually willing to support. Youngkin exposed this reality during his first month in office.

Rather than a wholesale rejection of his predecessor's deeply politicized DEI initiative, Youngkin embraced it. There is nothing wrong with diversity. What's wrong is the notion that only reliably Democrat-voting constituencies are worthy of protection. Youngkin rejected that premise, as well as the assertion that "equity" requires government to secure equality of results for all.

Upon being sworn in, he immediately reorganized the state's DEI initiative, taking down preceding governor Ralph Northam's DEI website and replacing the existing staff. Then he appointed the Heritage Foundation's Angela Sailor, a Black woman with an impressive history of opposition to politicized school curriculum such as Critical Race Theory and the 1619 Project. Sailor would head up the new Diversity, *Opportunity* & Inclusion office. The substitution of the word *opportunity* for the word *equity* signaled a sea change in the way diversity and inclusion would be sought.[2] It highlights one of the key contrasts between left and right in America.

When government sets out to secure equality of opportunity, we preserve the very American pursuit of excellence by incentivizing and rewarding merit. But when government tries to secure equality of result (equity), excellence and merit have to be suppressed and discriminated against. In this way, *equity* is nothing more than a euphemism for discrimination.

Created as a cabinet-level position by Northam, presumably to atone for a scandal involving a blackface photo in his medical school yearbook, the DEI office was a first-in-the-nation statewide effort to develop a plan to "help 100 Virginia government agencies work toward an equitable future."[3]

But the Democrats' plan for inclusiveness was, not surprisingly, somewhat exclusive. It seemed the word *equity* was just a euphemism for racism, as it could be used to exclude qualified people from state jobs purely on the basis of their skin color or sexual preference. An equitable system, by progressive standards, was one that excluded merit as a basis for achievement and substituted immutable or preferential characteristics.

Though goal number one of Northam's plan was to "recruit and retain a diverse workforce," the execution was almost singularly focused on what it called historically "underrepresented" populations of Black and other minorities. Northam's One Virginia plan was a "strategic blueprint to institutionalize equity across state government," but only certain kinds of equity—such as skin color equity and gender equity.[4]

Under Youngkin's executive order, the office would take "a stronger and more focused role on promoting ideas, policies, and economic opportunities for disadvantaged Virginians, including Virginians living with disabilities and bringing Virginians of different faiths together."[5]

This was a dramatic departure from the previous Democratic administration's focus on race and sexual orientation, instead prioritizing the creation of opportunities for the disabled, the endangered, and the suppressed. Youngkin's order directed that assistance for marginalized groups should include the most marginalized group of all—the one you could still legally murder in this country—unborn children. The department's revised mission was expanded to "promote free speech and civil discourse," to "be an ambassador for unborn children," and to promote viewpoint diversity in higher education.[6]

That change elicited a livid response. Planned Parenthood Advocates of Virginia tweeted, Virginia now has a DEI officer encouraged to spout and defend anti-abortion legislation, some of the least inclusive and equitable policy on the books.[7] (As if abortion were in any way inclusive or equitable for the child involved.)

In Youngkin's administration, a conservative applying for a position at a predominantly liberal university could be a diversity hire, regardless of skin color. In a five-page letter to university presidents during the May 2022 graduation season, Youngkin reiterated this commitment, urging schools to hire faculty of "diverse political perspectives." The letter specifically asked universities to develop a framework that will guide their efforts "to nurture a culture that prioritizes civil discourse and debate, both inside and outside the classroom."[8]

Suffice to say, this is not what the left had in mind when they created the DEI initiative. It preserves the values of diversity and inclusion but removes the political advantages this pretext was intended to create.

Youngkin, whose surprise victory came on a wave of opposition to progressive classroom curriculum, further sought to purge from public schools "inherently divisive concepts," which were arguably rooted in Critical Race Theory. In a report identifying "discriminatory and divisive concepts" compiled by the commonwealth's superintendent of public instruction, the administration identified "numerous resources" that "employ the concept that current discrimination is needed to address past discrimination."[9]

Youngkin had deftly called the Democrats' bluff.

The hail of criticism he received exposed an ugly reality. For the left, diversity means political conformity, equity legitimizes discrimination, and inclusion is achieved only by exclusion. By keeping the DEI office initiative and adopting a more inclusive direction, Youngkin predictably earned the indignation of Virginia Democrats, who apparently cared more about preserving the political advantages than the actual values of diversity and inclusion.

In the time since these changes were made, the shallowness of the left's DEI rhetoric has only become more apparent. In a video produced in compliance with state-mandated diversity training for new state government employees, the narrator quoted from Youngkin's executive order in which he acknowledged, "every one of us is made in the image of our Creator."[10]

Apparently, the left's tolerance for diverse perspectives has limits. Though the Pew Research Center finds that 90 percent of Americans believe in either God or a higher power, and references to the Creator are found in America's founding documents, Virginia Democrats were furious at Youngkin's reference to one. One agnostic employee, apparently ignorant to the irony of the previous program's political goals, griped, "[T]his is just all his agenda being forced into government employee training."[11] We can argue whether a position held by 90 percent of Americans reflects an agenda, but even if we concede the point, the fact remains that leftists pioneered the politicization of DEI training. They're fine with it when the agenda being pushed is their own.

Indeed, Youngkin's strategy probably wouldn't pass muster in a deeply conservative state, where this kind of diversity initiative might be seen as government overreach. But in a very divided commonwealth of Virginia, Youngkin is giving the left a taste of its own medicine. They don't like it.

The Advantage of Truth

In addition to state pushback, the right holds another advantage that could prove to be insurmountable for globalists in the long run: truth. While neither party has a corner on the truth, America's power players have made a critical mistake in attempting to align themselves against what is real and what is true.

You can fool some of the people all of the time and all of the people some of the time, Abraham Lincoln is widely believed to have commented. But as the famous saying goes, you cannot fool all the people all the time. Despite heavy restrictions on free speech throughout the pandemic, the dam is beginning to break. Powerful truths are beginning to be revealed. From Elon Musk's Twitter files to Pfizer's COVID vaccine trial data, the truth has a way of busting the myths and revealing the conspiracy theories.

Likewise, good public policy works. And conservative economic policies have a long history of leading to growth and prosperity. Managed economies like the one being built by the Biden administration have no such track record. Ultimately, we never want to see America fail. But individual policies will fail. And the right has a certain advantage—we are not required to fool all of the people all of the time.

Youngkin's changes on DEI are likely to result in a more ideologically diverse workforce, better futures for innocent unborn children, and less divisive curriculum in classrooms. They'll still take criticism because his policies do not create progressive jobs, result in lucrative contracts, or shift the balance of power leftward. Without those elements, the left has little use for diversity and inclusion—a reality that may become apparent the longer Youngkin is able to expose it.

Only DEI policies that promote political goals get any traction, regardless of whether they actually work. Policies that don't grow government, control the flow of money, or produce a political advantage get no support, even if they promote principles like diversity, opportunity, and inclusion.

As this example illustrates, the underlying principles of the leftist agenda are not where the political disagreements lie. It's in the policies that flow from them. Diversity, access to a quality education, upward mobility for the underprivileged, environmental stewardship of our lands and waters—these are not controversial values. What is controversial is the assertion that they can only be solved with more ineffective bureaucrats, more bloated federal contracts, and more government-subsidized markets that aren't profitable in a free market system. The fact is, these leftist solutions don't work.

This dichotomy shows up in education policy, energy policy, election reform, environmental regulations, and even intelligence operations. Only when we recognize the true goal can we understand how priorities get set. That's why, for example, the demand to defund the police is deafening when it means taking a top-down federal approach to hiring more leftists to do more training to do more crime "prevention." But when it comes to conservatives protesting at the Capitol, Canadian truckers protesting in Ottawa, lawful gun owners exercising their Second Amendment rights, or energy companies meeting critical demand, suddenly justice and law enforcement become critical priorities and no punishment is harsh enough.

These inherent contradictions are important. They help us distinguish genuine concern from political opportunism. We can answer a lot of questions by looking at public policy through the prism of corrupted institutions and counterfeit democracy. If we can recognize which solutions are intended to solve problems for all of us and which ones are intended to solve problems only for the B Team, we can unite to reject counterfeit institutions and restore a real representative republic. We can expose the puppeteers for what they are doing and how they're trying to do it.

This will require a massive undertaking by the states' elected representatives and ultimately the public. Perhaps one of the most important things we can do to flush out the system and start anew is to starve the beast. There is an insatiable desire for more money, and consequently more government. Unfortunately, in today's world the federal government has its tentacles in everything we do. That's not what freedom looks like. We simply have to starve the beast.

Looking Forward

Through the process of developing this book, I felt the weight of our national situation and the gravity of its consequences.

Personally, I'm an eternal optimist. I like to engage in the fight, but I try to do so with a smile on my face. Trey Gowdy, who represented South Carolina when we served together in Congress, used to regularly tease me about smiling while I was sticking a dagger in someone's gut. (Not literally, of course. He was referring to my interrogations of witnesses in committee hearings. And I only did this to those who deserved it.) If they couldn't answer the questions, then we had illuminated a problem, which was my job.

As I conclude my fourth book, I think this is an important point. The United States of America is the greatest country on the face of the planet. Period. No other country has offered more opportunity and brought such prosperity to so many. Our collective opportunity to pursue happiness is unparalleled anywhere else on this planet. I have so much admiration and gratitude for those who have gone before us and paved the way so we could have so much.

But each generation needs to step up and do its part. For most, they look at Washington, D.C., and say, "It is such a mess. Can't they all just get along?" Unfortunately, not everyone is fighting for prosperity, freedom, liberty, and equal justice under the law. For example, I find that often those who are preaching tolerance are the least tolerant of all. They work hard to subvert our cohesiveness and would rather divide us by race, ethnicity, economics, geography, etc.

So to those who attempt to oversimplify the complexity of our world, I would hope they would join the fight for less government, less regulation, and help us all pursue more freedom and liberty. There are also well-funded people and organizations who like to operate in darkness to manipulate the process to ensure that only they can select the winners and losers in society. As this book has shown, these puppeteers are clever and cunning. Like cockroaches, they flee from the light. This book sheds light where they don't want it.

Policy decisions made in Washington almost always involve taking money from one person and giving it to someone else. This is power. Power also manifests itself in laws, regulations, executive orders, and bureaucracy.

This entire equation is upside down and backward. The fundamental foundation of our country was based on the idea that the government works for the people. Unfortunately, there are far too many who believe government is all-powerful. They don't believe as I do, that our freedom and rights come from God, not government.

Rarely if ever do you find people who are willing to give away power and return it to where it rightfully belongs—with the people of the United States. I still have the optimism and positive approach that I heard from Rush Limbaugh. Even though I was young, I also felt it with President Reagan.

The election of 2022 was encouraging. While I still don't understand why some of these races were as close as they were, I think it was a strong acknowledgment from the people that our country was offtrack and they wanted a course correction. Americans are giving us a mandate to return to our core principles.

Certainly, the issues of fiscal discipline, justice/crime, energy policy, uniform immigration as per our Constitution, foreign affairs, and the off-the-rails wokeism all need to be addressed.

When you stack up all the problems and challenges, and look at how heavily fortified is the system that perpetuates them, it is daunting. I hope we remember we don't have to do this alone. It is not as if any one individual can unilaterally turn things around.

What we need is a cavalry of committed people who collectively identify the problem and seek to provide the changes needed. What I learned along the way in writing this book is that simply electing people to Congress will not change things fast enough. I am not here to negate or diminish the role and responsibility of the men and women who are elected to office, but it's going to take more than that.

We all have the responsibility to uphold the Constitution. That's not just up to the courts. We shouldn't assume that Congress will fix all things. They never have. The answers to our most complex problems are found outside of Washington, D.C. They are found in our homes, in our communities, and with our friends and neighbors.

This is what makes the United States of America so unique. As Rush said, it is never time to give up on America, nor is it time to give up on yourself.

Believe in America with a smile on your face. You live in the greatest country in the world. But let's fortify our state and local governments, seek and spread truth, and gather the like-minded around us to solve these problems. It is the best way to make sure the next generation can achieve immense prosperity, peace, and happiness without the puppeteers controlling their destiny.

Acknowledgments

Your willingness to buy a book that dives into the hard truths of our political predicament means so much to me. I know it's not easy to face the reality that the people we elect are not generally the people running the show. No one wants to believe puppeteers have taken over our government.

I have hope because I know you are not fooled. I know there are many Americans who simply will not accept the reality being foisted upon us. And I know change is possible. Thank you for taking the time to purchase, download, read, or listen to this book, which is the culmination of a lot of work, experience, and collaboration.

I would be remiss if I didn't immediately acknowledge the power of prayer in my life and my work. My faith and belief in Jesus Christ informs, inspires, and strengthens me in everything I do.

I was very fortunate to be entrusted to author this, my fourth book, for Broadside Books, an imprint of HarperCollins. I remember negotiating the terms of the first book, *Deep State*, and suggesting I could produce a finished product faster than the outline in the contract. Eric Nelson, the vice president and editorial director for Broadside, responded by saying, "You haven't seen our edits yet. We do this for a living. This is your first book. Trust us, this is going to take a lot longer than you think it will."

Oh, he was right!

By the time we mutually agreed (thanks to the professionalism and experience of my agent, David Larabell, of Creative Artists

Agency) to do book number four, we were asking for more time, not less.

There is a tremendous amount of research that goes into crafting a book worthy of your time. Behind the effort is always a team of people to produce a quality book. First there was Eric Nelson and his team from Broadside for having the vision and belief in me to write these books, and David Larabell to make sure we were thinking through all the issues. Many, many thanks to both for their ongoing support, direction, and pushing me to dive deeper and present the findings of our research in a coherent manner. They are the best in the business, and I am thrilled to be associated with them.

Not every story makes it to the final draft. The experiences of Sal DiCiccio as a city councilman for Phoenix, Arizona, is a worthy story I hope to share further in another setting. His story is reflective of elected officials trying to do the right thing and being pushed back by a bureaucracy determined not to cede power to someone who was elected.

None of this would have happened without the talents and passion of my long-time colleague and friend Jennifer Scott. She was my first campaign manager, worked with me during my service in Congress, and stayed on after I departed Congress in 2017. Jennifer is exceptionally capable, and her knowledge of the issues of the day is without parallel. I have leaned on her perspective daily for years. Her contributions and creativity have helped me every step of the way. She is a close friend and a confidant. Without her, this book would not have become what it is. Thank you, Jennifer!

Another source for research and insight has been the Government Accountability Institute (GAI), where I am a compensated Distinguished Fellow. Led by Peter Schweizer, this organization shares my passion for true oversight, accountability, and exposure of the truth. In particular, Steve Stewart, Steve Post, and Corey Adamyk were instrumental in helping us do primary research, brainstorm ideas, and proofread the final book. It is with great appreciation I thank

GAI and their resources and talents. They engage in meaningful endeavors and do so with a love of our country.

From my home state of Utah, our Utah state treasurer Marlo Oaks was tremendously generous with his time, sharing his perspective and experiences. In conjunction with his wife, Elaine Oaks, he has dived in with both feet to fight the puppeteers on a critical battlefront. He was insightful in helping me expand my understanding of the political weaponization of financial markets.

Along the way we were also aided by Utah attorney Jesse Trentadue, attorney Cassidy Wadsworth, Marianne Downing, Phoenix city councilman Sal DiCiccio, and others who would rather keep their input anonymous. For all of their contributions, I am most grateful. Thank you!

To my family, especially my wife, Julie. I love you. Words cannot adequately express my infinite devotion and endless gratitude. Every aspect of my life is positively impacted by you, and I thank you!

And thank you for taking the time to be involved and engaged with our country and its future. There is more that unites us than divides us. We all need to be involved and engaged. I believe in American Exceptionalism. The United States of America is the greatest country on the face of the planet, but we all must be vigilant and a participant.

By reading this book or listening to this audio, you are doing that. Now go out and do your part! And thank you for allowing me, and the above-mentioned team, to share these thoughts and perspectives. I hope you enjoyed it. I hope it was illuminating, because we can all confront and expose the puppeteers who are trying to impose their own counterfeit democracy.

Notes

Preface

1. https://www.natlawreview.com/article/cfpb-dead-now-fifth-circuit-correctly-holds-cfpb-s-funding-was-unconstitutional.

INTRODUCTION Establishing Perpetual Power

1. https://rollcall.com/2022/08/26/biden-rally-blasts-gop-but-real-midterm-effect-will-come-on-the-road/.

2. Xinhua News Agency, "Democracy in China," December 2021, http://www.gov.cn/zhengce/2021-12/04/content_5655823.htm; Mareike Ohlberg, "Why China Is Freaking Out over Biden's Democracy Summit," *Foreign Policy*, December 10, 2021, https://foreignpolicy.com/2021/12/10/china-response-biden-democracy-summit/.

3. https://www.nytimes.com/2020/06/30/world/asia/hong-kong-security-law-explain.html (see paragraph 18).

4. "China's Xi Allowed to Remain 'President for Life' as Term Limits Removed," BBC News, March 11, 2018, https://www.bbc.com/news/world-asia-china-43361276.

5. "Peace, Dignity and Equality on a Healthy Planet," United Nations, accessed July 11, 2022, https://www.un.org/en/global-issues/democracy.

6. "The Essence of Putin's Managed Democracy," Carnegie Endowment for International Peace, October 18, 2005, https://carnegieendowment.org/2005/10/18/essence-of-putin-s-managed-democracy-event-819.

7. https://www.heritage.org/education/report/correcting-carters-mistake-removing-cabinet-status-the-us-department-education.

8. National Federation of Independent Business v. Osha, 142 S.Ct. 661 (2022), https://www.law.cornell.edu/supremecourt/text/21A244.

9. https://nypost.com/2022/08/24/fbi-warned-agents-off-hunter-biden-laptop-due-to-election-whistleblowers/?utm_campaign=iphone_nyp&utm_source=twitter_app.

10. Eric Katz, "Federal Employees Are Donating Almost Exclusively to Hillary Clinton," *Government Executive*, October 26, 2016, https://www.govexec.com

/pay-benefits/2016/10/federal-employees-are-donating-almost-exclusively
-hillary-clinton/132667/.

11. https://www.opensecrets.org/political-action-committees-pacs/national
-treasury-employees-union/C00107128/candidate-recipients/2022.

CHAPTER 1 America's New Social Credit System

1. Reuters, "Beijing Pioneering Citizens' 'Points' System Critics Brand 'Orwellian,'"
Epoch Times, November 20, 2018, https://www.theepochtimes.com/beijing
-pioneering-citizens-points-system-critics-brand-orwellian_2719927.html.

2. Katie Canales, "China's 'Social Credit' System Ranks Citizens and Punishes
Them with Throttled Internet Speeds and Flight Bans if the Communist Party
Deems Them Untrustworthy," *Business Insider*, last updated December 24, 2021,
https://www.businessinsider.com/china-social-credit-system-punishments-and
-rewards-explained-2018-4.

3. Drew Donnelly, PhD, "An Introduction to the China Social Credit System,"
Horizons, last updated July 13, 2022, https://nhglobalpartners.com/china
-social-credit-system-explained/.

4. Dan Sanchez, "Elon Musk's Threat to the 'Current Thing' Monoculture,"
FEE Stories, April 15, 2022, https://fee.org/articles/elon-musks-threat-to-the
-current-thing-monoculture/; Disha Kandpal, "Elon Musk's 'I Support the Current Thing' Meme Sparks Twitter Debate," HITC, accessed July 16, 2022, https://
www.hitc.com/en-gb/2022/03/15/elon-musk-i-support-the-current-thing/.

5. Paul Kupiec, "Socially Responsible Investing Is Turning into a Covert War on
Fossil Fuels," *Hill*, March 11, 2022, https://thehill.com/opinion/finance/59
7837-socially-responsible-investing-is-turning-into-a-covert-war-on-fossil
-fuels/.

6. Newt Gingrich, "The Woke Industrial Complex and a Crisis of American Identity," Gingrich 360, August 15, 2021, https://www.gingrich360.com/2021/08/15
/the-woke-industrial-complex-and-a-crisis-of-american-identity/.

7. Klaus Schwab, "Now Is the Time for a 'Great Reset,'" World Economic Forum,
June 3, 2020, https://www.weforum.org/agenda/2020/06/now-is-the-time-for
-a-great-reset.

8. Ibid.

9. Mark Segal, "Harvard Moves to Complete Fossil Fuel Investment Exit, Invests
in Green Economy Solutions," ESG Today, September 13, 2021, https://www
.esgtoday.com/harvard-moves-to-complete-fossil-fuel-investment-exit-invests
-in-green-economy-solutions/; Mark P. Mills, "Mines, Minerals, and 'Green'
Energy: A Reality Check," Manhattan Institute, July 9, 2020, https://www.man
hattan-institute.org/mines-minerals-and-green-energy-reality-check.

10. James Mackintosh, "Is Tesla or Exxon More Sustainable? It Depends Whom You

Ask," *Wall Street Journal*, September 17, 2018, https://www.wsj.com/articles/is-tesla-or-exxon-more-sustainable-it-depends-whom-you-ask-1537199931.

11. https://www.texaspolicy.com/pushed-to-the-brink-the-2021-electric-grid-crisis-and-how-texas-is-responding/.

12. Michael Posner, "ESG Investing Needs More Rigorous Standards to Evaluate Corporate Conduct," *Forbes*, February 1, 2022, https://www.forbes.com/sites/michaelposner/2022/02/01/esg-investing-needs-more-rigorous-standards-to-evaluate-corporate-conduct/?sh=8dea47073578.

13. Mark S. Bergman et al., "Introduction to ESG," Harvard Law School Forum on Corporate Governance, August 1, 2020, https://corpgov.law.harvard.edu/2020/08/01/introduction-to-esg/.

14. Statista Research Department, "ESG Scores of the Worlds' Largest Companies 2021, by Provider," Statista, May 23, 2022, https://www.statista.com/statistics/1268534/comparison-esg-scores-largest-companies-provider-worldwide/.

15. "Moody's—ESG Credit Impact Scores Expanded to Autos, Oil & Gas, Utilities, and More Sectors," Moody's, December 7, 2021, https://www.moodys.com/research/Moodys-ESG-credit-impact-scores-expanded-to-autos-oil-gas—PBC_1313409.

16. Richard Morrison, "Environmental, Social, and Governance Theory," Competitive Enterprise Institute, May 5, 2021, https://cei.org/studies/environmental-social-and-governance-theory/.

17. Tristan Justice, "15 States Threaten to Pull $600 Billion from Banks That Won't Give Equal Service to Energy Industry," *Federalist*, November 30, 2021, https://thefederalist.com/2021/11/30/15-states-threaten-to-pull-600-billion-from-banks-that-wont-give-equal-service-to-energy-industry/.

18. https://www.latimes.com/world-nation/story/2020-07-03/germany-first-major-economy-phase-out-coal-nuclear-energy.

19. https://townhall.com/tipsheet/katiepavlich/2022/03/08/flashback-trump-warned-germany-against-becoming-energy-dependent-on-russia-n2604265.

20. https://www.cnbc.com/2018/07/13/trump-is-exaggerating-germanys-reliance-on-russia-for-energy.html.

21. https://www.pbs.org/newshour/world/trump-scolded-germany-for-buying-gas-from-russia-heres-what-we-know.

22. https://oilprice.com/Latest-Energy-News/World-News/Energy-Prices-Trigger-Deindustrialization-In-Germany.html.

23. "Tucker Carlson—Utah Treasurer Discusses How ESG Investing Sparked Inflation—6/14/22," YouTube video, posted by "jburma," June 14, 2022, https://www.youtube.com/watch?v=ftWYgpUzDaM.

24. Democratic Treasurers Association 2022 Corporate Benefits Package.

25. https://www.washingtonpost.com/opinions/2022/10/16/maryland-comptroller
-barry-glassman-endorsement/.

26. Ibid.

27. Wayne Winegarden, "The Empty Case for Stakeholder Capitalism and ESG Investing," *National Review*, February 10, 2022, https://www.nationalreview.com
/2022/02/the-empty-case-for-stakeholder-capitalism-and-esg-investing/.

28. Kent Lassman, "Not One Dollar: One-Third of Voters Unwilling to Spend Anything to Counter Climate Change," Competitive Enterprise Institute, October 13,
2021, https://cei.org/citations/not-one-dollar-one-third-of-voters-unwilling-to
-spend-anything-to-counter-climate-change/.

29. Mike Pence, "Republicans Can Stop ESG Political Bias," *Wall Street Journal*,
May 26, 2022, https://www.wsj.com/articles/only-republicans-can-stop-the-esg
-madness-woke-musk-consumer-demand-free-speech-corporate-america-11653
574189.

CHAPTER 2 Farewell Free Markets, Hello Stakeholder Capitalism

1. Citizens United v. FEC, Federal Election Commission, accessed July 18, 2022,
https://www.fec.gov/legal-resources/court-cases/citizens-united-v-fec/.

2. Kenny Xu, "Critical Race Theory Has No Idea What to Do with Asian Americans," *Newsweek*, July 13, 2021, https://www.newsweek.com/critical-race-theory
-has-no-idea-what-do-asian-americans-opinion-1608984.

3. "From Ambition to Action—the Path to Net Zero," BlackRock, accessed July 18,
2022, https://www.BlackRock.com/us/individual/about-us/road-to-net-zero.

4. Matt Egan, "BlackRock and the $15 Trillion Fund Industry Should Be Broken
Up, Antimonopoly Group Says," CNN Business, November 24, 2020, https://
www.cnn.com/2020/11/24/business/BlackRock-vanguard-state-street-biden
/index.html.

5. "80% of Equity Market Cap Held by Institutions," Pensions & Investments,
April 25, 2017, https://www.pionline.com/article/20170425/INTERACTIVE
/170429926/80-of-equity-market-cap-held-by-institutions; Jacob Greenspon,
"How Big a Problem Is It That a Few Shareholders Own Stock in So Many Com-
peting Companies?" *Harvard Business Review*, last updated February 22, 2019,
https://hbr.org/2019/02/how-big-a-problem-is-it-that-a-few-shareholders-own
-stock-in-so-many-competing-companies.

6. Citizens United v. FEC; Tim Lau, "Citizens United Explained," Brennan Center for Justice, December 12, 2019, https://www.brennancenter.org/our-work
/research-reports/citizens-united-explained.

7. Daniel I. Weiner, "Citizens United Five Years Later," Brennan Center for Justice,
January 15, 2015, https://www.brennancenter.org/our-work/research-reports
/citizens-united-five-years-later.

8. Igor Derysh, "The Citizens United Ruling Broke American Democracy at the Start of the Decade. It Never Recovered," Salon, December 29, 2019, https://www .salon.com/2019/12/29/the-citizens-united-ruling-broke-american-democracy -at-the-start-of-the-decade-it-never-recovered/.

9. Franco Ordoñez, "Biden Is Under Pressure on Gas Prices. So He's Putting Pressure on Oil Companies," NPR, June 15, 2022, https://www.npr.org/2022 /06/15/1105138903/biden-is-under-pressure-on-gas-prices-so-hes-putting-pres sure-on-oil-companies.

10. Steve Peoples, "In Intimate Moment, Biden Vows to 'End Fossil Fuel,'" ABC News, September 6, 2019, https://abcnews.go.com/Politics/wireStory/intimate -moment-biden-vows-end-fossil-fuel-65442382.

11. "ExxonMobil to Triple Permian Production by 2025, Expand Transportation Infrastructure," ExxonMobil, news release, January 30, 2018, https://corporate .exxonmobil.com/News/Newsroom/News-releases/2018/0130_ExxonMobil -to-triple-Permian-production-by-2025-expand-transportation-infrastructure.

12. Jennifer Hiller and Svea Herbst-Bayliss, "Engine No. 1 Extends Gains with a Third Seat on Exxon Board," Reuters, June 2, 2021, https://www.reuters.com /business/energy/engine-no-1-win-third-seat-exxon-board-based-preliminary -results-2021-06-02/.

13. Eric Rosenbaum, "Oil Giant Exxon Mobil Pushes New Climate Change Plan as Activist Investors Circle," CNBC, December 14, 2020, https://www.cnbc.com /2020/12/14/exxon-mobil-begins-to-mount-defense-of-itself-and-a-bigas-act ivists-circle.html.

14. Sergio Chapa, "Chevron Investors Back Climate Proposal in Rebuke to Management," BNN Bloomberg, May 26, 2021, https://www.bnnbloomberg.ca /chevron-investors-back-climate-proposal-in-rebuke-to-management-1.1608831.

15. "Exxon Board Debates Dropping Several Major Oil and Gas Projects—WSJ," Reuters, October 20, 2021, https://www.reuters.com/business/energy/exxon -board-debates-dropping-several-major-oil-gas-projects-wsj-2021-10-20/.

16. Nick Visser, "Climate Activists Win Bid to Put New Members on Exxon's Board," Huffington Post, last updated May 27, 2021, https://www.huffpost.com/entry /exxon-mobil-climate-change-board-members_n_60af0443e4b0d56a83f2bfdd.

17. Hiller and Herbst-Bayliss, "Engine No. 1 Extends Gains with a Third Seat on Exxon Board."

18. As You Sow, home page, accessed July 18, 2022, https://www.asyousow.org; "Current Resolutions," As You Sow, accessed July 18, 2022, https://www.asyou sow.org/resolutions-tracker.

19. Robert Stilson, "Record Number of ESG Shareholder Resolutions in 2022," Capital Research Center, April 11, 2022, https://capitalresearch.org/article/record -number-of-esg-shareholder-resolutions-in-2022/.

20. "Current Resolutions."

21. "In Broad Daylight: Uyghur Forced Labour and Global Solar Supply Chains," Sheffield Hallam University, accessed July 18, 2022, https://www.shu.ac.uk /helena-kennedy-centre-international-justice/research-and-projects/all-projects /in-broad-daylight.

22. "ESG Litigation Risk: Climate Lawsuits Dominate, but Scope Is Widening," Mining Review America, February 21, 2022, https://www.miningreview.com /health-and-safety/esg-litigation-risk-climate-lawsuits-dominate-but-scope-is -widening/.

23. "BlackRock Opposed Re-election of 800 Company Directors in Q3—Report," Reuters, photograph, October 21, 2021, https://www.reuters.com/news/picture /BlackRock-opposed-re-election-of-800-com-idUSKBN2HB1FF.

24. Orla McCaffrey, "Charlie Munger Expects Index Funds to Change the World— and Not in a Good Way," *Wall Street Journal*, February 16, 2022, https://www .wsj.com/articles/charlie-munger-expects-index-funds-to-change-the-world -and-not-in-a-good-way-11645055334.

25. Larry Fink, "Larry Fink's 2022 Letter to CEOs: The Power of Capitalism," BlackRock, accessed July 18, 2022, https://www.blackrock.com/corporate/in vestor-relations/larry-fink-ceo-letter.

26. Ira Kay, Chris Brindisi, and Blaine Martin, "The Stakeholder Model and ESG," Harvard Law School Forum on Corporate Governance, September 14, 2020, https://corpgov.law.harvard.edu/2020/09/14/the-stakeholder-model-and-esg/; Klaus Schwab and Peter Vanham, "What Is Stakeholder Capitalism?" World Economic Forum, January 22, 2021, https://www.weforum.org/agenda/2021/01 /klaus-schwab-on-what-is-stakeholder-capitalism-history-relevance/.

27. Witold Henisz, Tim Koller, and Robin Nuttall, "Five Ways That ESG Creates Value," McKinsey & Company, November 14, 2019, https://www.mckinsey .com/business-functions/strategy-and-corporate-finance/our-insights/five-ways -that-esg-creates-value.

28. M. B. Mathews, "Conservatives Are Playing Defense in an Offensive Cul- ture," American Thinker, April 20, 2022, https://www.americanthinker.com /blog/2022/04/onservatives_are_playing_defense_in_an_offensive_culture .html.

29. Fink, "Larry Fink's 2022 Letter to CEOs: The Power of Capitalism."

30. Ibid.

CHAPTER 3 The Progressive Catch-22

1. "ESG and Credit Rating Agencies: The Pressure Accelerates," ING Bank N.V., February 22, 2021, https://think.ing.com/articles/esg-and-credit-ratings-the -pressure-has-accelerated.

2. https://www.manhattan-institute.org/the-energy-transition-delusion.

3. Mark John, "Cost of a Net-zero World 'Much Higher' Than Estimated," BusinessDay, January 25, 2022, https://www.businesslive.co.za/bd/world/2022-01 -25-cost-of-a-net-zero-world-much-higher-than-estimated/.

4. Letter from State of Utah to S&P Global Ratings President and CEO Douglas L. Peterson and President Martina L. Cheung, Re: ESG Credit Indicators—State of Utah, April 21, 2022, https://treasurer.utah.gov/wp-content/uploads/04-21-22 -Utah-Letter_SP-Global_ESG-Indicators.pdf.

5. Kelcie Moseley-Morris, "Idaho Republicans Concerned over Environmental, Social Investment Standards," *Idaho Capital Sun*, June 7, 2022, https://idaho capitalsun.com/2022/06/07/idaho-republicans-concerned-over-environ mental-social-investment-standards/.

6. Khalid Azizuddin, "West Virginia Attacks S&P for 'Politically Subjective' ESG Ratings," *Responsible Investor*, April 26, 2022, https://www.responsible -investor.com/west-virginia-attacks-sp-for-politically-subjective-esg-ratings/; Skylar Woodhouse, "West Virginia Blasts S&P ESG Scoring as 'Politically Subjective,'" BNN Bloomberg, April 27, 2022, https://www.bnnbloomberg.ca/west -virginia-blasts-s-p-esg-scoring-as-politically-subjective-1.1757890.

7. Riley Moore, West Virginia State Treasurer, "Treasurer Moore Announces Board of Treasury Investments Ends Use of BlackRock Investment Fund," press release, January 17, 2022, https://www.wvtreasury.com/About-The-Office/Press -Releases/ID/406/Treasurer-Moore-Announces-Board-of-Treasury-Invest ments-Ends-Use-of-BlackRock-Investment-Fund.

8. "Report: China Emissions Exceed All Developed Nations Combined," BBC News, May 7, 2021, https://www.bbc.com/news/world-asia-57018837; Diksha Madhok, "Chinese Investors Pour $1 Billion into BlackRock's New Fund," CNN Business, September 8, 2021, https://www.cnn.com/2021/09/08/investing/Black Rock-china-fund-intl-hnk/index.html.

9. Moore, "Treasurer Moore Announces Board of Treasury Investments Ends Use of BlackRock Investment Fund."

10. Ben Weingarten, "It's Conservative David vs. the Woke Corporate Green Giant," RealClear Investigations, May 17, 2022, https://www.realclearinvestigations .com/articles/2022/05/17/its_conservative_david_vs_the_woke_corporate _green_giant_832255.html.

11. Bryan Bashur, "New ESG Tracker-States Divesting from BlackRock," Americans for Tax Reform, 12/13/2022, https://www.atr.org/esgradar/.

12. Rachel Adams-Heard, "Texas Targets Wall Street in Fight over ESG Investing (2)," Bloomberg Law, June 14, 2021, https://news.bloomberglaw.com/private -equity/texas-targets-wall-street-in-fight-over-esg-investing-1.

13. "Governor Ron DeSantis Takes Action Against Communist China and Woke Corporations," Ron DeSantis, news release, December 20, 2021, https://www .flgov.com/2021/12/20/governor-ron-desantis-takes-action-against-communist -china-and-woke-corporations/.

14. Mark Brnovich, "ESG May Be an Antitrust Violation," *Wall Street Journal*, opinion, March 6, 2022, https://www.wsj.com/articles/esg-may-be-an-antitrust-violation-climate-activism-energy-prices-401k-retirement-investment-political-agenda-coordinated-influence-11646594807.

15. https://secureservercdn.net/50.62.194.59/xxe.347.myftpupload.com/wp-content/uploads/2022/06/SFOF-Press-Release-SFOF-Highlights-Key-Concerns-with-Controversial-Proposed-ESG-Disclosure-Rule.pdf.

16. https://www.foxbusiness.com/politics/19-states-investigate-major-us-banks-pushing-esg-policies-killing-american-companies.

17. Jonah Goldberg, "Climate-Change Fearmongering Has Turned Totally Unhinged," *New York Post*, July 14, 2017, https://nypost.com/2017/07/14/climate-change-fearmongering-has-turned-totally-unhinged/.

CHAPTER 4 The End of the World Justifies Any Sacrifice

1. "Biden's Reckless Budget," House GOP, March 29, 2022, https://www.gop.gov/bidens-reckless-budget/.

2. https://www.budget.senate.gov/imo/media/doc/58357-Graham.pdf;https://www.democrats.senate.gov/imo/media/doc/inflation_reduction_act_one_page_summary.pdf.

3. https://finance.yahoo.com/news/1-9-trillion-american-rescue-234144507.html; https://www.cnn.com/2021/11/05/politics/house-votes-infrastructure-build-back-better/index.html.

4. Representative Ken Ivory, "America's National Debt: A Rendezvous with Reality?" American Legislative Exchange Council, April 22, 2021, https://alec.org/article/americas-national-debt-a-rendezvous-with-reality/.

5. https://www.whitehouse.gov/briefing-room/statements-releases/2021/01/27/fact-sheet-president-biden-takes-executive-actions-to-tackle-the-climate-crisis-at-home-and-abroad-create-jobs-and-restore-scientific-integrity-across-federal-government/.

6. "Release: Quarterly Retirement Market Data," Investment Company Institute, on Internet Archive, March 28, 2022, https://web.archive.org/web/20220614030122/https:/www.ici.org/statistical-report/ret_21_q4 (the screenshot of the site was captured on June 14, 2022); "Average, Median, Top 1%, and All United States Retirement Savings Percentile," dqydj.com, accessed July 18, 2022, https://dqydj.com/average-retirement-savings/.

7. Mekala Krishnan et al., "Six Characteristics Define the Net-Zero Transition," McKinsey Insights, January 25, 2022, https://www.mckinsey.com/business-functions/sustainability/our-insights/six-characteristics-define-the-net-zero-transition.

8. https://www.climatedepot.com/2022/10/21/goldman-sachs-jeff-currie-3-8

-trillion-of-investment-in-renewables-moved-fossil-fuels-from-82-to-81-of
-overall-energy-consumption-in-10-years/.

9. "Executive Order on Catalyzing Clean Energy Industries and Jobs Through Federal Sustainability," The White House, December 8, 2021, https://www.white house.gov/briefing-room/presidential-actions/2021/12/08/executive-order-on -catalyzing-clean-energy-industries-and-jobs-through-federal-sustainability/.

10. Megan Darby, "Net Zero: The Story of the Target That Will Shape Our Future," Climate Home News, September 16, 2019, https://www.climatechangenews .com/2019/09/16/net-zero-story-target-will-shape-future/.

11. David Rose, "World's Top Climate Scientists Confess: Global Warming Is Just QUARTER What We Thought—and Computers Got the Effects of Green-house Gases Wrong," *Daily Mail*, last updated September 19, 2013, https:// www.dailymail.co.uk/news/article-2420783/Worlds-climate-scientists-confess -Global-warming-just-QUARTER-thought—computers-got-effects-greenhou se-gases-wrong.html; Paul C. "Chip" Knappenberger and Patrick J. Michaels, "The IPCC AR5 Is in Real Trouble," Cato Institute, July 26, 2013, https://www .cato.org/blog/ipcc-ar5-real-trouble.

12. Whiting, "Snow in Ancient Greece and the Net-Zero Budget."

13. "Summary: Actuarial Status of the Social Security Trust Funds," Social Security Administration, June 2022, https://www.ssa.gov/policy/trust-funds-summary .html.

14. "U.S. Department of Labor Announces Final Rule to Protect Americans' Retirement Investments," U.S. Department of Labor, news release, accessed July 18, 2022, https://www.dol.gov/newsroom/releases/ebsa/ebsa20201030.

15. "U.S. Department of Labor Proposes Rule to Remove Barriers to Considering Environmental, Social, Governance Factors in Plan Management," U.S. Department of Labor, news release, accessed July 18, 2022, https://www.dol.gov/news room/releases/ebsa/ebsa20211013.

16. Tariq Fancy, "The Secret Diary of a 'Sustainable Investor'—Part 1," Medium, August 2021, https://medium.com/@sosofancy/the-secret-diary-of-a-sustainable -investor-part-1-70b6987fa139.

17. Patrick Temple-West and Kristen Talman, "ESG Shares Underperform Oil and Gas in 2021," *Financial Times*, December 30, 2021, https://www.ft.com /content/70984a9e-ab65-4905-a2fa-83202e3db68b.

18. "ESG Investing Is Heading for a Reckoning, Says One Veteran Manager," *Pensions & Investments*, June 6, 2022, https://www.pionline.com/esg/esg-investing -heading-reckoning-says-one-veteran-manager.

19. "Your New Woke 401(k)," *Wall Street Journal*, opinion, October 20, 2021, https:// www.wsj.com/articles/your-new-woke-401-k-retirement-savings-esg-erisa-biden -administration-department-of-labor-proposal-11634753095?page=1.

20. Michael Wursthorn, "Tidal Wave of ESG Funds Brings Profit to Wall Street,"

Wall Street Journal, March 16, 2021, https://www.wsj.com/articles/tidal-wave
-of-esg-funds-brings-profit-to-wall-street-11615887004.

21. https://www.azag.gov/sites/default/files/2022-08/BlackRock%20Letter.pdf.

22. https://video.foxbusiness.com/v/6311059098112#sp=show-clips.

23. Utah State Treasurer Marlo M. Oaks, "Attorney General Sean Reyes, State Treasurer Marlo Oaks and State Auditor John Dougall Lead 23 States in Letter Opposing Proposed Department of Labor Rule That Puts Retirement Savings at Risk,"
Utah Office of State Treasurer, accessed July 19, 2022, https://treasurer.utah
.gov/featured-news/attorney-general-sean-reyes-state-treasurer-marlo-oaks
-and-state-auditor-john-dougall-lead-23-states-in-letter-opposing-proposed-de
partment-of-labor-rule-that-puts-retirement-savings-at-risk/.

24. Peggy Hollinger, "Ukraine War Prompts Investor Rethink of ESG and the De-
fence Sector," *Financial Times*, March 8, 2022, https://www.ft.com/content
/c4dafe6a-2c95-4352-ab88-c4e3cdb60bba.

25. Stephen Moore, "Follow the (Climate Change) Money," Heritage Foundation, December 18, 2018, https://www.heritage.org/environment/commentary
/follow-the-climate-change-money.

26. Chris Martin, "Wind Turbine Blades Can't Be Recycled, So They're Piling Up in
Landfills," Bloomberg, last updated February 7, 2020, https://www.bloomberg
.com/news/features/2020-02-05/wind-turbine-blades-can-t-be-recycled-so
-they-re-piling-up-in-landfills.

27. Jackson Hickel, "The Limits of Clean Energy," *Foreign Policy*, September 6,
2019, https://foreignpolicy.com/2019/09/06/the-path-to-clean-energy-will-be
-very-dirty-climate-change-renewables/.

28. "The Growing Role of Minerals and Metals for a Low Carbon Future,"
World Bank Group, June 2017, https://documents1.worldbank.org/curated
/en/207371500386458722/pdf/117581-WP-P159838-PUBLIC-ClimateSmart
MiningJuly.pdf.

29. Jackson Hickel, "The Limits of Clean Energy," *Foreign Policy*, September 6,
2019, https://foreignpolicy.com/2019/09/06/the-path-to-clean-energy-will-be
-very-dirty-climate-change-renewables/; Stefan Bringezu, "Possible Target Cor-
ridor for Sustainable Use of Global Material Resources," *Resources* 4, no. 1 (February 11, 2015), https://www.mdpi.com/2079-9276/4/1/25.

30. Matthew Mosk, Brian Ross, and Ronnie Greene, "Solyndra Collapse a 'Waste'
of Half a Billion by Obama, GOP Critics Say," ABC News, August 31, 2011,
https://abcnews.go.com/Blotter/solyndra-collapse-waste-half-billion-obama
-gop-critics/story?id=14424323.

31. Alex Diaz, "Remember Solyndra? Loss of Taxpayer Millions Now Seems Forgotten, Expert Says," Fox News, March 20, 2019, https://www.foxnews.com/pol
itics/remember-solyndra-loss-of-taxpayer-millions-seems-forgotten-expert-says.

32. "Ten Lessons of the Solyndra Failure," House Energy and Commerce Commit-

tee, September 14, 2012, https://republicans-energycommerce.house.gov/news
/blog/ten-lessons-solyndra-failure/.

33. https://www.nytimes.com/2022/09/02/climate/john-podesta-climate-biden
.html?smtyp=cur&smid=tw-nytimes.

34. https://www.foxnews.com/politics/republicans-slam-bidens-new-clean-energy
-czar-john-podesta-ties-ccp-official.

35. https://www.nytimes.com/2022/09/02/climate/john-podesta-climate-biden
.html?smtyp=cur&smid=tw-nytimes.

36. https://www.npr.org/sections/goatsandsoda/2017/06/09/532106567/a-little
-known-climate-fund-is-suddenly-in-the-spotlight.

37. https://trumpwhitehouse.archives.gov/briefings-statements/statement
-president-trump-paris-climate-accord/.

38. https://thenewamerican.com/top-scientist-un-climate-finance-is-subsidy-for
-kleptocracy/.

39. "Follow the Money: How the Department of Justice Funds Progressive Activists,"
Government Accountability Institute, Consent Order Report, pp. 5–6, https://g-a-i
.org/wp-content/uploads/2016/10/Follow-the-Money-How-the-Department-of
-Justice-Funds-Progressive-Activists1.pdf; Josh Gerstein, "Eric Holder: 'I'm Still
the President's Wingman,'" *Politico*, April 4, 2013, https://www.politico.com
/blogs/politico44/2013/04/eric-holder-im-still-the-presidents-wingman-160861.

40. "Executive Order on Protecting Public Health and the Environment and Restoring Science to Tackle the Climate Crisis," The White House, January 20, 2021,
https://www.whitehouse.gov/briefing-room/presidential-actions/2021/01/20
/executive-order-protecting-public-health-and-environment-and-restoring
-science-to-tackle-climate-crisis/.

41. "DOJ Ends Holder-era 'Slush Fund' Payouts to Outside Groups," Fox News,
June 8, 2017, https://www.foxnews.com/politics/doj-ends-holder-era-slush-fund
-payouts-to-outside-groups.

42. https://www.justice.gov/ag/page/file/1499241/download.

43. Michelle Malkin, "The ACORN Obama Knows," *National Review*, June 25,
2008, https://www.nationalreview.com/2008/06/acorn-obama-knows-michelle
-malkin/; "Follow the Money: How the Department of Justice Funds Progressive
Activists," pp. 5–6.

44. Sean Higgins, "Obama's Big Bank 'Slush Fund,'" *Washington Examiner*, on Internet Archive, accessed July 19, 2022, https://web.archive.org/web/20201207163911/
https://www.washingtonexaminer.com/tag/barack-obama?source=%2Fobamas
-big-bank-slush-fund%2Farticle%2F2580431 (the screenshot of the site was captured on December 7, 2020).

45. Vivek Ramaswamy, *Woke, Inc.: Inside Corporate America's Social Justice Scam*
(New York: Center Street, 2021), 150.

46. "Attorney General Holder Speaks at the Announcement of the Financial Fraud Enforcement Task Force's New Residential Mortgage-Backed Securities Working Group," U.S. Department of Justice, speech, January 27, 2012, https://www.justice.gov/opa/speech/attorney-general-holder-speaks-announcementof-financial-fraud-enforcement-task-force-s.

47. Jeff Carlson, "The Department of Justice's Slush Fund," *themarketswork* (blog), March 2, 2017, https://themarketswork.com/2017/03/02/the-department-of-justices-slush-fund/.

48. Christina Rexrode, "Big Banks Paid $110 Billion in Mortgage-Related Fines. Where Did the Money Go?" *Wall Street Journal*, last updated March 9, 2016, https://www.wsj.com/articles/big-banks-paid-110-billionin-mortgage-related-fines-where-did-the-money-go-1457557442.

49. House Judiciary Committee, Stop Settlement Slush Funds Act of 2016, H.R. Rep. No. 114-694 (2016), https://www.congress.gov/congressional-report/114th-congress/house-report/694/1.

50. "Holder Cut Left-Wing Groups In on $17 Bil BofA Deal," *Investor's Business Daily*, August 27, 2014, https://www.investors.com/politics/editorials/holders-bank-of-america-settlement-includes-payoffs-to-democrat-groups/.

51. https://www.justice.gov/ag/page/file/1499241/download.

52. https://www.rubio.senate.gov/public/_cache/files/a4c4c80c-f912-4625-8aee-74f4b3174df7/635E6AEC50E8972B2127F8F2868289A2.public-comment-letter-opposing-settlement-agreements-involving-payments-to-non-governmental-third-parties-final71.pdf.

53. Elizabeth Warren, "Unsafe at Any Rate," *Democracy: A Journal of Ideas,* no. 5 (Summer 2007), https://democracyjournal.org/magazine/5/unsafe-at-any-rate/.

54. David A. Graham, "The Fight over the CFPB Reveals the Broken State of American Politics," *Atlantic*, November 28, 2017, https://www.theatlantic.com/politics/archive/2017/11/the-cfpb-and-the-loss-of-faith-in-politics/546833/.

55. Ronald L. Rubin, "Donald Trump Evicted Elizabeth Warren from the Consumer Financial Protection Bureau," *Washington Examiner*, January 3, 2018, https://www.washingtonexaminer.com/weekly-standard/donald-trump-evicted-elizabeth-warren-from-the-consumer-financial-protection-bureau.

56. Ronald L. Rubin, "The Tragic Downfall of the Consumer Financial Protection Bureau," *National Review*, December 21, 2016, https://www.nationalreview.com/2016/12/consumer-financial-protection-bureau-tragic-failures/.

57. Bill McMorris, "100% of CFPB Donations Went to Democrats," *Washington Free Beacon*, November 23, 2016, https://freebeacon.com/politics/100-cfpb-donations-went-democrats/.

58. Rubin, "The Tragic Downfall of the Consumer Financial Protection Bureau."

59. Eric Grover, "Mick Mulvaney Has Ignited a Firestorm to Rein in the CFPB," *Hill*,

February 15, 2018, https://thehill.com/opinion/finance/373977-mick-mulvaney-has-ignited-a-firestorm-to-rein-in-the-cfpb/.

60. Seila Law LLC v. Consumer Financial Protection Bureau, 140 S. Ct. 2183 (2020), https://www.scribd.com/document/467358959/Seila-Law-LLC-v-Consumer-Financial-Protection-Bureau.

61. "Consumer Financial Protection Bureau," Elizabeth Warren's website, accessed July 19, 2022, https://2020.elizabethwarren.com/cfpb.

62. "Civil Penalty Fund: Consumer Education and Financial Literacy," Consumer Financial Protection Bureau, accessed July 19, 2022, https://www.consumerfinance.gov/enforcement/payments-harmed-consumers/civil-penalty-fund/consumer-education-financial-literacy/.

63. "CFPB Joins Justice in Shaking Down Banks for Democrat Activist Groups," *Investor's Business Daily*, June 17, 2015, https://www.investors.com/politics/editorials/cfpb-diverts-civil-penalty-funds-to-democrat-activist-groups/.

64. Paul Sperry, "Trump Is Finally Fixing This Economy-Killing Agency," *New York Post*, December 2, 2017, https://nypost.com/2017/12/02/trump-is-finally-fixing-this-economy-killing-agency/.

CHAPTER 5 "Most Power, Least Famous": The Shadow Government Power Players

1. "Poll: Voters See Biden as More Moderate Than Trump," *Hill*, May 7, 2020, https://thehill.com/hilltv/what-americas-thinking/496596-poll-voters-see-biden-as-more-moderate-than-trump/.

2. Chris Cillizza, "Joe Biden Has a *Major* Independents Problem," CNN Politics, last updated October 8, 2021, https://www.cnn.com/2021/10/08/politics/joe-biden-independents-polling/index.html.

3. Lisa Mascaro, "Once Rivals, Biden and Sanders Are Now Partners in Power," Associated Press, July 15, 2021, https://apnews.com/article/joe-biden-business-government-and-politics-election-2020-4874e02f7fea1f5f44d144753212cc57.

4. Mark Segal, "Biden Taps Brian Deese, Global Head of Sustainable Investing at BlackRock, to Lead National Economic Council," ESG Today, December 4, 2020, https://www.esgtoday.com/biden-taps-brian-deese-global-head-of-sustainable-investing-at-blackrock-to-lead-national-economic-council/.

5. Michael Shellenberger, "Biden Climate Plan Risks Putting China and BlackRock Before the American People," *Forbes*, December 3, 2020, https://www.forbes.com/sites/michaelshellenberger/2020/12/03/biden-climate-plan-risks-putting-china-and-blackrock-before-the-american-people/.

6. David Dayen, "How BlackRock Rules the World," *American Prospect*, September 27, 2018, https://prospect.org/economy/blackrock-rules-world/.

7. Ryan Tracy and Sarah Krouse, "One Firm Getting What It Wants in Washington:

BlackRock," *Wall Street Journal*, April 20, 2016, https://www.wsj.com/articles /one-firm-getting-what-it-wants-in-washington-blackrock-1461162812.

8. "Washington's Most Powerful, Least Famous People," *New Republic*, October 11, 2011, https://newrepublic.com/article/96131/washingtons-most-powerful -least-famous-people.

9. Segal, "Biden Taps Brian Deese, Global Head of Sustainable Investing at Black-Rock, to Lead National Economic Council."

10. Juliet Eilperin and Greg Jaffe, "Obama Taps Senior Adviser Brian Deese to Run Supreme Court Nomination Process," *Washington Post*, February 29, 2016, https://www.washingtonpost.com/news/powerpost/wp/2016/02/29/obama -taps-senior-adviser-brian-deese-to-run-supreme-court-nomination-process/; David E. Sanger, "The 31-Year-Old in Charge of Dismantling G.M.," *New York Times*, May 31, 2009, https://www.nytimes.com/2009/06/01/business/01deese .html.

11. "Washington's Most Powerful, Least Famous People."

12. Eilperin and Jaffe, "Obama Taps Senior Adviser Brian Deese to Run Supreme Court Nomination Process."

13. Brian Deese and Christy Goldfuss, "What They're Saying: Environmental Advocates Point to the Trans-Pacific Partnership as a Historic Opportunity to Protect Our Oceans, Forests, and Wildlife," Obama White House, archives, March 31, 2015, https://obamawhitehouse.archives.gov/blog/2015/03/31/what-theyre-say ing-environmental-advocates-point-trans-pacific-partnership-historic-.

14. Eilperin and Jaffe, "Obama Taps Senior Adviser Brian Deese to Run Supreme Court Nomination Process"; Kevin Liptak, "How Obama Made His Supreme Court Pick," CNN Politics, March 17, 2016, https://www.cnn.com/2016/03/17 /politics/obama-supreme-court-merrick-garland/index.html.

15. Brian Deese, "That Rosy Unemployment Rate," Center for American Progress, September 13, 2004, https://www.americanprogress.org/article/that-rosy -unemployment-rate/; Martin Longman, "The Overwrought Opposition to Brian Deese," *Washington Monthly*, December 4, 2020, https://washingtonmonthly .com/2020/12/04/the-overwrought-opposition-to-brian-deese/.

16. Franco Ordoñez, "Biden Names BlackRock's Brian Deese as His Top Economic Aide," NPR, December 3, 2020, https://www.npr.org/sections/biden-transition -updates/2020/12/03/942205555/biden-names-blackrocks-brian-deese-as-his -top-economic-aide.

17. https://nypost.com/2022/06/04/bidens-inflator-in-chief-brian-deese-is-an -awful-pick/.

18. "Climate Corner Office: BlackRock's Brian Deese Talks Sustainable Investing with Neil Katz," YouTube video, posted by "The Weather Channel," October 16, 2019, https://www.youtube.com/watch?v=tXB-OYUxO20; Shellenberger, "Biden Climate Plan Risks Putting China and BlackRock Before the American People."

19. Kelly Pickerel, "The U.S. Solar Industry Has a Chinese Problem," Solar Power World, August 9, 2021, https://www.solarpowerworldonline.com/2021/08/u-s-solar-china-polysilicon-battle/.

20. Henry Wu, "The United States Can't Afford the Brutal Price of Chinese Solar Panels," *Foreign Policy*, July 14, 2021, https://foreignpolicy.com/2021/07/14/us-chinese-solar-panels-green-tech-strategy/.

21. George Soros, "BlackRock's China Blunder," *Wall Street Journal*, opinion, September 6, 2021, https://www.wsj.com/articles/blackrock-larry-fink-china-hkex-sse-authoritarianism-xi-jinping-term-limits-human-rights-ant-didi-global-national-security-11630938728.

22. Shellenberger, "Biden Climate Plan Risks Putting China and BlackRock Before the American People."

23. Ibid.

24. Simon Jessop and Ross Kerber, "BlackRock Raises $673 Mln for Climate-Focused Infrastructure Fund," Reuters, November 2, 2021, https://www.reuters.com/business/sustainable-business/exclusive-blackrock-raises-673-mln-climate-focused-infrastructure-fund-2021-11-02/.

25. https://www.sec.gov/news/statement/gensler-climate-disclosure-20220321.

26. Jessica DiNapoli, "PwC Planning to Hire 100,000 over Five Years in Major ESG Push," Reuters, June 15, 2021, https://www.reuters.com/business/sustainable-business/pwc-planning-hire-100000-over-five-years-major-esg-push-2021-06-15/.

27. "Agency Rule List—Spring 2022," Office of Information and Regulatory Affairs, Office of Management and Budget, accessed July 19, 2022, https://www.reginfo.gov/public/do/eAgendaMain?operation=OPERATION_GET_AGENCY_RULE_LIST&currentPub=true&agencyCode=&showStage=active&agencyCd=3235&csrf_token=7CE97CC2D49C9B6B70868F7B2752E582C86F1945A4A46F34426C18AF1ABE101E611318F64B67159C3A36E7556BD0FB872C8F.

28. "The SEC's Private Market Takeover," *Wall Street Journal*, opinion, March 15, 2022, https://www.wsj.com/articles/the-secs-private-market-takeover-gary-gensler-hester-peirce-11647375870?page=1.

29. Matthew Goldstein, Lauren Hirsch, and Andrew Ross Sorkin, "Gary Gensler Is Picked to Lead S.E.C.," *New York Times*, January 17, 2021, https://www.nytimes.com/2021/01/17/business/gary-gensler-sec-rohit-chopra-cfpb.html.

30. Michael S. Schmidt and Amy Chozick, "Hillary Clinton Hiring of C.F.O. Is Called Signal to Possible Donors," *New York Times*, April 17, 2015, https://www.nytimes.com/2015/04/18/us/politics/hillary-clinton-hiring-gary-gensler-is-called-signal-to-possible-donors.html.

31. "Chair Gary Gensler," U.S. Securities and Exchange Commission, biography, accessed July 19, 2022, https://www.sec.gov/biography/gary-gensler.

32. Ibid.

33. "Officials," AllGov.com, accessed July 19, 2022, http://www.allgov.com/officials /gensler-gary?officialid=28869; "Maryland Financial Consumer Protection Commission," Maryland Manual On-Line, on Internet Archive, accessed July 19, 2022, https://web.archive.org/web/20201031201003/https://msa.maryland.gov /msa/mdmanual/26excom/defunct/html/14financialcons.html (the screenshot of the site was captured on October 31, 2020).

34. Courtney McBride, "Commodity Future Trading Commission: Gary Gensler, Chairman," *National Journal*, on Internet Archive, accessed July 19, 2022, https://web.archive.org/web/20141030042750/http://www.nationaljournal .com/decision-makers/finance-economy/gary-gensler-chairman-20130714 (the screenshot of the site was captured on October 30, 2014).

35. Schmidt and Chozick, "Hillary Clinton Hiring of C.F.O. Is Called Signal to Possible Donors."

36. https://www.pbs.org/newshour/economy/sec-proposes-new-rules-for-compan ies-to-monitor-climate-risks.

37. https://heritageaction.com/toolkit/block-bidens-climate-regulation.

38. Ibid.

39. Gary Gensler, "Statement on Proposed Mandatory Climate Risk Disclosures," U.S. Securities and Exchange Commission, March 21, 2022, https://www.sec .gov/news/statement/gensler-climate-disclosure-20220321.

40. Ibid.

41. Ordoñez, "Biden Names BlackRock's Brian Deese as His Top Economic Aide."

42. Catherine Clifford, "Treasury Secretary Yellen: The U.S. Should Have Moved Faster Toward Renewable Energy," CNBC, March 25, 2022, https://www.cnbc .com/2022/03/25/yellen-the-us-should-have-moved-faster-toward-renewable -energy.html.

43. Letter from Sarah Bloom Raskin to the President, March 15, 2022, https:// s3.documentcloud.org/documents/21417717/sarahbloomraskinletter.pdf.

44. Mitch McConnell, "Federal Reserve Needs Nominees Without Radical Far-Left Ideologies and Ethical Questions," Mitch McConnell's website, speech, February 15, 2022, https://www.republicanleader.senate.gov/newsroom/remarks/fed eral-reserve-needs-nominees-without-radical-far-left-ideologies-and-ethical -questions.

45. Senator Pat Toomey (@SenToomey), "The Senate's bipartisan rejection of Sarah Bloom Raskin's nomination sends a powerful message to the Fed . . . ," Twitter post, March 15, 2022, 1:15 p.m., https://twitter.com/SenToomey/status /1503827205188636695?s=20&t=_P1HatxtmBw6lZKfPhI9oA.

CHAPTER 6 Government Needs More Racism

1. Alina Ptaszynski, "Redfin Hosts Race and Real Estate Symposium," Redfin, September 7, 2018, https://www.redfin.com/news/redfin-hosts-race-and-real-estate-symposium/.

2. Dana Anderson, "Redlining's Legacy of Inequality: $212,000 Less Home Equity, Low Homeownership Rates for Black Families," Redfin, last updated October 15, 2020, https://www.redfin.com/news/redlining-real-estate-racial-wealth-gap/.

3. Michele Lerner, "Housing Groups Sue Redfin, Alleging Federal Discrimination Violations," *Washington Post*, November 2, 2020, https://www.washingtonpost.com/business/2020/11/02/housing-groups-sue-redfin-alleging-federal-discrimination-violations/.

4. "After Collecting $16 Million in Grants from Housing Department in Obama Era, Liberal Group Sues Agency Now," Amac, June 4, 2018, https://beta.amac.us/after-collecting-16-million-in-grants-from-housing-department-in-obama-era-liberal-group-sues-agency-now/.

5. "Statement of the National Fair Housing Alliance in Response to Trump's SCOTUS Pick," National Fair Housing Alliance, press release, September 26, 2020, https://nationalfairhousing.org/statement-of-the-national-fair-housing-alliance-in-response-to-trumps-scotus-pick/; "Act Now: Demand That the Senate Deliver for the American Public and Pass the Build Back Better Act NOW!" National Fair Housing Alliance, accessed July 21, 2022, https://nationalfairhousingalliance.salsalabs.org/bbbacta20dec21/index.html; "National Fair Housing Alliance Response to DACA Termination," National Fair Housing Alliance, press release, September 5, 2017, https://nationalfairhousing.org/national-fair-housing-alliance-response-to-daca-termination/.

6. "After Collecting $16 Million in Grants from Housing Department in Obama Era, Liberal Group Sues Agency Now."

7. Noah Manskar, "Redfin Policy Makes It Harder to Sell Homes in Minority Neighborhoods, Lawsuit Claims," *New York Post*, November 2, 2020, https://nypost.com/2020/11/02/redfin-accused-of-redlining-in-federal-housing-lawsuit/.

8. Peter Robison and Noah Buhayar, "A Progressive Real Estate Firm Faces Accusations of Discrimination," Bloomberg, January 18, 2022, https://www.bloomberg.com/news/features/2022-01-18/progressive-real-estate-firm-redfin-faces-accusations-of-housing-discrimination.

9. Manskar, "Redfin Policy Makes It Harder to Sell Homes in Minority Neighborhoods, Lawsuit Claims."

10. Robison and Buhayar, "A Progressive Real Estate Firm Faces Accusations of Discrimination."

11. "Federal Eviction Moratoriums in Response to the COVID-19 Pandemic,"

Congressional Research Service, last updated March 30, 2021, https://crs reports.congress.gov/product/pdf/IN/IN11516.

12. "HUD Releases More Than $13 Million in American Rescue Plan Funds to Assist Victims of Housing Discrimination Related to the Coronavirus Pandemic," U.S. Department of Housing and Urban Development, press release, November 3, 2021, https://www.hud.gov/press/press_releases_media_advisories/HUD _No_21_182; "HUD Makes Additional $5.7 Million in American Rescue Plan Funds Available to Fight Housing Discrimination Related to the Coronavirus Pandemic," U.S. Department of Housing and Urban Development, press release, December 2, 2021, https://www.hud.gov/press/press_releases_media_advisories /HUD_No_21_199; "NCSHA Summary of Coronavirus Relief Legislation," National Council of State Housing Agencies, March 26, 2020, https://www.nc sha.org/ncsha-news/ncsha-summary-of-coronavirus-relief-legislation/.

13. "Waters and 29 Democrats Work to Protect Fair Housing Regulations During COVID-19 Crisis," U.S. House Committee on Financial Services, press release, March 20, 2020, https://financialservices.house.gov/news/documentsingle.aspx ?DocumentID=406443; Katy O'Donnell, "Maxine Waters Ready to Battle over Potential Cuts to Housing Aid," *Politico*, October 7, 2021, https://www.politico .com/news/2021/10/07/housing-aid-cuts-battle-515588.

14. James Taranto, "'Riot Is the Voice of the Unheard,'" *Wall Street Journal*, opinion, April 6, 2010, https://www.wsj.com/articles/SB1000142405270230341160 4575168041790910582.

15. Chandelis Duster, "Waters Calls for Protesters to 'Get More Confrontational' if No Guilty Verdict Is Reached in Derek Chauvin Trial," CNN Politics, April 20, 2021, https://edition.cnn.com/2021/04/19/politics/maxine-waters -derek-chauvin-trial/index.html.

16. Tim Hains, "Maxine Waters: 'God Is on Our Side,' if You See a Member of Trump Cabinet, 'Push Back,'" RealClearPolitics, June 25, 2018, https://www.realclear politics.com/video/2018/06/25/maxine_waters_god_is_on_our_side.html.

17. The Sunday Show with Jonathan Capehart (@TheSundayShow), "Is it important to maybe discuss issues of sexuality the way one talks about a mom and a dad? . . ." Twitter post, April 17, 2022, 8:50 a.m., https://twitter.com/TheSun dayShow/status/1515719322253017098.

18. Congresswoman Maxine Waters, biography, accessed July 21, 2022, https:// waters.house.gov/about-maxine/biography.

19. Callie Patteson, "Maxine Waters Campaign Paid Daughter $81K in FY 2021," *New York Post*, October 18, 2021, https://nypost.com/2021/10/18/maxine -waters-campaign-paid-daughter-81k-in-fy-2021/; Caitlin McFall, "Maxine Waters Has Given over $1 Million in Campaign Cash to Daughter," Fox News, January 30, 2021, https://www.foxnews.com/politics/maxine-waters-has-given -over-1-million-in-campaign-cash-to-daughter.

20. Rusty Weiss, "Maxine Waters Wants Reparations if Democrats Take Back the

House and Senate in 2018," Political Insider, March 5, 2018, https://thepolitical insider.com/maxine-waters-reparations/.

21. "Black Lives Matter News," *Washington Examiner*, accessed July 21, 2022, https://www.washingtonexaminer.com/washington-secrets/mayors-back-reparations-could-cost-6-2-quadrillion-151m-per-descendant.

22. Richard Hanania, "The Law That Banned Everything," Richard Hanania's Newsletter, April 11, 2022, https://richardhanania.substack.com/p/the-law-that-banned-everything.

23. Jason L. Riley, "Let's Talk About the Black Abortion Rate," *Wall Street Journal*, opinion, July 10, 2018, https://www.wsj.com/articles/lets-talk-about-the-black-abortion-rate-1531263697.

24. Diana Chandler, "Alabama Baby Q Lawsuit Tackles Roe v. Wade from Eugenics and States' Rights Argument," Baptist Press, February 10, 2021, https://www.baptistpress.com/resource-library/news/alabama-baby-q-lawsuit-tackles-roe-v-wade-from-eugenics-and-states-rights-argument/.

25. Derrick Hollie, "'Green New Deal' Would Hit Minorities the Hardest," Daily Signal, March 7, 2019, https://www.dailysignal.com/2019/03/07/green-new-deal-would-hit-minorities-the-hardest/.

26. David Kreutzer et al., "The State of Climate Science: No Justification for Extreme Policies," Heritage Foundation, April 22, 2016, https://www.heritage.org/environment/report/the-state-climate-science-no-justification-extreme-policies/.

27. Kery Murakami, "Pelosi Backs Removing Deduction Cap on State and Local Taxes," *Washington Times*, April 1, 2021, https://www.washingtontimes.com/news/2021/apr/1/pelosi-backs-removing-deduction-cap-state-and-loca/.

28. Howard Gleckman and Leonard E. Burman, "How an $80,000 SALT Cap Stacks Up Against a Full Deduction for Those Making $400,000 or Less," Tax Policy Center, Urban Institute and Brookings Institution, November 18, 2021, https://www.taxpolicycenter.org/taxvox/how-80000-salt-cap-stacks-against-full-deduction-those-making-400000-or-less.

29. Sandy Baum and Adam Looney, "Who Owes the Most in Student Loans: New Data from the Fed," Brookings Institution, October 9, 2020, https://www.brookings.edu/blog/up-front/2020/10/09/who-owes-the-most-in-student-loans-new-data-from-the-fed/.

30. Rav Arora, "See No Murder," *City Journal*, December 1, 2021, https://www.city-journal.org/violent-crimes-disparate-racial-impact.

31. Barton Gellman and Sam Adler-Bell, "The Disparate Impact of Surveillance," Century Foundation, December 21, 2017, https://tcf.org/content/report/disparate-impact-surveillance/.

32. "Landmark Legislation: The Civil Rights Act of 1964," United States Senate, accessed July 21, 2022, https://www.senate.gov/artandhistory/history/common/generic/CivilRightsAct1964.htm.

33. Gail L. Heriot, "Title VII Disparity Impact Liability Makes Almost Everything Presumptively Illegal," *New York University Journal of Law & Liberty* 14, no. 1 (2020), https://papers.ssrn.com/sol3/papers.cfm?abstract_id=3482015.

34. "EEOC Releases Fiscal Year 2020 Enforcement and Litigation Data," U.S. Equal Employment Opportunity Commission, press release, February 26, 2021, https://www.eeoc.gov/newsroom/eeoc-releases-fiscal-year-2020-enforcement-and-litigation-data; "Fiscal Year 2020 Annual Performance Report," U.S. Equal Employment Opportunity Commission, accessed July 21, 2022, https://www.eeoc.gov/fiscal-year-2020-annual-performance-report#h_3448817464131611083639655.

35. Heriot, "Title VII Disparate Impact Liability Makes Almost Everything Presumptively Illegal."

36. Richard Lapchick, "The 2018 Racial and Gender Report Card: National Football League," Institute for Diversity and Ethics in Sport, January 23, 2019, p. 8, https://perma.cc/U4GA-DBPW (the screenshot of the site was captured on October 25, 2019).

37. Heriot, "Title VII Disparate Impact Liability Makes Almost Everything Presumptively Illegal," p. 34.

38. Hansi Lo Wang, "Native Americans on Tribal Land Are 'The Least Connected' to High-Speed Internet," NPR, Dec. 6, 2018, https://perma.cc/6JHJ-WVY5 (the screenshot of the site was captured on October 28, 2019).

39. "Equal Employment Opportunity Commission," Cornell Law School, Legal Information Institute, accessed July 21, 2022, https://www.law.cornell.edu/wex/equal_employment_opportunity_commission; Equal Employment Opportunity Act of 1972, Pub. L. No. 92-261, 86 Stat. 103 (1972) (codified as amended at 42 U.S.C. § 2000e et seq. (2018)).

40. Hanania, "The Law That Banned Everything."

41. https://www.federalregister.gov/documents/2020/09/24/2020-19887/huds-implementation-of-the-fair-housing-acts-disparate-impact-standard.

42. https://news.bloomberglaw.com/banking-law/huds-anti-discrimination-rule-rewrite-put-on-hold.

43. Pema Levy, "Sorry, Liberals, but the Roberts Court Is Still Conservative," *Mother Jones*, July 1, 2015, https://www.motherjones.com/politics/2015/07/supreme-court-liberal-conservative/.

44. Roger Clegg, "HUD Proposes Good New Regulations," *National Review*, July 30, 2019, https://www.nationalreview.com/corner/hud-proposes-good-new-regulations/.

45. Katy O'Donnell, "HUD Moves to Restore Fair Housing Rules Weakened Under Trump," *Politico*, April 13, 2021, https://www.politico.com/news/2021/04/13/hud-housing-rules-481209.

46. Max Abelson, "Bankers Rush to Settle Redlining Suits as They Chase Big Paydays," Bloomberg Law, October 27, 2021, https://news.bloomberglaw.com/mergers-and-acquisitions/bankers-rush-to-settle-redlining-suits-as-they-chase-big-paydays.

47. Neil Haggerty, "House Dems Call on HUD to Rescind Changes to Disparate Impact Standard," *American Banker*, November 22, 2019, https://www.americanbanker.com/news/house-dems-call-on-hud-to-rescind-disparate-impact-changes.

CHAPTER 7 Inventing Discrimination to Redirect Capital

1. Paul Ingram, "Man Convicted in 'Fast and Furious' Murder of U.S. Border Agent Sentenced to Life," Reuters, January 8, 2020, https://www.reuters.com/article/us-usa-crime-border/man-convicted-in-fast-and-furious-murder-of-u-s-border-agent-sentenced-to-life-idUSKBN1Z72S0.

2. Jane Ann Morrison, "Program to Help the Needy Squandered Federal Dollars in Nevada," *Las Vegas Review-Journal*, December 16, 2017, https://www.reviewjournal.com/news/news-columns/jane-ann-morrison/program-to-help-the-needy-squandered-federal-dollars-in-nevada/.

3. Josh Hicks, "HUD Paid $37 Million a Month in Subsidies to Ineligible Households," *Washington Post*, February 19, 2015, https://www.washingtonpost.com/news/federal-eye/wp/2015/02/19/hud-paid-37-million-a-month-in-subsidies-to-ineligible-households/.

4. Floor Statement of Senator Chuck Grassley Before the United States Senate, Oversight at the U.S. Department of Housing and Urban Development, "Grassley: HUD Oversight of Housing Dollars Is Lacking," Chuck Grassley's Senate page, January 28, 2014, https://www.grassley.senate.gov/news/news-releases/grassley-hud-oversight-housing-dollars-lacking.

5. Kathryn Watson, "HUD Can Fix $520 Billion in Accounting Errors, but Still Can't Document Its Spending," Daily Caller, March 7, 2017, https://dailycaller.com/2017/03/07/hud-can-fix-520-billion-in-accounting-errors-but-still-cant-document-its-spending/.

6. Letter from Senator Charles E. Grassley, Senate Committee on the Judiciary, to the Honorable Dr. Ben Carson, Secretary, U.S. Department of Housing and Urban Development, March 24, 2017, https://www.grassley.senate.gov/imo/media/doc/constituents/2017-3-24%20CEG%20to%20HUD%20%28New%20Core%20Project%29.pdf.

7. Kamala Harris (@KamalaHarris), "There's a big difference between equality and equity," Twitter post, November 1, 2020, 10:06 a.m., https://twitter.com/KamalaHarris/status/1322963321994289154.

8. "The Biden-Harris Administration Immediate Priorities," The White House, accessed July 22, 2022, https://www.whitehouse.gov/priorities/.

9. Adam Shaw, "Biden Administration Rolls Out 'Equity Action Plans' Across Gov't Agencies," Fox News, April 16, 2022, https://www.foxnews.com/politics/biden-administration-equity-actions-plans-across-govt-agencies.

10. "Executive Order on Promoting Access to Voting," The White House, March 7, 2021, https://www.whitehouse.gov/briefing-room/presidential-actions/2021/03/07/executive-order-on-promoting-access-to-voting/.

11. "Hatch Act Overview," U.S. Office of Special Counsel, accessed July 22, 2022, https://osc.gov/Services/Pages/HatchAct.aspx.

12. "Executive Order on Promoting Access to Voting."

13. Erin Duffin, "Presidential Election Exit Polls: Share of Votes by Ethnicity U.S. 2020," Statista, June 21, 2022, https://www.statista.com/statistics/1184425/presidential-election-exit-polls-share-votes-ethnicity-us/.

14. Anna V. Smith, "How Indigenous Voters Swung the 2020 Election," *High Country News*, November 6, 2020, https://www.hcn.org/articles/indigenous-affairs-how-indigenous-voters-swung-the-2020-election.

15. Paul Bedard, "Jail Survey: 7 in 10 Felons Register as Democrats," *Washington Examiner*, January 1, 2014, https://www.washingtonexaminer.com/jail-survey-7-in-10-felons-register-as-democrats.

16. Jonathan Swan, "Government Workers Shun Trump, Give Big Money to Clinton," *Hill*, October 26, 2016, https://thehill.com/homenews/campaign/302817-government-workers-shun-trump-give-big-money-to-clinton-campaign/.

17. https://www.foxnews.com/politics/doj-stonewalling-requests-details-implementation-bidens-federal-election-scheme.

18. Tarren Bragdon and Stewart Whitson, "Voter Registration Drive: What's Biden Hiding?" *Wall Street Journal*, opinion, April 19, 2022, https://www.wsj.com/articles/voter-drive-whats-biden-hiding-justice-department-freedom-of-information-foia-transparency-corruption-lawsuit-foundation-for-government-accountability-11650403740.

19. https://www.whitehouse.gov/briefing-room/statements-releases/2021/09/28/fact-sheet-biden-administration-promotes-voter-participation-with-new-agency-steps/.

20. Fred Lucas, "HUD Pushes Voter Registration Drives in Public Housing Under Biden's Executive Order," Daily Signal, April 27, 2022, https://www.dailysignal.com/2022/04/27/hud-pushes-voter-registration-drives-in-public-housing-under-bidens-executive-order/.

21. Stephen Fastenau, "Mayoral Candidate Objects After Columbia Housing Chairman Directs Agency to Turn Out Vote," *Post and Courier*, November 10, 2021, https://www.postandcourier.com/columbia/news/mayoral-candidate-objects-after-columbia-housing-chairman-directs-agency-to-turn-out-vote/article_23845592-4254-11ec-85bc-7b240fd79270.html.

22. "Justice Department Announces New Initiative to Combat Redlining," U.S. De-

partment of Justice, press release, October 22, 2021, https://www.justice.gov /opa/pr/justice-department-announces-new-initiative-combat-redlining; Paul F. Hancock et al., "Banks and Non-banks Beware: New Types of Redlining Claims Are on the Horizon," K&L Gates, October 26, 2021, https://www.klgates.com /Banks-and-Non-Banks-Beware-New-Types-of-Redlining-Claims-are-on-the -Horizon-10-26-2021.

23. Letter from the Human Capital Management Coalition to Chairman Gary Gens- ler, U.S. Securities and Exchange Commission, "Re: SEC's Climate Change Disclo- sure Request—Letter to Financial Accounting Standards Board (FASB) on Human Capital Management Disclosures—Workforce Costs," November 13, 2021, https:// www.sec.gov/comments/climate-disclosure/cll12-9376981-262167.pdf.

24. Ibid.; Bob Pisani, "SEC Chair Gensler Is Taking a Deeper Look at ESG Investing Issues," CNBC, June 23, 2021, https://www.cnbc.com/2021/06/23/sec-chair-gen sler-is-taking-a-deeper-look-at-esg-investing-issues.html.

25. Joseph A. Wulfsohn, "Kamala Harris Panned for Offering 'Word Salad' at WH Event with Jamaican Prime Minister: 'Is She Punking Us?'" Fox News, March 31, 2022, https://www.foxnews.com/media/kamala-harris-word-salad-white-house -event-jamaican-prime-minister-andrew-holness.

26. David Dayen, "Kamala Harris Celebrates Her Role in the Mortgage Crisis Set- tlement. The Reality Is Quite Different," Intercept, March 13, 2019, https://the intercept.com/2019/03/13/kamala-harris-mortage-crisis/.

27. Phil Hall, "Calif. Gov. Signs Law to Circumvent Mortgage Settlement Fund Usage," National Mortgage Professional, September 11, 2018, https://national mortgageprofessional.com/news/68445/calif-signs-circumvent-mortgage -settlement-fund-usage.

28. "U.S. Department of Education Announces Richard Cordray as Chief Operating Officer of Federal Student Aid," U.S. Department of Education, press release, May 3, 2021, https://www.ed.gov/news/press-releases/us-department-education -announces-richard-cordray-chief-operating-officer-federal-student-aid.

29. Ronald L. Rubin, "The Tragic Downfall of the Consumer Financial Protection Bureau," National Review, December 21, 2016, https://www.nationalreview.com /2016/12/consumer-financial-protection-bureau-tragic-failures/.

30. "CFPB Acting Director Dave Uejio Nominated to Serve as HUD Assistant Sec- retary," Ballard CFS Group, June 29, 2021, https://www.consumerfinancemon itor.com/2021/06/29/cfpb-acting-director-dave-uejio-nominated-to-serve-as -hud-assistant-secretary/.

31. Dave Uejio, "The Bureau Is Taking Much-Needed Action to Protect Consumers, Particularly the Most Economically Vulnerable," Consumer Financial Protection Bureau, January 28, 2021, https://www.consumerfinance.gov/about-us/blog /the-bureau-is-taking-much-needed-action-to-protect-consumers-particularly -the-most-economically-vulnerable/.

32. https://www.ca5.uscourts.gov/opinions/pub/21/21-50826-CV0.pdf.

33. Lisa Rowan, "Rohit Chopra Is the New Head of the CFPB. What Does That Mean for You?" Nasdaq, September 30, 2021, https://www.nasdaq.com/articles/rohit-chopra-is-the-new-head-of-the-cfpb.-what-does-that-mean-for-you-2021-09-30.

34. "Toomey Opening Statement During Chopra, Gensler Nomination Hearing," United States Senate Committee on Banking, Housing, and Urban Affairs, March 2, 2021, https://www.banking.senate.gov/newsroom/minority/toomey-opening-statement-during-chopra-gensler-nomination-hearing.

35. "Rohit Chopra Is Coming After You," *Wall Street Journal*, opinion, April 7, 2022, https://www.wsj.com/articles/rohit-chopra-is-coming-after-you-consumer-financial-protection-bureau-discrimination-businesses-11649192089.

36. "Tennessee Presidential Results," *Politico*, last updated January 6, 2021, https://www.politico.com/2020-election/results/tennessee/.

37. "Justice Department Announces New Initiative to Combat Redlining."

38. https://republicans-financialservices.house.gov/news/documentsingle.aspx?DocumentID=407311.

39. "How to Calculate Your Individual ESG Score," Impact Investor, last updated February 7, 2022, https://theimpactinvestor.com/calculate-individual-esg-score/.

40. "Waters at Hearing on Overhauling Credit Reporting System: We Need Big, Bold Legislative Solutions," U.S. House Committee on Financial Services, June 29, 2021, https://financialservices.house.gov/news/documentsingle.aspx?DocumentID=408090.

41. Amy Traub, "Establish a Public Credit Registry," Demos, report, March 2019, https://www.demos.org/sites/default/files/2019-03/Credit%20Report_Full.pdf; "The Biden Plan for Investing in Our Communities Through Housing," Joe Biden's web page, accessed July 22, 20222, https://joebiden.com/housing/; Emma Newbery, "Why Biden Wants to Replace the Credit Bureaus," Ascent, last updated July 21, 2021, https://www.fool.com/the-ascent/credit-cards/articles/why-biden-wants-to-replace-the-credit-bureaus/.

42. "The Coming Transformation of the CFPB in the Biden Administration: What to Expect and How to Prepare," Paul, Weiss, February 1, 2021, https://www.paulweiss.com/media/3980813/the_coming_transformation_of_the_cfpb_in_the_biden_administration_what_to_expect_and_how_to_prepare.pdf.

CHAPTER 8 Unions: The Education B Team

1. "LCS Lesbian, Gay, Bisexual, Transgender, Gender Nonconforming and Questioning Support Guide," Leon County (Florida) Schools, October 18, 2021, https://www.politico.com/f/?id=0000017f-d30b-d9e9-a57f-d38b05900000.

2. "'How Gender Ideology Almost Destroyed My Family'—January Littlejohn," YouTube video, posted by "Florida Family Policy Council," November 18, 2021, https://www.youtube.com/watch?v=adjvnvv8rV4.

3. https://g-a-i.org/wp-content/uploads/2022/10/GAI-Teachers-Union-Report.pdf.

4. https://www.nationalreview.com/news/connecticut-teachers-union-circles-the-wagons-after-undercover-video-reveals-anti-catholic-discrimination/.

5. https://epe.brightspotcdn.com/be/2b/1bc98850470e9fecf8f8085a3284/educator-political-perceptions-education-week-12-12-2017.pdf, p. 7.

6. Madeline Will, "NEA's Lily Eskelsen García Talks Racial Justice, COVID Layoffs, and Leaving Office," *Education Week*, July 1, 2020, https://www.edweek.org/teaching-learning/neas-lily-eskelsen-garcia-talks-racial-justice-covid-layoffs-and-leaving-office/2020/07.

7. "Black Lives Matter at School," National Education Association, accessed July 22, 2022, https://neaedjustice.org/black-lives-matter-at-school/.

8. NEA Center for Social Justice, "Racial Justice in Education Resource Guide," National Education Association, January 2021, https://www.nea.org/professional-excellence/student-engagement/tools-tips/racial-justice-education-resource-guide.

9. Erica L. Green, "New Leader Pushes Teachers' Union to Take On Social Justice Role," *New York Times*, December 12, 2021, https://www.nytimes.com/2021/12/12/us/politics/teachers-union-becky-pringle.html.

10. Lauren Camera, "Teachers Union Backs Clinton for President," *U.S. News & World Report*, October 3, 2015, https://www.usnews.com/news/articles/2015/10/03/powerful-nea-teachers-union-endorses-hillary-clinton-for-president; Eric Jotkoff, "Educators Congratulate President-elect Joe Biden and Vice President–elect Kamala Harris," National Education Association, November 7, 2020, https://www.nea.org/about-nea/media-center/press-releases/educators-congratulate-president-elect-joe-biden-and-vice.

11. Will, "NEA's Lily Eskelsen García Talks Racial Justice, COVID Layoffs, and Leaving Office."

12. Cassidy Morrison, "Teachers Union Influenced CDC School Masking Guidance, Emails Show," *Washington Examiner*, September 8, 2021, https://www.washingtonexaminer.com/news/watchdog-group-shows-union-influence-over-cdc-school-masking-guidance.

13. Sonia Chaabane et al., "The Impact of COVID-19 School Closure on Child and Adolescent Health: A Rapid Systematic Review," *Children (Basel)* 8, no. 5 (May 19, 2021), https://www.ncbi.nlm.nih.gov/pmc/articles/PMC8159143/.

14. "Randi Weingarten," American Federation of Teachers, accessed July 22, 2022, https://www.aft.org/about/leadership/randi-weingarten.

15. "The Miseducation of Randi Weingarten: AFT's Number One Policy Pusher," Drill Down with Peter Schweizer, January 19, 2022, https://thedrilldown.com/newsroom/the-miseducation-of-randi-weingarten-afts-number-one-policy-pusher/; "Randi Weingarten," Influence Watch, accessed July 22, 2022, https://www.influencewatch.org/person/randi-weingarten/.

16. "American Federation of Teachers," OpenSecrets.org, accessed July 22, 2022, https://www.opensecrets.org/orgs/american-federation-of-teachers/totals?id=D000000083.

17. Houston Keene, "AFT Head Randi Weingarten Makes over $560,000 Per Year, 9 Times Average Teacher Salary, Records Show," Fox News, July 9, 2021, https://www.foxnews.com/politics/aft-president-randi-weingarten-salary.

18. Freedom Foundation, "AFT's Weingarten in a Conundrum of Her Own Making," RedState, May 11, 2022, https://redstate.com/freedom-foundation/2022/05/11/afts-weingarten-in-a-conundrum-of-her-own-making-n562677.

19. Betsy McCaughey, "Teachers Unions Are Indoctrinating Kids—with Biden's Support," *New York Post*, May 3, 2022, https://nypost.com/2022/05/03/teachers-unions-are-indoctrinating-kids-with-bidens-support/.

20. Government Accountability Office report, *Teachers Unions: From Academics to Activists*, January 10, 2022, https://thedrilldown.com/wp-content/uploads/2022/01/2022_Teachers_Union_Report.pdf, p. 7.

21. https://g-a-i.org/wp-content/uploads/2022/10/GAI-Teachers-Union-Report.pdf.

22. Isaac Schorr, "Students Will Be an Afterthought Under Biden," *National Review*, November 2, 2020, https://www.nationalreview.com/corner/students-will-be-an-afterthought-under-biden/.

23. "Teachers Unions: From Academics to Activists," Government Accountability Institute, January 10, 2022, https://thedrilldown.com/wp-content/uploads/2022/01/2022_Teachers_Union_Report.pdf.

24. Ibid.; Alex Samuels and Amelia Thomson-DeVeaux, "Democrats Have Been Souring on Biden Since Last Summer," FiveThirtyEight, February 22, 2022, https://fivethirtyeight.com/features/democrats-have-been-souring-on-biden-since-last-summer/.

25. "Biden's Covid Death Milestone," *Wall Street Journal*, opinion, November 25, 2021, https://www.wsj.com/articles/bidens-covid-death-milestone-biden-administration-trump-11637708781.

26. "Teachers Unions: From Academics to Activists."

27. "Take Action," American Federation of Teachers, accessed July 22, 2022, https://www.aft.org/action.

28. "Remarks by President Biden at the 2022 National and State Teachers of the Year Event," The White House, speech, April 27, 2022, https://www.whitehouse.gov/briefing-room/speeches-remarks/2022/04/27/remarks-by-president-biden-at-the-2022-national-and-state-teachers-of-the-year-event/.

29. Selim Algar, "Florida Officials Say Math Textbooks Rife with 'Woke' Political Content," *New York Post*, May 6, 2022, https://nypost.com/2022/05/06/florida-officials-textbook-rife-with-woke-political-content/.

30. Hannah Natanson, "Parental Say in Schools, Resonant in Va. Governor's Race, Bound for GOP National Playbook," *Washington Post*, November 3, 2021, https://www.washingtonpost.com/local/education/parent-control-schools-republican-virginia/2021/11/03/313e8a68-3cc3-11ec-a493-51b0252dea0c_story.html.

31. "AFT Resolution: Black Lives Matter at School Week—Feb. 1–5, 2021," American Federation of Teachers, accessed October 22, 2021, https://www.aft.org/resolution/black-lives-matter-school-week-feb-1-5-2021.

32. "Early Childhood & Elementary Resources," D.C. Area Educators for Social Justice, accessed October 22, 2021, https://www.dcareaeducators4socialjustice org/black-lives-matter/resources/early-childhood-elementary#lessons; "Materials from Teaching for Black Lives," Google Docs, accessed October 22, 2021, https://docs.google.com/document/d/1tDCYpIZFPa3UTowKTRGKWkCers PZk5ePwBp0IBNg-_A/edit.

33. "Black Panther Party Mixer," Google Drive, accessed October 22, 2021, https://drive.google.com/file/d/1SSXH6N2CpxBWChWtvxwhWoM0lpJjIy_N/view.

34. "About Us," Rethinking Schools, accessed October 22, 2021, https://rethinking schools.org/about-rethinking-schools/.

35. "Randi Weingarten," American Federation of Teachers; "Indigenous Peoples Lesson Plans and Resources," Share My Lesson, accessed July 22, 2022, https://sharemylesson.com/collections/indigenous-peoples; "Teaching About Race and Racism: Lesson Plans and Resources," Share My Lesson, accessed July 22, 2022, https://sharemylesson.com/collections/teaching-about-race-and-racism-lesson-plans-and-resources.

36. Rebecca S. Pringle, "NEA's Letter to Social Media Companies," National Education Association, October 8, 2021, https://www.nea.org/about-nea/leaders/president/from-our-president/neas-letter-social-media-companies.

37. Letter from National School Boards Association to the Honorable Joseph R. Biden, September 29, 2021, https://www.documentcloud.org/documents/21094 557-national-school-boards-association-letter-to-biden.

38. Tyler O'Neil, "NEA Urged Social Media Giants to Fight Anti-CRT 'Propaganda' Stoking 'Violent' 'Radicalized' Parents," Fox News, January 12, 2022, https://www.foxnews.com/politics/nea-teachers-union-social-media-crack-down-violent-radicalized-parents-crt.

39. "AFT Partners with NewsGuard to Combat Misinformation Online," American Federation of Teachers, January 25, 2022, https://www.aft.org/press-release/aft-partners-newsguard-combat-misinformation-online.

40. Jordan Boyd, "Left-Wing 'Misinformation' Group Will Help Teachers Union Indoctrinate Students with Corrupt Media Propaganda," *Federalist*, January 27, 2022, https://thefederalist.com/2022/01/27/left-wing-misinformation-group-will-help-teachers-union-indoctrinate-students-with-corrupt-media-propaganda/; Joseph Vazquez, "STUDY: NewsGuard Ratings System Heavily Skews in Favor

of Left-Wing Outlets," *NewsBusters* (blog), December 13, 2021, https://www
.newsbusters.org/blogs/free-speech/joseph-vazquez/2021/12/13/study-news
guard-ratings-system-heavily-skews-favor-left.

41. Catherine Salgado, "NewsGuard Gives Baby-Killing Planned Parenthood Posi-
    tive 'Credibility' Rating, Slams Pro-Life Sites," *NewsBusters* (blog), February 25,
    2022, https://newsbusters.org/blogs/free-speech/catherine-salgado/2022/02/25
    /newsguard-gives-baby-killing-planned-parenthood.

42. Brian Flood, "Conservative Watchdog Irked by Teachers Union–NewsGuard
    Pact to Combat 'Disinformation': 'Worse' Than CRT," Fox News, January 27,
    2022, https://www.foxnews.com/media/conservative-watchdog-teachers-union
    -newsguard-pact-aft.

43. Kira Davis, "Teachers Union Boss Randi Weingarten Lobbying Facebook to
    Crack Down on 'Disinformation' . . . for the Children," RedState, May 9, 2022,
    https://redstate.com/kiradavis/2022/05/09/teachers-union-boss-randi-wein
    garten-lobbying-facebook-to-crack-down-on-disinformation-for-the-child
    ren-n562061.

44. "Vaccines and Related Biological Products Advisory Committee Meeting,"
    FDA Briefing Document, June 15, 2022, https://www.fda.gov/media/159195
    /download; Tommaso Celeste Bulfone et al., "Outdoor Transmission of SARS-
    CoV-2 and Other Respiratory Viruses: A Systematic Review," *Journal of In-
    fectious Diseases* 223, no. 4 (2021): 550–61, https://pubmed.ncbi.nlm.nih.gov
    /33249484/; Dr. Joel Zinberg, "Studies Prove That Most Politicians and Ex-
    perts Handled COVID Terribly," *New York Post*, April 27, 2022, https://nypost
    .com/2022/04/27/studies-prove-that-most-politicians-experts-handled-covid
    -terribly/.

45. "LAUSD Community Schools," Reclaim Our Schools LA, accessed July 22,
    2022, https://www.utla.net/sites/default/files/community_schools_flyer_2021
    _eng_spa_final1.pdf.

46. Cindy Long, "Over-Policing in LAUSD Gives Way to Safe and Just Schools,"
    National Education Association, April 7, 2021, https://www.nea.org/advocating
    -for-change/new-from-nea/over-policing-lausd-gives-way-safe-and-just-schools.

47. Jack Ross, "Los Angeles Leads Growing Transition to 'Community Schools'
    Model," City Watch, November 15, 2021, https://www.citywatchla.com/index
    .php/cw/los-angeles/23051-los-angeles-leads-growing-transition-to-community
    -schools-model.

48. Larry Sand, "California's Misguided Education Spending," *City Journal*, Sep-
    tember 14, 2021, https://www.city-journal.org/california-misguided-education
    -spending.

49. Kalyn Belsha and Sarah Darville, "Biden Proposes Doubling Title I, Sending
    Even More Money to High-Poverty Schools," Chalkbeat, April 9, 2021, https://
    www.chalkbeat.org/2021/4/9/22375692/biden-proposes-doubling-title-i-send
    ing-high-poverty-schools; Senators Sherrod Brown, Chris Van Hollen, and

Kirsten Gillibrand, "The Full-Service Community School Expansion Act of 2021," accessed July 22, 2022, https://www.brown.senate.gov/imo/media/doc/Full-Service%20Community%20School%20Expansion%20Act%20-%20One-Pager.pdf.

50. "Successful and Sustainable Community Schools: The Union as an Essential Ingredient," American Federation of Teachers, accessed July 22, 2022, https://www.aft.org/sites/default/files/wysiwyg/sustainablecommunityschools.pdf.

51. "Community Schools and the 'Four Pillars' Resources," Minnesota Department of Education, July 19, 2021, https://education.mn.gov/mdeprod/groups/educ/documents/hiddencontent/bwrl/mdg3/~edisp/mde087166.pdf.

52. "No Child Left Unkempt," Pinellas Technical College, March 6, 2020, https://www.pcsb.org/Page/32705; https://co.chalkbeat.org/2022/3/10/22971803/lawmaker-community-schools-option-not-intended-for-adams-14; Theodora Chang, "Maximizing the Promise of Community Schools: Streamlining Wraparound Services for ESEA," Center for American Progress, April 2011, https://cdn.americanprogress.org/wp-content/uploads/issues/2011/04/pdf/wraparound_report.pdf.

53. Ross, "Los Angeles Leads Growing Transition to 'Community Schools' Model."

54. "Teachers Unions: From Academics to Activists."

55. "Frank Lieberman," LinkedIn profile, accessed July 22, 2022, https://www.linkedin.com/in/frank-lieberman-a313a420/.

56. "Franklin Lieberman," Business News, accessed July 22, 2022, https://www.businessnews.com.au/Person/Franklin-Lieberman.

57. "KNM Secures Major US Content Sales Catalyst with NAACP Partnership," KNeoMedia, June 12, 2018, https://www.kneomedia.com/pdf/KNeoMedia_Strategic_Alliance_with_NAACP_180612.pdf.

CHAPTER 9 The Unions Go Global

1. "To America's Educators," American Federation of Teachers, accessed July 25, 2022, https://www.aft.org/sites/default/files/taw-aft-nytimes.pdf.

2. "Over 200 Parent, Civil Rights and Student Groups, Other National and State-Level Advocates, Join American Federation of Teachers to Praise and Celebrate America's Teachers," American Federation of Teachers, press release, May 1, 2022, https://www.aft.org/press-release/over-200-parent-civil-rights-and-student-groups-other-national-and-state.

3. Jon Levine, "Powerful Teachers Union Influenced CDC on School Reopenings, Emails Show," *New York Post*, May 1, 2021, https://nypost.com/2021/05/01/teachers-union-collaborated-with-cdc-on-school-reopening-emails/.

4. "Investigation Reveals Biden's CDC Bypassed Scientific Norms to Allow Teachers Union to Re-Write Official Guidance," House Committee on Oversight and Reform, press release, March 30, 2022, https://republicans-oversight.house.gov

/release/investigation-reveals-bidens-cdc-bypassed-scientific-norms-to-allow
-teachers-union-to-re-write-official-guidance/.

5. Ibid.; Michael Sadowski, "More Than a Safe Space: How Schools Can Enable LGBTQ Students to Thrive," *American Federation of Teachers*, Winter 2016–17, https://www.aft.org/ae/winter2016-2017/sadowski; Randi Weingarten (@rwein garten), "Here's my statement on Russia's invasion of Ukraine . . . ," Twitter post, February 24, 2022, 1:28 p.m., https://twitter.com/rweingarten/status /1496960143300435974.

6. Hanna Panreck, "Randi Weingarten Suggests Not Getting Rid of Masks Until Zero Transmission in Schools," *Fox News*, February 9, 2022, https://www .foxnews.com/media/randi-weingarten-suggests-not-getting-rid-masks-zero -transmission-schools.

7. Lee Ohanian, "Teacher Union Demands Far-Left Economic Policies Before Reopening Classrooms," *Hoover Institution*, July 22, 2020, https://www.hoover .org/research/teachers-union-demands-far-left-policies-returning-classrooms.

8. Katie Lobosco, "Schools Still Have Billions of Federal Covid Relief Money to Spend," *CNN Politics*, September 5, 2021, https://www.cnn.com/2021/09/05 /politics/school-federal-covid-relief-money/index.html.

9. "Billions in Pandemic Relief Funds Used to Implement CRT: One Nation Research," One Nation America, April 28, 2022, https://www.onenationamerica.org /billions-in-pandemic-relief-funds-used-to-implement-crt-one-nation-research/; Jessica Chasmar, "California, New York, Illinois Used COVID-19 Relief Funds to Push CRT in Schools," *Fox News*, April 28, 2022, https://www.foxnews.com /politics/california-new-york-illinois-covid-19-relief-funds-crt-schools.

10. Ibid.

11. Annie Waldman and Bianca Fortis, "The Federal Government Gave Billions to America's Schools for COVID-19 Relief. Where Did the Money Go?" *ProPublica*, October 20, 2021, https://www.propublica.org/article/the-federal-government -gave-billions-to-americas-schools-for-covid-19-relief-where-did-the-money-go; Erin Einhorn, "Behind the Teacher Shortage, an Unexpected Culprit: Covid Relief Money," *NBC News*, October 1, 2021, https://www.nbcnews.com/news/educa tion/behind-teacher-shortage-unexpected-culprit-covid-relief-money-n1280491.

12. David Corn, "Trump Says There's Plenty of PPE. So Why Did This Union for Nurses Have to Find Its Own?" *Mother Jones*, May 8, 2020, https://www .motherjones.com/politics/2020/05/trump-ppe-failure-nurses-union-american -federation-of-teachers/.

13. Ibid.; Keith Bradsher and Liz Alderman, "The World Needs Masks. China Makes Them, but Has Been Hoarding Them," *New York Times*, last updated April 2, 2020, https://www.nytimes.com/2020/03/13/business/masks-china -coronavirus.html.

14. Corn, "Trump Says There's Plenty of PPE. So Why Did This Union for Nurses Have to Find Its Own?"

15. "Our Team," Empire Global Ventures, accessed July 25, 2022, https://egvllc.com/our-team/.

16. Daniel Greenfield, "A Biden Ally and J Street Vice Chair's Company Offers Access to Senior Chinese Officials," FrontPage Magazine, September 16, 2020, https://www.frontpagemag.com/fpm/2020/09/biden-ally-and-j-street-vice-chairs-company-offers-daniel-greenfield/.

17. "Empire Global Ventures LLC," LinkedIn profile, accessed July 25, 2022, https://www.linkedin.com/company/empire-global-venture-llc/about/; Blake Morgan, "20 Husbands Who Support Their Working Mom Spouses," *Forbes*, March 8, 2021, https://www.forbes.com/sites/blakemorgan/2021/03/08/20-husbands-who-support-their-working-mom-spouses/; Sam Natapoff used the email address snatapoff@rosemontcapital.com, while Alexandra Stanton used the email address astanton@rosemontseneca.com; Peter Schweizer, "Inside the Shady Private Equity Firm Run by Kerry and Biden's Kids," *New York Post*, March 15, 2018, https://nypost.com/2018/03/15/inside-the-shady-private-equity-firm-run-by-kerry-and-bidens-kids/.

18. Greenfield, "A Biden Ally and J Street Vice Chair's Company Offers Access to Senior Chinese Officials"; "Our Team," Empire Global Ventures.

19. "Teachers Unions: From Academics to Activists," Government Accountability Institute, report, January 10, 2022, https://thedrilldown.com/wp-content/uploads/2022/01/2022_Teachers_Union_Report.pdf; email from Eric Schwerin to Hunter Biden, "Policy Dinner," June 16, 2010, https://bidenlaptopemails.com/biden-emails/email.php?id=20100616-131155_55484; Jon Levine, "Hunter Biden Held Two Meetings with Ex–NY Gov. David Paterson," *New York Post*, May 29, 2021, https://nypost.com/2021/05/29/hunter-biden-held-two-meetings-with-ex-ny-gov-david-paterson/.

20. "Our Team," Empire Global Ventures.

21. "Board of Directors," J Street, accessed July 25, 2022, https://jstreet.org/about-us/board-of-directors/.

22. "Executive Committee," J Street, accessed July 25, 2022, https://jstreet.org/about-us/our-supporters/rabbinic-and-cantorial-cabinet/executive-committee/.

23. "Teachers Unions: From Academics to Activists"; email from Alexandra Stanton to Hunter Biden, "Checking In," May 6, 2010, https://bidenlaptopemails.com/biden-emails/email.php?id=20100506-103631_61754.

24. Corn, "Trump Says There's Plenty of PPE. So Why Did This Union for Nurses Have to Find Its Own?"

25. Emma-Jo Morris and Gabrielle Fonrouge, "Smoking-Gun Email Reveals How Hunter Biden Introduced Ukrainian Businessman to VP Dad," *New York Post*, October 14, 2020, https://nypost.com/2020/10/14/email-reveals-how-hunter-biden-introduced-ukrainian-biz-man-to-dad/.

26. "Overview," Empire Global Ventures, on Internet Archive, accessed July 25,

2020, https://web.archive.org/web/20200919183827/http://egvllc.com/overview / (the screenshot of the site was captured on September 19, 2020); "Overview," Empire Global Ventures, on Internet Archive, accessed July 25, 2020, https://web.archive.org/web/20201020085115/http://egvllc.com/overview/ (the screenshot of the site was captured on October 20, 2020).

27. Email from Eric Schwerin to Alexandra Stanton, "Re: Look and Feel," June 17, 2010, https://bidenlaptopemails.com/biden-emails/email.php?id=20100617-232 231_29165.

28. Corn, "Trump Says There's Plenty of PPE. So Why Did This Union for Nurses Have to Find Its Own?"

29. U.S. Department of Labor, Form LM-2 Labor Organization Annual Report, Teachers AFL-CIO, from July 1, 2019 to June 30, 2020, https://olmsapps.dol.gov/query/orgReport.do?rptId=736385&rptForm=LM2Form.

30. U.S. Department of Labor, Form LM-2 Labor Organization Annual Report, Teachers AFL-CIO, from July 1, 2020 to June 30, 2021, https://olmsapps.dol.gov/query/orgReport.do?rptId=783067&rptForm=LM2Form; "Our Founders," Little Lives PPE, accessed July 25, 2022, https://littlelivesppe.com/pages/our-founders.

31. "Mini Face Shield for Kids Ages 2–6," Little Lives PPE, accessed July 25, 2022, https://littlelivesppe.com/products/mini-face-shield-for-kids-ages-2-6.

32. "American Federation of Teachers Secures Personal Protective Equipment for Frontline Healthcare Providers," American Federation of Teachers, press release, May 7, 2020, https://www.aft.org/press-release/american-federation-tea chers-secures-personal-protective-equipment-frontline; U.S. Department of Labor, Office of Labor-Management Standards, LM Reports and Constitutions and Bylaws, accessed July 25, 2022, https://olmsapps.dol.gov/olpdr/?_ga= 2.227958301.1630405121.1633982406-1056998162.1633982406#Union%20Re ports/Payer/Payee%20Search/ (search Union Name "TEACHERS AFL-CIO" and Type/Classification "medical equipment").

33. "Responding to the Coronavirus Epidemic to Keep Families Healthy, Protect Frontline Providers and Save Our Economy," American Federation of Teachers, adopted March 22, 2020, https://www.aft.org/resolution/responding-corona virus-epidemic-keep-families-healthy-protect-frontline.

34. Randi Weingarten, Twitter, October 10, 2022, https://twitter.com/rweingarten/status/1579414707949096960?ref_src=twsrc%5Etfw%7Ctwcamp%5Etweet embed%7Ctwterm%5E1579457109913403392%7Ctwgr%5E04be996 779dd6bf1987332a1ade0444e8599bd44%7Ctwcon%5Es3_&ref_url= https%3A%2F%2Fwww.foxnews.com%2Fus%2Frandi-weingarten-takes-flak -social-media-ukraine-trip-us-schools-struggle.

35. https://about.burbio.com/school-opening-tracker.

36. https://www.nytimes.com/2021/07/28/us/covid-schools-at-home-learning -study.html.

37. https://www.edworkingpapers.com/ai21-355.

38. Phil Kerpen, Stephen Moore, and Casey Mulligan, "A Final Report Card on the States' Response to COVID-19," Committee to Unleash Prosperity, accessed July 25, 2022, https://committeetounleashprosperity.com/wp-content/uploads/2022/04/Which-States-Handled-the-Covid-Pandemic-Best.pdf.

39. https://www.nytimes.com/2022/09/01/us/national-test-scores-math-reading-pandemic.html.

40. Julie Kiefer, "Study: In Much of the U.S., Virtual School Did Not Lower Covid-19 Case Rates in Surrounding Communities," Covid-19 Central @THEU, October 27, 2021, https://coronavirus.utah.edu/research-news/study-in-much-of-the-u-s-virtual-school-did-not-lower-covid-19-case-rates-in-surrounding-communities/.

41. "CDC: Schools with Mask Mandates Didn't See Statistically Significant Different Rates of COVID Transmission from Schools with Optional Policies," Foundation for Economic Education, August 25, 2021, https://fee.org/articles/cdc-schools-with-mask-mandates-didn-t-see-statistically-significant-different-rates-of-covid-transmission-from-schools-with-optional-policies/.

42. "Education and COVID-19: Focusing on the Long-Term Impact of School Closures," Organisation for Economic Co-operation and Development, June 29, 2020, https://www.oecd.org/coronavirus/policy-responses/education-and-covid-19-focusing-on-the-long-term-impact-of-school-closures-2cea926e/.

43. Angela Nelson, "How COVID-19 Has Affected Special Education Students," Tufts Now, September 29, 2020, https://now.tufts.edu/articles/how-covid-19-has-affected-special-education-students.

44. David Leonhardt, "'Not Good for Learning,'" *New York Times*, May 5, 2022, https://www.nytimes.com/2022/05/05/briefing/school-closures-covid-learning-loss.html; Dan Goldhaber et al., "The Consequences of Remote and Hybrid Instruction During the Pandemic," Center for Education Policy Research, Harvard University, May 2022, https://cepr.harvard.edu/files/cepr/files/5-4.pdf?m=1651690491.

45. Matt Grossmann et al., "All States Close but Red Districts Reopen: The Politics of In-Person Schooling During the COVID-19 Pandemic," Annenberg Institute for School Reform at Brown University, working paper, February 2021, https://www.edworkingpapers.com/ai21-355.

46. Chelsea Coffin, "Racial and Ethnic Diversity over Time in D.C.'s Schools," D.C. Policy Center, February 6, 2019, https://www.dcpolicycenter.org/publications/racial-and-ethnic-diversity-over-time-in-d-c-s-schools/; "San Francisco Unified School District," Public School Review, accessed July 25, 2022, https://www.publicschoolreview.com/california/san-francisco-unified-school-district/634410-school-district; Joel B. Pollak, "20% of San Francisco Teachers Skip School to Protest Reopening Conditions," Breitbart, January 7, 2022, https://www.breitbart.com/education/2022/01/07/20-of-san-francisco-teachers-skip-school-to-protest-reopening-conditions/.

47. Howard Blume and Stephanie Chavez, "No Quick Path to Reopening L.A. Unified Is Emerging as School Year Slips Away," *Los Angeles Times*, February 21, 2021, https://www.latimes.com/california/story/2021-02-21/la-teachers-union-vaccination-demand-school-reopening.

48. Los Angeles Times, "Teachers Union Resists Parents' Push to Reopen L.A. Schools," KTLA, February 23, 2021, https://ktla.com/news/local-news/teachers-union-resists-parents-push-to-reopen-l-a-schools/.

49. Andrew Kerr, "LA Teachers Union Demands Defunding of Police, Medicare-for-All and Ban on New Charter Schools as Conditions for Reopening Schools," Daily Caller, July 13, 2020, https://dailycaller.com/2020/07/13/la-teachers-union-demands-reopen-schools/.

50. Lucas Manfredi, "Chicago Teachers Union Deletes Tweet Claiming School Reopening Push 'Rooted' in Sexism, Racism, Misogyny," Fox News, December 6, 2020, https://www.foxnews.com/us/chicago-teachers-union-deletes-tweet-school-reopening-sexism-racism-misogyny.

51. "Building Resilient Communities," *AFT Healthcare* 2, no. 2 (Fall 2021), https://www.aft.org/sites/default/files/media/documents/2022/HC-fall2021-lores.pdf.

52. "Learning Beyond COVID-19: A Vision for Thriving in Public Education," National Education Association, accessed July 25, 2022, p. 9, https://www.nea.org/sites/default/files/2021-03/Learning_Beyond_COVID_web.pdf.

53. Ibid., p. 10.

54. Ibid.

55. Ibid.

56. Ibid.

57. Ibid., p. 11.

58. Ibid., p. 12.

59. Ibid., p. 14.

60. Ibid.

61. Ibid.

62. Ibid., p. 16.

63. Robert Pondiscio, "How Randi Weingarten Is Actually Undermining Trust in Public Schools," *New York Post*, May 5, 2022, https://nypost.com/2022/05/05/how-randi-weingarten-is-actually-undermining-trust-in-public-schools/.

64. Edmund DeMarche, "McAuliffe's Decision to Have Weingarten Speak at Rally Mocked by Republicans," Fox News, November 2, 2021, https://www.foxnews.com/politics/mcauliffes-decision-to-have-weingarten-speak-at-rally-mocked-by-republicans; Mark Moore, "Youngkin's Victory in Virginia Seen as Win for 'Parental Rights' in Education," *New York Post*, November 3, 2021, https://ny

post.com/2021/11/03/glenn-youngkin-win-seen-as-victory-for-virginia-school
-parents/.

65. Ian Schwartz, "VA Gov. Candidate McAuliffe: 'I Don't Think Parents Should
Be Telling Schools What They Should Teach,'" RealClear Politics, September 28, 2021, https://www.realclearpolitics.com/video/2021/09/28/va_gov_candi
date_mcauliffe_i_dont_think_parents_should_be_telling_schools_what
_they_should_teach.html.

66. https://www.fcps.edu/news/social-studies-teachers-collaborate-colleagues-state
wide-create-anti-racist-culturally; https://www.dailywire.com/news/exclusive-vir
ginia-mother-who-delivered-fiery-takedown-of-critical-race-theory-speaks-out.

67. https://www.justice.gov/ag/page/file/1438986/download.

68. https://news.yahoo.com/fbi-whistleblower-claims-doj-used-210523832.html.

69. https://www.cruz.senate.gov/imo/media/doc/202110.08crtlettertoaggarland
.pdf.

70. https://www.grassley.senate.gov/news/news-releases/judiciary-republicans-to
-garland-are-concerned-parents-domestic-terrorists-or-not.

CHAPTER 10 Hunting Hatred to Silence Dissent

1. Wendy S. Painting, *Aberration in the Heartland of the Real: The Secret Lives of
Timothy McVeigh* (Walterville, OR: TrineDay, 2016), p. 370. See also pages 555
and 654.

2. Lexi Lonas, "Men Accused of Whitmer Kidnapping Plot Say FBI Set Them Up:
Report," *Hill*, July 20, 2021, https://thehill.com/homenews/state-watch/563902
-men-accused-of-whitmer-kidnapping-plot-say-fbi-set-them-up-report/.

3. "The Department of Justice's Operation Fast and Furious: Accounts of ATF
Agents," House Committee on Oversight and Reform, June 14, 2011, https://
republicans-oversight.house.gov/report/the-department-of-justices-operation
-fast-and-furious-accounts-of-atf-agents/.

4. *Epoch Times*, "PATCON Explored Records Provide Glimpse of FBI Right-Wing
Infiltration Ops," March 22, 2022, https://www.theepochtimes.com/patcon
-explored-records-provide-glimpse-of-fbi-right-wing-infiltration-ops_4344148
.html.

5. Painting, *Aberration in the Heartland of the Real*, p. 261.

6. Ken Silva, "FBI's Operation to Infiltrate Right-Wing Extremist Groups Lies at
Center of Transparency Lawsuit," *Epoch Times*, February 23, 2022, https://
www.theepochtimes.com/fbis-operation-to-infiltrate-right-wing-extremist
-groups-lies-at-center-of-transparency-lawsuit-2_4292365.html.

7. Ibid.; R. M. Schneiderman, "My Life as a White Supremacist," *Newsweek*, November 21, 2011, https://www.newsweek.com/my-life-white-supremacist-475032.

8. Painting, *Aberration in the Heartland of the Real*, p. 534.

9. *Epoch Times*, "PATCON Explored Records Provide Glimpse of FBI Right-Wing Infiltration Ops."

10. Ibid.; Silva, "FBI's Operation to Infiltrate Right-Wing Extremist Groups Lies at Center of Transparency Lawsuit."

11. Schneiderman, "My Life as a White Supremacist."

12. https://libertarianinstitute.org/documents/MAG-2011_11_28-Newsweek-I _Was_an_Undercover_White_Supremacist_PATCON_ORIGINAL_UNRED ACTED_COPY.pdf. The Libertarian Institute hosts an archive of more than 2,000 documents and news reports on this case to include FBI 302 reports, transcripts, Secret Service documents, affidavits, DOJ reports, studies, and other source material. This archive was created over a five-year period by Richard Booth in collaboration with Jesse Trentadue and journalist Roger Charles, who provided many of the never-before-published documents on the archive. This archive can be found at https://libertarianinstitute.org/okc.

13. John Kline, "It's Time We Get Answers About the FBI's Involvement in the OKC Bombing," Libertarian Institute, April 27, 2022, https://libertarianinstitute .org/articles/its-time-we-get-answers-about-the-fbis-involvement-in-the-okc -bombing/.

14. Pamela Manson, "Magistrate to Investigate Witness Tampering Claims in Utah Man's Oklahoma City Bombing Records Case," *Salt Lake Tribune*, April 30, 2015, https://archive.sltrib.com/article.php?id=2462146&itype=CMSID.

15. Silva, "FBI's Operation to Infiltrate Right-Wing Extremist Groups Lies at Center of Transparency Lawsuit."

16. Bill Malugin and Landon Mion, "September Migrant Encounters Hit Record High, 20 Suspected Terrorists Arrested," Fox News, October 22, 2022, https:// www.foxnews.com/us/southern-border-migrant-encounters-surpass-record -227k-september.

17. "Portman: March CBP Numbers Show 33 Percent Increase in Unlawful Migrant Encounters at Southern Border," U.S. Senate Committee on Homeland Security and Governmental Affairs, April 19, 2022, https://www.hsgac.senate.gov /media/minority-media/portman-march-cbp-numbers-show-33-percent-in crease-in-unlawful-migrant-encounters-at-southern-border; William La Jeunesse, "US-Mexico Border Traffickers Earned as Much as $14M a Day Last Month: Sources," Fox News, March 22, 2021, https://www.foxnews.com/politics/us -mexico-border-traffickers-million-february; John B. Washington, "Trump's Big Border Wall Is Now a Pile of Rusting Steel," *Atlantic*, December 20, 2021, https://www.theatlantic.com/politics/archive/2021/12/steel-trump-border-wall -rusting-desert/621005/.

18. Andy Ngo (@MrAndyNgo), "The @SeattleParks property in the former CHAZ that was vandalized with #Antifa graffiti this week is now filled with more extremist messages . . . ," Twitter post, April 29, 2022, 12:01 a.m., https://twitter

.com/MrAndyNgo/status/1519934888337715201; Yaron Steinbuch, "Waukesha Parade Rampage Suspect Darrell Brooks Once Wrote Anti-Trump Rap," *New York Post*, November 23, 2021, https://nypost.com/2021/11/23/waukesha-parade-suspect-darrell-brooks-wrote-anti-trump-rap/; Taylor Penley, "Antifa Mob Wreaks Havoc on GOP Candidate's Portland Rally: 'From Roses to Riots,'" Fox News, May 2, 2022, https://www.foxnews.com/media/antifa-portland-rally-gop-candidate-police-pulliam.

19. Marisa Schultz, "Mayorkas Says White Supremacists Pose 'Most Prominent Threat' to US Homeland," Fox News, April 8, 2022, https://www.foxnews.com/politics/mayorkas-white-supremacists-poise-most-prominent-threat.

20. "WATCH: White supremacy is 'most lethal threat to the homeland today,' Biden says," YouTube video, posted by "PBS NewsHour," April 28, 2021, https://www.youtube.com/watch?v=cYJd2VFtHDM.

21. Liz George, "Video: Biden Again Says 'White Supremacist Domestic Terrorism' Is 'Most Lethal Terrorist Threat' to US," American Military News, October 21, 2021, https://americanmilitarynews.com/2021/10/video-biden-again-says-white-supremacist-domestic-terrorism-is-most-lethal-terrorist-threat-to-us/.

22. Chad F. Wolf and James Jay Carafano, "Biden Tries to Turn Domestic Security into Partisan Witch Hunt," Heritage Foundation, June 25, 2021, https://www.heritage.org/homeland-security/commentary/biden-tries-turn-domestic-security-partisan-witch-hunt.

23. Matt Zapotosky, "Garland Emphasizes Need for Funding on Domestic Terrorism and Civil Rights Work," *Washington Post*, May 4, 2021, https://www.washingtonpost.com/national-security/merrick-garland-hearing-justice-department-budget/2021/05/03/4024cb18-ac28-11eb-b476-c3b287e52a01_story.html.

24. Spencer Brown, "Mayorkas Calls Domestic Terrorism Greatest Threat, but Can't Cite an Example," Townhall, April 29, 2022, https://townhall.com/tipsheet/spencerbrown/2022/04/29/mayorkas-couldnt-cite-one-case-of-1-threat-domestic-terrorism-referred-to-doj-n2606542.

25. "About Us," Center for Strategic and International Studies, accessed July 30, 2022, https://www.csis.org/programs/about-us.

26. Jason Wilson, "Violence by Far Right Is Among US's Most Dangerous Terrorist Threats, Study Finds," *Guardian*, June 27, 2020, https://www.theguardian.com/world/2020/jun/27/us-far-right-violence-terrorist-threat-analysis.

27. Robert O'Harrow Jr., Andrew Ba Tran, and Derek Hawkins, "The Rise of Domestic Extremism in America," *Washington Post*, April 12, 2021, https://www.washingtonpost.com/investigations/interactive/2021/domestic-terrorism-data/.

28. Joey Pellegrino, "Anti-Abortion Protestors Arrested at South Fort Myers Planned Parenthood," Wink News, January 27, 2022, https://www.winknews.com/2022/01/27/anti-abortion-protestors-arrested-at-south-fort-myers-planned-parenthood/; Andrew Ba Tran, "Right-Wing Domestic Terrorism Incidents

Since 2015," GitHub, March 31, 2021, https://wpinvestigative.github.io/csis _domestic_terrorism/output/docs/04_exploratory_map.html.

29. Mitchell Byars, "Man Accused of Threatening Longmont Protesters with Hatchet Takes Plea Deal," Daily Camera, December 22, 2020, https://www.daily camera.com/2020/12/22/man-accused-of-threatening-longmont-protesters -with-hatchet-takes-plea-deal/.

30. "Examining Extremism: Antifa," Center for Strategic and International Studies, June 24, 2021, https://www.csis.org/blogs/examining-extremism/examining-ex tremism-antifa.

31. Kay Jones et al., "A Sixth Victim Has Died After the Waukesha Christmas Parade Crash, Prosecutors Say," CNN, November 23, 2021, https://www.cnn .com/2021/11/23/us/waukesha-car-parade-crowd-tuesday/index.html.

32. Stephan Dinan, "Mayorkas: Black Lives Matter Isn't Domestic Terrorism Threat," *Washington Times*, April 28, 2022, https://www.washingtontimes.com /news/2022/apr/28/dhs-secretary-alejandro-mayorkas-black-lives-matte/.

33. https://www.whitehouse.gov/briefing-room/statements-releases/2022/08/19 /statement-by-press-secretary-karine-jean-pierre-on-the-white-house-united -we-stand-summit/.

34. https://m.washingtontimes.com/news/2022/sep/14/biden-host-white-house -summit-combat-racism-violen/?utm_campaign=shareaholic&utm_medium =twitter&utm_source=socialnetwork.

35. https://republicans-judiciary.house.gov/press-release/republicans-release-1000 -page-report-on-fbi-doj-politicization/.

36. Jessica McBride, "Lyndon McLeod: Social Media Posts, Books by Denver Gun- man," Heavy, last updated December 28, 2021, https://heavy.com/news/lyndon -mcleod-social-media-books/.

37. Alyssa Pone et al., "5 Dead in Denver 'Killing Spree' by Suspect with Ex- tremist Views, Police Sources Say," ABC News, December 28, 2021, https:// abcnews.go.com/US/dead-officer-injured-killing-spree-denver-police/story ?id=81966638.

38. "DA Rollins: Winthrop Shooting Suspect Nathan Allen Had 'Troubling White Supremacist Rhetoric,' Targeted Black Victims," CBS Boston, June 27, 2021, https://www.cbsnews.com/boston/news/winthrop-crash-shooting-nathan -allen-dave-green-ramona-cooper/.

39. Deroy Murdock, "Democrats Who Claim White Supremacy Is Top Prob- lem Ignore Black Racist Killers," *New York Post*, April 17, 2022, https://ny post.com/2022/04/17/democrats-who-claim-white-supremacy-is-top-prob lem-ignore-black-racist-killers/.

40. Erin Doherty, "Biden: Jan. 6 Capitol Riot 'Was About White Supremacy,'" Ax- ios, October 21, 2021, https://www.axios.com/2021/10/21/biden-jan-6-capitol -riot-white-supremacy.

CHAPTER 11 Criminalizing Dissent

1. Joey Garrison, "Biden Takes Steps to Confront Domestic Violent Extremism Following Capitol Riot," *USA Today*, January 22, 2021, https://www.usatoday.com/story/news/politics/2021/01/22/biden-orders-threat-assessment-domestic-violent-extremism/6676776002/; "Fact Sheet: National Strategy for Countering Domestic Terrorism," The White House, June 15, 2021, https://www.whitehouse.gov/briefing-room/statements-releases/2021/06/15/fact-sheet-national-strategy-for-countering-domestic-terrorism/; Eric Tucker, "Joe Biden Orders Review of Domestic Violent Extremism Threat in U.S.," Huffington Post, January 22, 2021, https://www.huffpost.com/entry/joe-biden-review-domestic-violent-extremism_n_600b522dc5b6f401aea45e04.

2. "Fact Sheet: National Strategy for Countering Domestic Terrorism."

3. Ibid.; Roger Koppl and Abigail Devereaux, "Biden Establishes a Ministry of Truth," *Wall Street Journal*, opinion, May 1, 2022, https://www.wsj.com/articles/biden-establishes-a-ministry-of-truth-disinformation-governance-board-partisan-11651432312.

4. "Summary of Terrorism Threat to the U.S. Homeland," U.S. Department of Homeland Security, National Terrorism Advisory System, February 7, 2022, https://www.dhs.gov/ntas/advisory/national-terrorism-advisory-system-bulletin-february-07-2022.

5. Ibid.

6. "Fact Sheet: Biden-Harris Administration Releases Agency Equity Action Plans to Advance Equity and Racial Justice Across the Federal Government," The White House, April 14, 2022, https://www.whitehouse.gov/briefing-room/statements-releases/2022/04/14/fact-sheet-biden-harris-administration-releases-agency-equity-action-plans-to-advance-equity-and-racial-justice-across-the-federal-government/.

7. Ibid.; https://nypost.com/2022/05/12/you-couldnt-have-picked-a-worse-minister-of-truth-than-nina-jankowicz/; https://nypost.com/2022/04/28/bidens-disinformation-czar-is-latest-assault-on-free-speech/.

8. https://news.yahoo.com/nina-jankowicz-resigns-dhs-disinformation-194030339.html.

9. https://theintercept.com/2022/10/31/social-media-disinformation-dhs/.

10. https://nypost.com/2022/09/17/government-censorship-should-scare-us-as-much-as-covid-did/.

11. https://www.heritage.org/progressivism/report/president-bidens-equity-action-plans-reveal-radical-divisive-agenda.

12. https://www.cnn.com/2020/08/06/opinions/susan-rice-vice-president-joe-biden-psaki/index.html.

13. Edmund DeMarche, "Grenell Calls Susan Rice the 'Shadow President' and 'No

One Is Paying Attention,'" Fox News, May 13, 2021, https://www.foxnews.com /politics/grenell-calls-susan-rice-the-shadow-president-and-no-one-is-paying -attention.

14. Michael Barone, "Biden's 'Racial Justice' Agenda: Judge Everyone by the Color of Their Skin," *New York Post*, January 29, 2021, https://nypost.com/2021/01/29 /bidens-racial-justice-agenda-judge-everyone-by-the-color-of-their-skin/.

15. Carol E. Lee, "Biden Looks to Susan Rice to Elevate Low-Profile Domestic Policy Council," NBC News, December 21, 2020, https://www.nbcnews.com /politics/politics-news/biden-looks-susan-rice-elevate-low-profile-domestic -policy-council-n1251851.

16. Peter Schweizer, *Red Handed: How American Elites Get Rich Helping China Win* (New York: HarperCollins, 2022).

17. Charles Krauthammer, "The Iran Deal: Anatomy of a Disaster," *Washington Post*, opinion, April 9, 2015, https://www.washingtonpost.com/opinions /the-iran-deal-anatomy-of-a-disaster/2015/04/09/11bdf9ee-dee7-11e4-a1b8 -2ed88bc190d2_story.html; Adam Rachman, "Jake Sullivan, Architect of the Iran Deal, National Security Adviser to Biden, and Key Clinton Aide, on Trump's Withdrawal from the Agreement, North Korea, and What Happened in 2016," Cambridge Globalist, May 11, 2018, https://cambridgeglobalist.org/2018/05/11 /jake-sullivan-architect-of-the-iran-deal-national-security-adviser-to-biden -and-key-clinton-aide-on-trumps-withdrawal-from-the-agreement-north-korea -and-what-happened-in-2016/.

18. Rachael Bade, "Top Clinton Adviser Sent 'Top Secret' Messages to Her Private Account," *Politico*, February 10, 2016, https://www.politico.com/story/2016/02 /hillary-clinton-email-jake-sullivan-secret-219013; Andy Ngo (@MrAndyNgo), "The @SeattleParks property in the former CHAZ that was vandalized with #Antifa graffiti this week is now filled with more extremist messages . . . ," Twitter post, April 29, 2022, 12:01 a.m., https://twitter.com/MrAndyNgo/status /1519934888337715201.

19. Steven Nelson and Bruce Golding, "Biden NSA Jake Sullivan's Future Questioned over Russia Hoax 'Role,'" *New York Post*, November 9, 2021, https://nypost .com/2021/11/09/biden-nsa-jake-sullivans-future-questioned-over-russia-hoax -role/.

20. Jeff Mordock, "Durham Says Clinton Campaign Funded Surveillance of Trump Tower, White House," *Washington Times*, February 12, 2022, https://www .washingtontimes.com/news/2022/feb/12/durham-says-clinton-campaign -funded-surveillance-t/.

21. Soo Rin Kim and Libby Cathey, "Obama-era Officials Return to White House Worth Millions," ABC News, March 21, 2021, https://abcnews.go.com/US /obama-era-officials-return-white-house-worth-millions/story?id=76582015.

22. Emilee Larkin, "Susan Rice Tapped for Biden Cabinet Post That Won't Need Senate Nod," Courthouse News Service, December 10, 2020, https://www

.courthousenews.com/susan-rice-tapped-for-biden-cabinet-post-that-wont
-need-senate-nod/.

23. "Flashback: What Susan Rice Said About Benghazi," *Wall Street Journal*, last
    updated November 16, 2012, https://www.wsj.com/articles/BL-WB-36921;
    Jake Miller, "Susan Rice: No Regrets on Benghazi Description," CBS News,
    February 23, 2014, https://www.cbsnews.com/news/susan-rice-no-regrets-on
    -benghazi-description/.

24. David French, "Did Susan Rice Lie, Again?" *National Review*, September 14,
    2017, https://www.nationalreview.com/2017/09/susan-rice-devin-nunes-unmask
    ing-controversy-did-rice-lie/.

25. "Judicial Watch: Obama NSC Advisor Susan Rice's Unmasking Material Is
    at Obama Library," Judicial Watch, press release, June 19, 2017, https://www
    .judicialwatch.org/judicial-watch-obama-nsc-advisor-susan-rices-unmasking
    -material-obama-library/.

26. Rebecca Shabad, "Susan Rice Says Unmasking of Names Wasn't for Political
    Purposes," CBS News, last updated April 4, 2017, https://www.cbsnews.com
    /news/susan-rice-says-unmasking-of-names-wasnt-for-political-purposes/.

27. Andrew C. McCarthy, "Susan Rice's White House Unmasking: A Watergate-Style
    Scandal," *National Review*, April 4, 2017, https://www.nationalreview.com/2017
    /04/susan-rice-unmasking-trump-campaign-members-obama-administration-fbi
    -cia-nsa/.

28. Eric Felten, "Susan Rice's Testimony on Being Out of Russiagate Loop Doesn't
    Add Up," RealClear Investigations, July 30, 2020, https://www.realclearinvesti
    gations.com/articles/2020/07/30/susan_rices_strained_relationship_with_the
    _truth_strikes_again_124660.html.

29. Michael Sinclair, "Under Susan Rice, Will There Be Increased Overlap Between
    the Domestic Policy Council and the National Security Council?" Brookings
    Institution, January 5, 2021, https://www.brookings.edu/blog/order-from
    -chaos/2021/01/05/under-susan-rice-will-there-be-increased-overlap-between
    -the-domestic-policy-council-and-the-national-security-council/.

30. DeMarche, "Grenell Calls Susan Rice the 'Shadow President' and 'No One Is
    Paying Attention.'"

31. Lora Ries and GianCarlo Canaparo, "Biden's New Domestic Terrorism Unit
    Bad for Freedom-Loving Americans," Heritage Foundation, January 20, 2022,
    https://www.heritage.org/terrorism/commentary/bidens-new-domestic-ter
    rorism-unit-bad-freedom-loving-americans.

32. Statement of Merrick B. Garland, Attorney General, Department of Justice, Be-
    fore the Committee on Appropriations, U.S. Senate, at a Hearing Entitled "Do-
    mestic Violent Extremism in America," presented May 12, 2021, https://www
    .appropriations.senate.gov/imo/media/doc/Merrick%20Garland%20SFR%20
    for%20SAC%20DVE%20Hearing%2005-12-2021.pdf.

33. Ibid.

34. Mulligan et al., "A National Policy Blueprint to End White Supremacist Violence."

CHAPTER 12 Justifying Surveillance

1. Hina Shamsi and Hugh Handeyside, "Biden's Domestic Terrorism Strategy Entrenches Bias and Harmful Law Enforcement Power," American Civil Liberties Union, July 9, 2021, https://www.aclu.org/news/national-security/bidens-domestic-terrorism-strategy-entrenches-bias-and-harmful-law-enforcement-power.

2. Anne Henochowicz, "Translation: What Happened When My Health Code Turned Yellow," China Digital Times, November 26, 2021, https://chinadigitaltimes.net/2021/11/translation-what-happened-when-my-health-code-turned-yellow/.

3. Dorothy Li, "Chinese City Uses COVID-19 App to Prevent Bank Protestors from Gathering, Depositors Say," Epoch Times, last updated June 16, 2022, https://www.theepochtimes.com/chinese-city-uses-covid-19-app-to-prevent-bank-protestors-from-gathering-depositors-say_4535955.html?utm_source=ai&utm_medium=search.

4. Ibid.; Mary Hong, "Nearly 1 Million Chinese Customers Unable to Access Their Bank Deposits: Report," Epoch Times, last updated May 25, 2022, https://www.theepochtimes.com/millions-of-chinese-customers-unable-to-access-their-bank-deposits_4486878.html.

5. Ibid.

6. Adrian Shahbaz and Allie Funk, "False Panacea: Abusive Surveillance in the Name of Public Health," Freedom House, accessed August 11, 2022, https://freedomhouse.org/report/report-sub-page/2020/false-panacea-abusive-surveillance-name-public-health.

7. Ibid.

8. Alexandra Kelley, "Federal Ability to Buy Citizen Data Worries Lawmakers and Experts Alike," Nextgov, July 20, 2022, https://www.nextgov.com/analytics-data/2022/07/federal-ability-buy-citizen-data-worries-lawmakers-and-experts-alike/374719/.

9. "Wyden, Chaffetz Stand Up for Privacy with GPS Act," United States Senator for Oregon Ron Wyden's web page, press release, January 22, 2015, https://www.wyden.senate.gov/news/press-releases/wyden-chaffetz-stand-up-for-privacy-with-gps-act; Adam Mazmanian, "Chaffetz Wants Answers from US-CERT, OPM, on Hack," FCW, August 20, 2015, https://fcw.com/security/2015/08/chaffetz-wants-answers-from-us-cert-opm-on-hack/207066/; "Committee to Review Law Enforcement's Policies on Facial Recognition Technology," House Committee on Oversight and Reform, hearing, March 22, 2017,

https://republicans-oversight.house.gov/hearing/law-enforcements-use-facial-recognition-technology/.

10. United States Government Accountability Office, Report to the Ranking Member, Subcommittee on Privacy, Technology and the Law, Committee on the Judiciary, U.S. Senate, "Face Recognition Technology: FBI Should Better Ensure Privacy and Accuracy," May 2016, pp. 47–48, https://www.gao.gov/assets/gao-16-267.pdf.

11. United States Government Accountability Office, Report to Congressional Requesters, "Facial Recognition Technology: Federal Law Enforcement Agencies Should Better Assess Privacy and Other Risks," June 2021, pp. 12, 60, https://www.gao.gov/assets/gao-21-518.pdf; Gerrit De Vynck, "Federal Agencies Need Stricter Limits on Facial Recognition to Protect Privacy, Says Government Watchdog," *Washington Post*, June 29, 2021, https://www.washingtonpost.com/technology/2021/06/29/gao-facial-recognition-blm/.

12. Law Enforcement's Use of Facial Recognition Technology: Hearing Before the Committee on Oversight and Government Reform, House of Representatives, 115th Cong. (March 22, 2017), pp. 105–6, https://docs.house.gov/meetings/GO/GO00/20170322/105757/HHRG-115-GO00-Transcript-20170322.pdf.

13. Vynck, "Federal Agencies Need Stricter Limits on Facial Recognition to Protect Privacy, Says Government Watchdog."

14. Jordan Liles, "What Is USPS's Internet Covert Operations Program (iCOP)?" Snopes, February 7, 2022, https://www.snopes.com/articles/393823/usps-icop/.

15. Ibid.

16. Betsy Woodruff Swan, "Covert Postal Service Unit Probed Jan. 6 Social Media," *Politico*, September 27, 2021, https://www.politico.com/news/2021/09/27/covert-postal-service-514327.

17. Jana Winter, "The Postal Service Is Running a 'Covert Operations Program' That Monitors Americans' Social Media Posts," Yahoo! News, April 21, 2021, https://news.yahoo.com/the-postal-service-is-running-a-running-a-covert-operations-program-that-monitors-americans-social-media-posts-160022919.html.

18. Ibid.

19. Jana Winter, "Chief Postal Inspector Tells Lawmakers That Social Media Monitoring Began After George Floyd Protests," Yahoo! News, April 30, 2021, https://news.yahoo.com/chief-postal-inspector-tells-lawmakers-that-social-media-monitoring-began-after-george-floyd-protests-145116660.html.

20. United States Postal Inspection Service, FY 2020 Annual Report, accessed August 11, 2022, https://www.uspis.gov/wp-content/uploads/2021/07/FY2020-annual-report-web-FINAL.pdf; Aaron Kliegman, "Postal Service Hacking into Hundreds of Seized Mobile Devices, Tracking Users' Social Media Posts," Just the News, February 2, 2022, https://justthenews.com/government/federal-agencies/postal-service-accused-violating-americans-privacy-civil-liberties.

21. "11 Jan. 2021 USPIS iCOP Bulletin re Coordination of Militia Groups and Threat to Nancy Pelosi," Property of the People, September 25, 2021, https://prop ertyofthepeople.org/document-detail/?doc-id=21069041.

22. Elizabeth Nolan Brown, "The USPS' Semi-Secret Internet Surveillance Appa- ratus," *Reason*, August/September 2021, https://reason.com/2021/07/12/the -usps-semi-secret-internet-surveillance-apparatus/.

23. Woodruff Swan, "Covert Postal Service Unit Probed Jan. 6 Social Media."

24. Brown, "The USPS' Semi-Secret Internet Surveillance Apparatus."

25. Megan Cassidy, "San Francisco Police Linked a Woman to a Crime Using DNA from Her Rape Exam, D.A. Boudin Says," *San Francisco Chronicle*, last updated February 15, 2022, https://www.sfchronicle.com/sf/article/San-Francisco-police -linked-a-woman-to-a-crime-16918673.php.

26. Laura Hecht-Felella, "Federal Agencies Are Secretly Buying Consumer Data," Brennan Center for Justice, April 16, 2021, https://www.brennancenter.org/our -work/analysis-opinion/federal-agencies-are-secretly-buying-consumer-data.

27. Carpenter v. United States, 138 S. Ct. 2206 (2018), https://www.supremecourt .gov/opinions/17pdf/16-402_h315.pdf.

28. Letter from J. Russell George, Inspector General, to Senator Ron Wyden and Senator Elizabeth Warren, February 18, 2021, https://s.wsj.net/public/resources /documents/Response.pdf.

29. Hecht-Felella, "Federal Agencies Are Secretly Buying Consumer Data."

30. Joseph Cox, "Secret Service Bought Phone Location Data from Apps, Contract Confirms," *Vice*, August 17, 2020, https://www.vice.com/en/article/jgxk3g /secret-service-phone-location-data-babel-street.

31. Trevor Aaronson, "A Declassified Court Ruling Shows How the FBI Abused NSA Mass Surveillance Data," Intercept, October 10, 2019, https://theintercept .com/2019/10/10/fbi-nsa-mass-surveillance-abuse/.

32. Byron Tau and Michelle Hackman, "Federal Agencies Use Cellphone Location Data for Immigration Enforcement," *Wall Street Journal*, February 7, 2020, https://www.wsj.com/articles/federal-agencies-use-cellphone-location-data-for -immigration-enforcement-11581078600.

33. Kelly Cohen, "Jason Chaffetz: Use Facial Recognition Technology to Track Illegal Immigrants," *Washington Examiner*, March 22, 2017, https://www .washingtonexaminer.com/jason-chaffetz-use-facial-recognition-technology-to -track-illegal-immigrants.

34. Caroline Haskins, "Almost 17,000 Protesters Had No Idea a Tech Company Was Tracing Their Location," BuzzFeed News, June 25, 2020, https://www.buzz feednews.com/article/carolinehaskins1/protests-tech-company-spying.

35. "Wyden, Chaffetz Stand Up for Privacy with GPS Act"; Mazmanian, "Chaffetz

Wants Answers from US-CERT, OPM, on Hack"; "Committee to Review Law Enforcement's Policies on Facial Recognition Technology."

36. Jason Chaffetz, "Jason Chaffetz: Apple's Tim Cook Is Right: Americans' Privacy Should Be Treated as a Fundamental Right," Fox News, October 29, 2018, https://www.foxnews.com/opinion/jason-chaffetz-apples-tim-cook-is-right-privacy-should-be-treated-as-a-fundamental-right.

37. Isabelle Qian, Muyi Xiao, Paul Mozur, and Alexander Cardia, "Four Takeaways from a Times Investigation into China's Expanding Surveillance State," *New York Times*, last updated July 26, 2022, https://www.nytimes.com/2022/06/21/world/asia/china-surveillance-investigation.html.

38. Shamsi and Handeyside, "Biden's Domestic Terrorism Strategy Entrenches Bias and Harmful Law Enforcement Power."

39. Malia Wollan and Charlie Savage, "Holder Calls Terrorism Sting Operations 'Essential,'" *New York Times*, December 11, 2010, https://www.nytimes.com/2010/12/12/us/politics/12holder-1.html.

40. Trevor Aaronson, "Spy in Disguise," Intercept, September 12, 2021, https://theintercept.com/2021/09/12/fbi-informant-surveillance-muslims-supreme-court-911/.

41. "Attorney General Eric Holder Speaks at the Muslim Advocates' Annual Dinner," U.S. Department of Justice, Office of Public Affairs, December 10, 2010, https://www.justice.gov/opa/speech/attorney-general-eric-holder-speaks-muslim-advocates-annual-dinner.

42. Trevor Aaronson, "The Informants," *Mother Jones*, September/October 2011, https://www.motherjones.com/politics/2011/07/fbi-terrorist-informants/.

43. Trevor Aaronson, *Terror Factory* (Brooklyn: IG, 2013), https://readsbookonline.com/the-terror-factory-f; Trevor Aaronson, "Inside the Terror Factory," *Mother Jones*, January 11, 2013, https://www.motherjones.com/politics/2013/01/terror-factory-fbi-trevor-aaronson-book/.

44. Joseph Cox, "How the U.S. Military Buys Location Data from Ordinary Apps," *Vice*, November 16, 2020, https://www.vice.com/en/article/jgqm5x/us-military-location-data-xmode-locate-x.

45. Ibid.

46. Ibid.; Joseph Cox, "Private Intel Firm Buys Location Data to Track People to Their 'Doorstep,'" *Vice*, September 2, 2020, https://www.vice.com/en/article/qj454d/private-intelligence-location-data-xmode-hyas.

47. Tyler Sonnemaker, "Apple and Google Have Repeatedly Banned a Major Data Broker from Collecting Location Data from Users' Phones Amid Scrutiny over its National Security Work," Business Insider, December 9, 2020, https://www.businessinsider.com/apple-google-ban-developers-x-mode-collecting-location-tracking-data-2020-12?op=1.

48. Charlie Savage, "C.I.A. Is Collecting in Bulk Certain Data Affecting Americans, Senators Warn," *New York Times*, February 10, 2022, https://www.nytimes.com/2022/02/10/us/politics/cia-data-privacy.html; "Committee Members," Senate Select Committee on Intelligence Responsibilities and Activities, accessed August 13, 2022, https://www.intelligence.senate.gov/about/committee-members-117th-congress-2020-2021.

49. Exec. Order No. 12333, United States Intelligence Activities, July 30, 2008, https://dpcld.defense.gov/Portals/49/Documents/Civil/eo-12333-2008.pdf.

50. Savage, "C.I.A. Is Collecting in Bulk Certain Data Affecting Americans, Senators Warn."

51. Ibid.

52. Aaronson, "A Declassified Court Ruling Shows How the FBI Abused NSA Mass Surveillance Data."

53. Ibid.; "2018 FISC Ruling Shows How FBI Abused NSA Mass Surveillance Powers," U.S. Foreign Intelligence Surveillance Court, October 18, 2018, https://www.documentcloud.org/documents/6464604-2018-FISC-Ruling-Shows-How-FBI-Abused-NSA-Mass.html.

54. Bradley A. Smith, "Bradley A. Smith: Connecting the Dots in the IRS Scandal," *Wall Street Journal*, opinion, February 26, 2014, https://www.wsj.com/articles/bradley-a-smith-connecting-the-dots-in-the-irs-scandal-1393458077; Bradley A. Smith, "Remember the IRS Targeting Scandal? No One Ever Got Punished for It," *Washington Examiner*, January 18, 2018, https://www.washingtonexaminer.com/remember-the-irs-targeting-scandal-no-one-ever-got-punished-for-it.

55. Eric Shawn, "EPA Accused of Singling Out Conservative Groups, Amid IRS Scandal," Fox News, December 21, 2015, https://www.foxnews.com/politics/epa-accused-of-singling-out-conservative-groups-amid-irs-scandal.

56. Jennifer G. Hickey and John Gizzi, "Dershowitz, Law Enforcement Experts Slam D'Souza Targeting," Newsmax, January 29, 2014, https://www.newsmax.com/Newsfront/DSouza-Dershowitz-targeting-selective/2014/01/29/id/549845/.

57. Aaron Bandler, "7 Times the Obama Administration Used Government to Target Its Political Opponents," Daily Wire, April 4, 2017, https://www.dailywire.com/news/7-times-obama-administration-used-government-aaron-bandler.

58. Adam Entous and Danny Yadron, "U.S. Spy Net on Israel Snares Congress," *Wall Street Journal*, December 29, 2015, https://www.wsj.com/articles/u-s-spy-net-on-israel-snares-congress-1451425210.

59. "Fact Sheet: National Strategy for Countering Domestic Terrorism," The White House, press release, June 15, 2021, https://www.whitehouse.gov/briefing-room/statements-releases/2021/06/15/fact-sheet-national-strategy-for-countering-domestic-terrorism/.

60. Frank Konkel, "HHS Needs Improved Data Breach Reporting, Watchdog Says,"

Government Executive, June 28, 2022, https://www.govexec.com/technology /2022/06/gao-hhs-needs-improved-data-breach-reporting/368688/.

61. Krishnadev Calamur, "The Real Illegal Immigration Crisis Isn't on the Southern Border," *Atlantic*, April 19, 2019, https://www.theatlantic.com/international /archive/2019/04/real-immigration-crisis-people-overstaying-their-visas/587 485/.

62. "Biometric Entry-Exit System: Legislative History and Status," Congressional Research Service, August 27, 2020, https://crsreports.congress.gov/product/pdf /IF/IF11634.

63. Blake Hall, "Why I Moved My Tech Startup to D.C.," *Wall Street Journal*, January 30, 2013, https://www.wsj.com/articles/BL-232B-452.

64. Ron Hurtibise, "Florida Continues to Require Identity Verification with ID .me," Governing, May 9, 2022, https://www.governing.com/security/florida-cont inues-to-require-identity-verification-with-id-me.

CHAPTER 13 How to Take On the Puppeteers and Win

1. Confidential memo to Rob Flaherty, April 22, 2021, available online: https://www .wsj.com/public/resources/documents/17289-0421.pdf?mod=article_inline.

2. Kendall Tietz, "Youngkin Appoints Critical Race Theory Foe Angela Sailor as Diversity Officer, Unborn Ambassador," Daily Signal, January 20, 2022, https:// www.dailysignal.com/2022/01/20/youngkin-appoints-critical-race-theory-foe -angela-sailor-as-diversity-officer-unborn-ambassador/.

3. Dan Merica, "The Political Revival of Ralph Northam: How an Ostracized Governor Became a Progressive Champion," CNN Politics, April 26, 2021, https:// www.cnn.com/2021/04/25/politics/ralph-northam-virginia-governor/index .html; Nicholas F. Benton, "Northam Unveils 'One Virginia' Inclusion Initiative," *Falls Church News-Press*, February 26, 2021, https://www.fcnp.com/2021/02/26 /northam-unveils-one-virginia-inclusion-initiative/; "Virginia Launches Country's First-Ever Statewide Diversity, Equity, and Inclusion Plan," Insight into Diversity, March 2, 2021, https://www.insightintodiversity.com/virginia-launches-countrys -first-ever-statewide-diversity-equity-and-inclusion-plan/.

4. Mel Leonor, "Northam Administration's Statewide Plan Seeks to Institutionalize Diversity at State Agencies," *Richmond Times-Dispatch*, March 7, 2021, https://richmond.com/news/state-and-regional/govt-and-politics/northam -administrations-statewide-plan-seeks-to-institutionalize-diversity-at-state-age ncies/article_527733f6-25a3-5bba-b8cb-abc1960e73b3.html; "Virginia Launches Country's First-Ever Statewide Diversity, Equity, and Inclusion Plan."

5. "Governor Youngkin Appoints Chief Diversity, Opportunity & Inclusion Officer," Governor of Virginia Glenn Youngkin, press release, January 19, 2022, https://www.governor.virginia.gov/news-releases/2022/january/name-9226 94-en.html.

6. "Focusing Virginia's Diversity, Equity, and Inclusion Office and Designating a Commonwealth Chief Diversity, Opportunity, & Inclusion Officer," Commonwealth of Virginia Office of the Governor, Executive Order No. 10 (2022), accessed July 29, 2022, https://www.governor.virginia.gov/media/governorvirginiagov/governor-of-virginia/pdf/74–eo/74–eo/EO-10—Focusing-Virginia's-Diversity,-Equity,-and-Inclusion-Office-.pdf.

7. Ian Miles Cheong, "Virginia Gov. Glenn Youngkin Changes 'Diversity Officer' Position to Focus on Free Speech and Unborn Children's Rights," Post Millennial, January 19, 2022, https://thepostmillennial.com/virginia-gov-glenn-youngkin-turns-diversity-officer-position-into-free-speech-and-unborn-childrens-rights-ambassador.

8. Michael Martz, "Youngkin Wants College Presidents to Hire Faculty with 'Diverse Political Perspectives,'" Richmond Times-Dispatch, May 12, 2022, https://richmond.com/news/state-and-regional/govt-and-politics/youngkin-wants-college-presidents-to-hire-faculty-with-diverse-political-perspectives/article_4c40bddf-d671-5286-8dc1-ec98ee9e41a9.html.

9. Sean Salai, "Youngkin Identifies Racially 'Divisive Concepts' in Schools Report," Washington Times, February 25, 2022, https://www.washingtontimes.com/news/2022/feb/25/youngkin-identifies-racially-divisive-concepts-sch/.

10. Kate Masters and Graham Moomaw, "Youngkin's 'Almighty Creator' Rhetoric in New Diversity Training Offends Some State Employees," NBC 12, May 12, 2022, https://www.nbc12.com/2022/05/12/youngkins-almighty-creator-rhetoric-new-diversity-training-offends-some-state-employees/; "Focusing Virginia's Diversity, Equity, and Inclusion Office and Designating a Commonwealth Chief Diversity, Opportunity, & Inclusion Officer."

11. Dalia Fahmy, "Key Findings About Americans' Belief in God," Pew Research Center, April 25, 2018, https://www.pewresearch.org/fact-tank/2018/04/25/key-findings-about-americans-belief-in-god/; Kate Masters, "Youngkin's 'Almighty Creator' Rhetoric in New Diversity Training Offends Some State Employees," Longview News-Journal, May 11, 2022, https://www.news-journal.com/youngkin-s-almighty-creator-rhetoric-in-new-diversity-training-offends-some-state-employees/article_98dab7d9-0efb-5fdd-bb3b-2197810b0a2c.html.

Index

About the Author

Jason Chaffetz is an American politician and Fox News contributor. He was elected as a U.S. representative from Utah in 2008 after spending sixteen years in the local business community. When he left Congress in 2017, he was the chairman of the United States House Committee on Oversight and Government Reform.